Delia Knipe

Uncle Herbert's Speaker and Autograph-Album Verses

A Choice Collection Carefully Selected and Arranged

Delia Knipe

Uncle Herbert's Speaker and Autograph-Album Verses
A Choice Collection Carefully Selected and Arranged

ISBN/EAN: 9783743419216

Manufactured in Europe, USA, Canada, Australia, Japa

Cover: Foto ©Thomas Meinert / pixelio.de

Manufactured and distributed by brebook publishing software (www.brebook.com)

Delia Knipe

Uncle Herbert's Speaker and Autograph-Album Verses

UNCLE HERBERT'S SPEAKER

AND

AUTOGRAPH-ALBUM VERSES.

A CHOICE COLLECTION CAREFULLY SELECTED

AND ARRANGED

BY

UNCLE HERBERT.

SOLD BY SUBSCRIPTION ONLY.

J. A. RUTH & CO.,

PHILADELPHIA AND CHICAGO.

1886.

PREFACE.

THE selections for this volume have been made with very great care. Nothing that could in the slightest degree prove objectionable has been admitted. All the pieces are pure in language, lofty in sentiment, pithy, bright, sparkling. None dull or prosy. Beginning with the short simple pieces for the "little prattlers," the book gradually runs into those for older children; thus about one-third of the Speaker is given to pieces suitable for children under eight years of age, one-third for children from eight to twelve years old, and the remainder for older ones.

The little ones will memorize the short pieces by hearing them read, and thus early acquire the love for reciting and the confidence and knowledge of ability to perform, so essential to their development and success in life. The large number and great variety afford suitable selections for children of all ages and for all occasions; and though especially designed for school and parlor recitations, will also prove a treasure around the fireside, affording instruction, amusement and recreation for young and old.

Who has not been at a loss for an appropriate subject when asked to contribute a line, verse or page to an Autograph-Album? Who is always ready to "take the facile pen and write as if with fairy's magic wand"? The verses of this collection are so numerous and varied that a suitable one may be readily found for any requirement. Here are Friendship, Affection, Wit, Miscellany; every verse, as given, is appropriate to precede a signature, or can, by a little ingenuity, be changed to an original form—"In thought the same, the language only changed."

The utility and necessity for a suitable collection of Recitations and Autograph-Album verses are too obvious to require argument or apology, and the Publishers feel the assurance that this little volume will meet with universal favor. The modesty of the Author prompts him to withhold his name, and he will be known to the world only as "Uncle Herbert." That he has performed his work conscientiously and well, and that he has added a valuable contribution to the standard literature of the time we submit to an indulgent, appreciative, albeit critical Public.

THE PUBLISHERS.

CONTENTS.

CONTENTS.

CONTENTS.

CONTENTS.

CONTENTS.

CONTENTS.

Uncle Herbert's Speaker.

SIX LITTLE MICE.

SIX merry little mice,
  As lively as you please,
Went out to take a walk one day,
  And came across a cheese.

Said Mousie Number One
  To Mousie Number Two,
"Let's go and take a nibble,"
  Said Number Three, "Oh, do!"

Said Number Four, "I never saw
  A cheese so very nice;
I think I'll take some morsels home
  To my three little mice!"

Said Number Five, "I'll think a while,
  Nor nibble here in haste,
Although I'm sure, this nice, large cheese,
  Must have delicious taste!"

But while the five were talking,
  Believe it, if you please.
Industrious little Number Six,
  Had carried off the cheese!

13

THE THRUSH.

SONGSTER of the russet coat,
Full and liquid is thy note;
Plain thy dress, but great thy skill,
Captivating at thy will.

Small musician of the field,
Near my bower thy tribute yield,
Little servant of the ear,
Ply thy task, and never fear.

I will learn from thee to praise
God, the Author of my days;
I will learn from thee to sing,
Christ, my Saviour and my King;
Learn to labor with my voice,
Make the sinking heart rejoice.

BABY.

WHERE did you come from baby dear?
Out of the everywhere into here.

Where did you get those eyes so blue?
Out of the sky as I came through.

What makes the light in them sparkle and spin?
Some of the starry spikes left in.

Where did you get that little tear?
I found it waiting when I got here.

What makes your forehead so smooth and high?
A soft hand stroked it as I went by.

What makes your cheek like a warm white rose?
I saw something better than any one knows.

Whence that three-cornered smile of bliss?
Three angels gave me at once a kiss.

Where did you get this pearly ear?
God spoke and it came out to hear.

Where did you get those arms and hands?
Love made itself into bonds and bands.

Feet, whence did you come, you darling things?
From the same box as the cherubs' wings.

How did they all just come to be you?
God thought about me, and so I grew.

But how did you come to us, you dear?
God thought about you, and so I am here.

George Macdonald.

BRIGHT LITTLE DANDELION.

BRIGHT little dandelion,
   Downy yellow-face,
Peeping up among the grass
   With such gentle grace.
Minding not the April wind
   Blowing rude and cold,
Brave little dandelion,
   With a heart of gold!

HALF-PAST EIGHT AND HALF-PAST FOUR.

HALF-PAST eight, half-past eight!
  School-bell's ringing—don't be late!
Get your books, and pens, and papers;
Don't be cutting truant capers.
Half-past eight, half-past eight!
School-bell's ringing—don't be late!

Half-past eight, half-past eight!
Who is he for whom we wait?
Lazy Jack!—why this folly!
Why d'ye look so melancholy?
Don't hang back—march out straight,
School-bell's ringing—school won't wait!

Half-past four, half-past four!
Bell is ringing—school is o'er!
Master Jack is blithe and ready:
Needn't hurry, Jack—march steady.
See the rogue, he runs about;
He's the very first boy out.
Half-past four, half-past four!
Bell is ringing—school is o'er.

SILLY LITTLE MARY.

SILLY little Mary,
  Sulking all the day,
While the other children
  Run about and play.

Silly little Mary
 Wears a peevish look,
When she sees the others
 Laughing at the brook.

Silly little Mary
 Will not skip or swing,
Won't at puss-in-corner play,
 Won't do anything.

Silly little Mary
 Hides behind the bank,
In among the roots and weeds,
 All so thick and rank.

FOR A SMALL GIRL.

THE other girls and boys in school
 All said I was too young
To stand up here, like them, and use
 My hands, and feet, and tongue.

But *now* I guess they'll own that I
 Am quite as smart as they,
For all my speech is not as long
 As some the rest may say.

WORDS OF WELCOME.

KIND friends and dear parents, we welcome you
    here
To our nice pleasant school-room, and teacher so
    dear;
We wish but to show how much we have learned,
And how to our lessons our hearts have been
    turned.

But hope you'll remember we all are quite young,
And when we have spoken, recited and sung,
You will pardon our blunders, which, as all are
    aware,
May even extend to the President's chair.

Our life is a school time, and till that shall end,
With our Father in heaven for teacher and friend,
O let us perform well each task that is given,
Till our time of probation is ended in heaven.

TO BED.

I KNOW a little boy,
    And have often heard it said
That he never was so tired
    That he wished to go to bed.
Though he scarcely can hold up
    His drowsy little head,
Yet this very foolish boy
    Cannot bear to go to bed.

When the big golden sun
　Has lain down to sleep;
When the lambs every one
　Are lying by the sheep;
When underneath its wing
　Every chick tucks its head,—
Still this odd little boy
　Does not like to go to bed.

FOR A VERY LITTLE BOY.

IT'S very hard, kind friends, for me
　To stand up here, with trembling knee,
And see so many people's eyes
Cast on a boy of my small size;
But then I thought I'd take my place,
And, soldier-like, the music face.
I've tried my hardest to please you,
You may believe me this is true;
Your kind attention (ere we part)
I thank you for with all my heart!

AN OPENING ADDRESS.

I am a very little boy (or girl), and I suppose that is why the teacher puts me first to-day. But I am big enough to tell you that we are very glad to see you.

I hope you will like our school very much. We will sing our best songs, and say our prettiest verses, and be just as good as we can all the time you stay, for we want you to come again.

WHERE IS MAMMA?

I CANNOT find my mamma!
    Where do you think she can be?
She said she was going down to the store,
    To buy a pound of tea.

And I'm sure she's been gone a hundred years,
    I'm as lonesome as I can be!
Please tell her if you see her,
    To hurry home to me.

I'm tired of my doll and the kitty,
    And the baby just cries and cries;
I've tried and tried to rock him to sleep,
    But he won't even shut his eyes.

So, please, if you see my mamma,
    Tell her to hurry home to me,
For I'm sure I want her very much more
    Than she wants a pound of tea.

LITTLE, BUT "SPUNKY."

I AM little, but I'm "spunky,"
    As you now may plainly tell;
All the session I have studied
    Every lesson very well.
Now I'm glad that school is over,
    And with books and work I'm done,
For I want to take vacation,
    And have "lots" of play and fun.

ONLY A BABY SMALL.

ONLY a baby small,
  Dropped from the skies;
Only a laughing face,
  Two sunny eyes;
Only two cherry lips,
  One chubby nose;
Only two little hands
  Ten little toes.

Only a golden head,
  Curly and soft;
Only a tongue that wags
  Loudly and oft;
Only a little brain,
  Empty of thought;
Only a little heart,
  Troubled with nought.

Only a tender flower
  Sent us to rear;
Only a life to love
  While we are here;
Only a baby small,
  Never at rest;
Small, but how dear to us,
  God knoweth best.

GOOD-NIGHT LITTLE STAR.

GOOD-NIGHT, little star!
    I will go to my bed
And leave you to burn
    While I lay down my head.

On my pillow I'll sleep
    Till the morning light,
Then you will be fading
    And I shall be bright.

WELCOME.

KIND friends, we welcome you to-day,
    With songs of merry glee,
Your loving smiles we strive to win,
    Each face we love to see.

Sweet welcomes then to one and all,
    And may your smiles approve;
And may we never miss the light
    Of faces that we love.

THROWING KISSES.

DON'T think, dear friends, that I'm too small
    To fill a place like this;
I'm big enough to love you all,
    And throw you all a kiss.

A little word, a look, a smile,
　　Will never come amiss;
Takes but a moment, as you see,
　　To throw you all a kiss.

It may be that you have at home
　　Some boy, or little sis,
Who laughs, and peeps, and when you go
　　Throws after you a kiss.

MAMMA'S KISSES.

A KISS when I wake in the morning,
　　A kiss when I go to bed,
A kiss when I burn my fingers,
　　A kiss when I bump my head.

A kiss when my bath is over,
　　A kiss when my bath begins;
My mamma is full of kisses,
　　As full as a nurse is of pins.

A kiss when I give her trouble,
　　A kiss when I give her joy;
There's nothing like mamma's kisses
　　To her own little baby boy!

THE TOAD.

I'VE heard a song about the frogs,
    And bees with pretty wings,
And what a very pleasant note
    The little robin sings.

But oh! no poet ever yet
    Has greatly praised the toad,
Oft seated on his haunches,
    A-winking in the road!

He's neither tall nor stately,
    And he looks very old; .
His skin all wrinkled, tough and brown—
    It keeps out wet and cold.

He's very strange, ugly and coarse,
    And surely very odd;
He sets all the children laughing
    When he leaps o'er the sod.

But the old toad is quite friendly,
    And he seems very wise
Coming out from the old door-stone
    To catch the little flies.

Lucy S. Ruggles.

FROWNS AND SNEERS.

FOOLISH things are frowns and sneers,
    For angry thoughts reveal them,
Rather drown them all in tears,
    Than let another feel them.

SPEECH FOR A SMALL BOY.

Nobody knows how hard I've tried
　　To learn a speech to say,
And be up with the other boys,
　　Who all show off to-day.

But now I'm here, I am afraid
　　I never will get through;
For I am badly scared, you see,
　　And scarce know what to do.

I haven't much to say, because
　　I am so very small,
But anything is better than
　　To make no speech at all.

TRIP LIGHTLY.

Trip lightly over trouble.
　　Trip lightly over wrong;
We only make it double,
　　By dwelling on it long.

Trip lightly over sorrow,
　　Though this day may be dark,
The sun may shine to-morrow,
　　And gayly sing the lark.

Fair hope has not departed,
　　Though roses may have fled;
Then never be down-hearted,
　　But look for joy instead.

A FIRST IMPRESSION.

I RECOLLECT a nurse called Ann
Who carried me about the grass,
And one fine day a fine young man
Came up and kissed the pretty lass.
She did not make the least objection.
Thinks I, "Ah,
When I can talk I'll tell mamma"—
And *that's my* earliest recollection.

FOR A VERY SMALL GIRL.

I AM a merry little girl,
And if I had my way,
I'd never go to school at all,
But with my dollies play.
I wish some one would come along
And steal the school-house key,
Then all the boys and girls could play—
How happy we would be!
I hope the audience will excuse
The shortness of my speech;
And now I'm done, I'll say good-bye,
And kiss my hand to each.

NO BABY IN THE HOUSE.

NO baby in the house I know,
'Tis far too nice and clean.

No toys, by careless fingers strewn,
    Upon the floors are seen.
No finger-marks are on the panes,
    No scratches on the chairs;
No wooden men set up in rows,
    Or marshalled off in pairs;
No little stockings to be darned,
    All ragged at the toes;
No pile of mending to be done,
    Made up of baby-clothes;
No little troubles to be soothed;
    No little hands to fold;
No grimy fingers to be washed;
    No stories to be told;
No tender kisses to be given;
    No nicknames "Dove," or "Mouse;"
No merry frolics after tea—
    No baby in the house.
          Clara G. Dolliver.

ALL THINGS LOVE ME.

O LITTLE flowers! you love me so,
    You could not do without me;
O little birds that come and go!
    You sing sweet songs about me;
O little moss, observed by few,
    That round the tree is creeping!
You like my head to rest on you,
    When I am idly sleeping.

MY KITTENS.

MY dear little kittens!—my five little darlings!—
　　I loved you—the gray ones, the spotted, the
　　　　white;
I brought you your breakfast of warm milk each
　　　　morning,
　　And saw you all lap it with keenest delight.

You played, too, so merry and cunning together;
　　Your mother would watch while she laid in the
　　　　straw
A-winking her eyes in the warm sunny weather,
　　And giving you sometimes a tap with her paw.

You would pull at her tail, at her ears you would
　　　　nibble;
　　You had no respect for her gray hairs at all;
I am sure, though, she liked it, but sometimes she
　　　　scolded,
　　And said, in cat-language, "Be off with you,
　　　　all!"

But one day poor Whitey, the prettiest darling
　　Of all these five kittens, grew sick and then died;
I never again could have such a sweet kitten,
　　And oh how I grieved, and how sadly I cried!

I went out and dug her a grave in the garden,
　　And lined it all softly with leaves and with
　　　　moss;

I brought to the burial her brothers and sisters,
  Thinking that they, too, would mourn for her
    loss.

But the heartless things capered and whisked all
    around me—
  They chased a bright butterfly, searched for a
    mouse,
Jumped for the bird that sang up in the pear tree;
  I whipped them and sent them all back to the
    house.

Then I filled up the grave and I rounded it over,
  And made it a border of white pearly stone,
And on it I planted a nice root of catnip,
  Then I left little Whitey to sleep all alone.

One day, Tom, the bad boy who lives round the
    corner,
  Stole Spotty and Grayback—I called help too
    late!
He never would tell where he carried the darlings,
  And I sigh when I think of their probable fate.

Then I had but two left me, and these a good
    neighbor
  Adopted and brought up with kindness and
    care;
Their mother and I were both sorry to lose them,
  But we knew it was best for them both to be
    there.

BIRDIE AND BABY.

WHAT does little birdie say,
In her nest at peep of day?
"Let me fly," says little birdie,
"Mother, let me fly away."

"Birdie, rest a little longer,
Till the little wings are stronger,"
So she rests a little longer,
Then she flies away.

What does little baby say,
In her bed at peep of day?
Baby says, like little birdie,
"Let me rise and fly away,"

"Baby, sleep a little longer,
Till the little limbs are stronger.
If she sleeps a little longer,
Baby, too, shall fly away."

FAULTS OF OTHERS.

WHAT are others' faults to me?
I've not a vulture's bill,
To peck at every flaw I see,
And make it wider still.

It is enough for me to know
I've follies of my own;
And on my heart the care bestow,
And let my friends alone.

SPEECH FOR A BOY.

NOBODY knows the nerve it takes
    To rise up in a crowd,
And speak out so that all can hear,
    With voice both clear and loud,
For often men of sense have failed,
    When *first* they'd try to speak,
And ere they could pronounce a word;
    Begin to feel quite weak.

So you, therefore, must not expect
    Great things from one so small;
I'd rather make a little speech
    Than to say none at all.
No man can ever get to be
    Renown'd, or great, or wise,
Unless, when he is small and young,
    He bravely strives to rise.

I've done my very best, kind friends,
    This to my credit score;
For you will readily agree,
    "Angels can do no more!"

THE BEE AND THE BUTTERFLY.

"DEAR me, dear me,"
    Said a busy bee;
"I'm always making honey.
    No time to play

But work all day;
    Isn't it very funny,
Very, very funny?"

"Oh, my, oh, my,"
    Said a butterfly,
"I'm always eating honey.
    And yet I play
The livelong day,
    Isn't it very funny,
Very, very funny?"

THE MORNING CALL.

*A young lady comes on stage, walks to front, stops.
Just then a knock is heard, and in walks a tiny
miss. (Young Lady.)*

    "WONDER who is knocking;
        Why, Mamie, is it you?
Walk, in, take off your bonnet,
    How does my darling do? (*Kissing her.*)

(*Little Miss.*)
    "I'se pitty well, I thank 'ou,
        But twasn't nice at all,
For 'ou to kiss me, auntie,
        Because I's come to call.

"My name is Mrs. Gookins—
    My husband he is dead—

I'se got twelve little chil'ren,
    They're all at home in bed.

"And now I must be going,
    I'se so much work, you see,
Next time I'll bring my babies,
    And then we'll stay to tea."

MR. TONGUE.

MY friend Mr. Tongue
    He lives in my mouth,
He's as red as a rose,
    And as warm as the south;
He has not a foot,
    Yet how quickly he goes,
My little friend Tongue,
    As red as a rose.

FOR A SMALL BOY.

THERE are some things that puzzle me,
    Boy as I am; these things I see—
For instance: Men who dress quite fine,
They smoke cigars and drink rich wine;
And others swill down lager beer,
Till on the street they scarce can steer;
And yet, when they go home, they swear,
They haven't got a cent to spare;
Their children need both bread and meat,

And shoes to cover naked feet;
Their wives don't have a copper cent,
Because *they* sew to pay the rent.
Now these are things I daily see,
And, as I said, they puzzle me.

LITTLE BLUE BELL.

UP where the meadow grass
    Leans toward the river,
Stood little blue bell,
    All in a shiver.

Oh, little blue bell,
    Do, then, look up;
Some kind cloud will give you
    A drop in your cup.

At dawn little blue bell
    Held gracefully up
Her silent thanksgiving—
    The dew in her cup!

BE PLEASANT.

WHEN little ones worry,
    Their parents are sorry,
And all who are near them look sad:
    But when they are good,
    And smile as they should,
Their friends are contented and glad.

How much better it is
  To be cheerful and sing,
Than to deserve to be called
  A cross old thing.

SPEECH FOR A LITTLE GIRL.

I NEVER made a speech before;
  But that's no reason why,
Because I never spoke before,
  I ought not now to try.

There are some silly little girls,
  Who are afraid to speak,
For fear some one will laugh at them;
  I think this very weak.

I hope I'll always have the sense
  To do as I am told;
Then people will not laugh at me,
  Or think I am too bold.

A LITTLE BOY'S SPEECH.

I AM a little boy, you see,
  Not higher much than pappy's knee;
Some of the big boys said that I,
  To make a speech ought not to try.
This raised my spunk, and I am here,
  Small as to you I may appear.
And though my voice, I know is weak,
  I'll show these boys that I *can* speak.

THE THREE LITTLE KITTENS.

THREE little kittens met one day,
  Right on top of a load of hay.

They were black and white and brindle gray,
And full of frolic, the livelong day.

They arched their backs, and hissed and spit,
And swelled their sides, till you'd think they'd split.

So there they stood with glaring eyes,
And tails like a dusting brush in size.

Then three small voices cried: Mew! Mew!
I don't know you, but how do you do!

Well, they all rubbed noses, and made up friends,
And so right here my story ends.

THE LITTLE DUTCHMAN.

OH, I'm a little Tuchman,
  My name is Van der Dose,
An' vat I cannot get to eat,
  I smells it mit my nose.

An' ven dey vill not let me blay,
  I takes it out in vork;
An' ven dey makes me vork too hard,
  I soon de job will shirk.

An' ven dey sends me off to ped,
  I lays avake all night;

An' ven. dey comes to vake me up,
    I shuts my eyes up tight.

For I'm a little Tuchman,
    My name is Van der Dose,
An' vat I do not know myself,
    I never vants to knows.

WHAT WILLIE SAID.

HEAR what a little child would say,
    Who comes to school each pleasant day,
And tries to learn his lessons well,
    A good report at home to tell.

I love the school, and teacher dear,
    And all the scholars gathered here;
To each I say in simple rhyme,
    Be careful and not waste your time.

For moments spent in life's young day,
    In useless or in thoughtless play,
Will cast a shade o'er future years,
    And cause you many sighs and tears.

SPRING HAS COME.

SPRING has come back to us, beautiful spring!
    Blue-birds and swallows are out on the wing;
    Over the meadows a carpet of green
Softer and richer than velvet are seen.

Up come the blossoms so bright and so gay,
    Giving sweet odors to welcome the May.
Sunshine and music are flooding the air,
    Beauty and brightness are everywhere.

THE LITTLE SHEPHERDESS.

MARY had a little lamb,
    Its fleece was white as snow,
"Oh, we know that so well," you say,
    "Say something we don't know!"

But you don't know this Mary,
    And though this lamb can play
He never followed her to school,
    Never a single day!

This Mary plays at shepherdess,
    And with her pretty crook,
She guides her sheep in pleasant paths,
    Down by the shaded brook.

ON TIME.

I'M the boy who's "on time" through by day-light. When the sun wakes up in the morning, he says, "Who's that 'round so early?" I guess he'd have to be spry to get his face washed before I do. As soon as the old roosters hear me up they all begin to crow. Who's afraid of a little snow or mud? They don't scare ME any; when the bell rings for school I'm THERE.

LITTLE TODDLEKINS.

POOR little Toddlekins,
 All full o' sketer-bites,
Bodder him awful,
 Baby can't sleep o'nights.
Buzzing all over him,
 Singing and tickling,
In and out, round about,
 Nipping and prickling.
Poor little Toddlekins,
 All full o' sketer-bites,
Bodder him awful,
 Can't even sleep o' nights.

PRESCRIPTION FOR SPRING FEVER.

TAKE the open air,
 The more you take the better
Follow Nature's laws,
 To the very letter.
Let the doctors go
 To the Bay of Biscay,
Let alone the gin,
 The brandy and the whisky.
Freely exercise;
 Keep your spirits cheerful;

Let no dread of sickness
　Make you ever fearful.
Eat the simplest food,
　Drink the pure cold water,
Then you will be well,
　Or at least you ought to.

------◆------

THE VIOLET.

DOWN in a green and shady bed
　　A modest violet grew;
Its stalk was bent, it hung its head
　As if to hide from view.

·And yet it was a lovely flower,
　Its colors bright and fair;
It might have graced a rosy bower
　Instead of hiding there.

Yet there it was content to bloom,
　In modest tints arrayed;
And there diffused its sweet perfume
　Within the silent glade.

Then let me to the valley go,
　This pretty flower to see,
That I may also learn to grow
　In sweet humility.

　　　　　　　　　　JANE TAYLOR.

NO GOOD REASON.

I NEVER could find a good reason
  Why sorrow, unbidden, should stay,
And all the bright joys of life's season
  Be driven unheeded away.
Our cares would make no more emotion
  Were we to our lot but resigned,
Than pebbles flung into the ocean,
  That leave scarce a ripple behind.

NOBODY'S DOG.

ONLY a dirty black and white dog!
  You can see him any day,
Trotting meekly from street to street.
  He almost seems to say,
As he looks in your face with wistful eye,
  "I don't mean to be in your way."

His tail hangs drooping between his legs;
  His body is thin and spare;
How he envies the sleek and well-fed dogs
  That thrive on their master's care!
And he wonders what they must think of him
  And grieves at his own hard fare.

Sometimes he sees a friendly face—
  A face that he seems to know;

And thinks he may be the master
    That he lost so long ago;
And even dares to follow him home,
    For he loved his master so.

Poor Jack! He's only mistaken again,
    And stoned and driven back;
But he's used to disappointment now,
    And takes up his beaten track;
Nobody's dog, for nobody cares
    For poor, unfortunate Jack.

FOR A SMALL BOY.

I AM quite small to go to school,
    But you can see I am no fool!
I've studied hard this speech to say,
    And now I'll bow and go away.

                          (Bows.)

A CHILD'S THOUGHT.

DEAR birdie, I love you,
    So blithely you sing;
Now perched on the tree-top,
    Now soaring on the wing.

You never seem weary,
  Though swiftly you fly,
So far—far away—
  Through the beautiful sky.

But then mamma says,
  Some day when I die—
My soul shall have wings
  And I'll find the blue sky.

HOE YOUR OWN ROW.

I THINK there are some maxims
    Under the sun,
Scarce worth preservation;
  But here, boys, is one
So sound and so simple
  'Tis worth while to know—
And all in the single line,
  "Hoe your own row!"

If you want to have riches, .
  And want to have friends,
Don't trample the means down
  And look for the ends;
But always remember,
  Wherever you go
The wisdom of practising
  "Hoe your own row!"

A LITTLE GIRL'S SPEECH.

MY pa and ma will be surprised
    To hear me speak to-day;
For neither of them thought that I
    Would have a word to say.

I hope they will be pleased, for oh,
    I've studied hard to make
This little speech, because I learned
    To say it for their sake.

———•———

MY LITTLE HUSBAND.

I HAVE a little husband,
    And he has gone to sea;
The winds that whistle round his ship
    Fly home to me.

———•———

"THEY SAY."

THE subject of my speech is one
    We hear of every day—
'Tis simply all about the fear
    We have of what "*they say!*"

How happy all of us could be,
    If—as we go our way—
We did not stop to think and care
    So much for what "*they say.*"

We never dress to go outside,
  To church, to ball, or play,
But everything we wear or do
  Is ruled by what "*they say.*"

Half of the struggles we each make
  To keep up a display,
Might be avoided, were it not
  For dread of what "*they say.*"

The half of those who leave their homes
  For Long Branch and Cape May
Would never go, if it were not
  For fear of what "*they say.*"

One reason why I'm now so scared
  (Pardon the weakness, pray!)
Is that I'm thinking all the while,
  "Of *me* what will ' *they say?*' "

But so 'twill be, I judge, as long
  As on the earth folks stay—
There'll always be, with wise and fools,
  That dread of what "*they say.*"

LITTLE WHIMPY.

WHIMPY, little Whimpy,
  Cried so much one day.
He was waiting by the window

When they all came home to tea,
And a gladder boy than Whimpy
You never need hope to see.

MISS TIDY.

LITTLE Miss Tidy
Is neat as a pin;
She wipes her feet neatly
Whene'er she comes in.

She folds her clothes smoothly
When going to rest ;
Of all little girls
She's the nicest and best.

FOR A LITTLE GIRL.

I LOVE my papa, that I do,
And mamma says she loves him too;
And both of them love me, I know,
A thousand ways their love they show.
But papa says he fears some day
With some mean scamp I'll run away.

SOUR GRAPES.

A FOX was trotting on one day,
And just above his head
He spied a vine of luscious grapes,
Rich, ripe, and purple-red;

Eager he tried to snatch the fruit,
　But, ah! it was too high!
Poor Reynard had to give it up,
　And, heaving a deep sigh,
He curl'd his nose and said, "Dear me!
　I would not waste an hour
Upon such mean and common fruit—
　I'm sure those grapes are sour!"
'Tis thus we often wish thro' life,
　When seeking wealth and pow'r;
And when we fail, say, like the fox,
　We're "*sure the grapes are sour!*"

HOLIDAY SPEECH.

WE hail our coming holiday,
　So full of frolic, fun and play.
'Tis true we love our teachers well,
They've taught us how to read and spell;
But children must from study rest,
E'en when they learn their very best;
All work, however, and no play,
Makes a dull boy of Jack, folks say.

AN ORATION FOR A BOY.

I RISE to make this short oration,
　Without the least equivocation,
Or any false exaggeration,
And hope to win your approbation—

If not your warmest admiration.
I want to make a revelation,
Just for the sake of exultation,
Without a long enumeration,
In reference to education;
For, since our school association
We feel a high appreciation
Of teachers' kind administration.
Whate'er may be our destination,
We'll have the pleasing consolation
Of living in high estimation
With all our teachers, in relation
With every day's assimilation.
I hope you'll have the penetration
To see this is my own creation,
And quite a novel adaptation.
Please pardon the conglomeration,
For I am scared like all the nation,
Therefore accept my resignation.

MAKE YOUR MARK.

IN the quarries should you toil,
    Make your mark;
Do not delve upon the soil,
    Make your mark;
In whatever path you go,

In whatever place you stand—
Moving swift or moving slow—
   With a firm but honest hand,
   Make your mark.

HURRAH!

HURRAH for the sunny day!
   Hurrah for the lovely flowers!
Hurrah for the happy way
   We spend our evening hours!
All the day we work or play
   Together with our might,
And when our bed-time comes,
   We say to all—GOOD-NIGHT!

BABY SISTER.

I'VE a baby sister,
   A wee thing and simple;
There's a dint in her cheek,
   They call it a dimple.

She has a little hand
   Doubled up in a fist,
And a red, rosy mouth,
   Sweet enough tc be kissed.

Her face, like an apple
   That is well baked and sweet,
Looks soft, red and wrinkled,
   So do her tiny feet.

Mamma says I must love
   This queer little stranger;
And when she runs about
   Keep her out of danger.

I don't need a sister!
   She's only in the way;
So don't bring another
   Here, good doctor, I pray!
                     Lucy S. Ruggles.

A BOY'S TROUBLES.

AUNT LIBBY patted me on the head the other day, and said, "George, my boy, this is the happiest part of your life." I guess Aunt Libby don't know much. I guess she never worked a week to make a kite, and the first time she went to fly it got the tail hitched to a tall tree, whose owner would not let her climb up to get it. I guess she never broke one of the runners of her sled some Saturday afternoon when it was prime coasting. I guess she never had to give her new humming-top to quiet the baby, and had the paint all sucked off. I guess she never saved all her pennies a whole winter to buy a trumpet, and then was told she must not blow it because it would make a noise. No; Aunt Libby don't know much. How should she? *She never was a boy.*

--------•-•---------

CHARLIE'S SPEECH.

BROTHER WILL has said his piece,
  I'll try my little hand,
Although I own it's pretty hard,
  Before so many folks to stand.

Little folks should not be heard,
  Only seen, some people say;
So I will end my little speech,
  Since you have all *seen me* to-day.

--------•-•---------

HAPPY IS MY NAME.

I'M a little Fairy,
  Dancing everywhere
In the children's faces,
  See me bright and fair

In their merry voices,
  In their romping play,
Children, don't you know me?
  I come every day.

If you will not take me,
  What have I to say?
I am always ready,
  For your work or play.

I have brought you sunshine,
  Every time I came,
I have lightened labor,
  Happy is my name!

DOING NOTHING.

WORTHLESS, wicked boys I've seen
  Doing nothing;
And they grew up worthless men,
  Doing nothing;
Life to them a failure proved,
As they spent it, all unloved,
  Doing nothing.

MORNING.

LET'S up and be doing,
  The morning is bright
We hail it with rapture,
  With sweetest delight.

The east is all dazzling,
　　With azure and gold,
The roses are fragrant,
　　And sweet to behold.

The sunlight is playing
　　On tree-top and hill,
And dew-drops are shining
　　Beside the dark rill.

The birds carol sweetly,
　　To hail the new spring,
And "May-day is coming,"
　　The school-children sing.

How bright is the morning,
　　How golden its hours!
All nature is glowing
　　With sunshine and flowers.

Let's up and be doing,
　　The dark night is past,
Cast bread on the waters,
　　'Twill come back at last.
　　　　　　　　LUCY S. RUGGLES.

TWO LITTLE MAGPIES SAT ON A WALL.

TWO magpies sat on a garden rail,
　　As it might be Wednesday week;
And one little magpie wagged his tail
　　In the other little magpie's beak.

And, doubling like a fist his little claw-hand,
  Said the other, "Upon my word,
This is more than flesh or blood can stand
  Of magpie or any bird."

So they pecked and they scratched each other's eyes,
  Till all that was left on the rail
Was the beak of one of the little magpies
  And the other little magpies tail!

THE EARLY BIRDS.

THE little birds are wide awake,
  So early in the morn;
Just think how funny it would be
  To see the robins yawn.

To hear the little sparrow say,
  "Oh dear! 'tis hardly light!
Mamma, I want to sleep some more,"—
  'Twould make you laugh outright.

They hop out of their little nest,
  So cosy and so warm,
And sing their merry morning song
  In sunshine and in storm.

A MITE SONG.

ONLY a drop in the bucket,
  But every drop will tell,
The bucket would soon be empty
  Without the drops in the well.

Only a poor little penny,
  It was all I had to give;
But as pennies make the dollars,
  It may help some cause to live.

A few little bits of ribbon
  And some toys that were not new,
But they made the sick child happy,
  Which has made me happy too

Only some outgrown garments,
  They were all I had to spare,
But they'll help to clothe the needy,
  And the poor are everywhere.

A word now and then of comfort
  That cost me nothing to say;
But the poor old man died happy,
  And it helped him on the way.

God loveth the cheerful giver,
  Though the gift be poor and small;
What doth he think of his children
  When they never give at all?

A BOY'S DREAM.

NINE grenadiers with bayonets on their guns;
Nine baker's baskets with hot cross buns;
Nine brown elephants standing in a row;
Nine new velocipedes—good ones to go;
Nine Knickerbocker suits with buttons all complete;
Nine pairs of skates with straps for the feet;
Nine little drummer boys beating on their drums;
Nine fat Aldermen sitting on their thumbs;
Nine times running—I dreamt it all plain.
With bread and cheese for supper I could dream it
    all again.

"YOURS TRULY, SIR."

A RICH old bachelor once asked
    A lady fair to see,
"If you were not yourself, dear Miss,
    Who would you rather be?"
Beneath his earnest gaze she dropp'd
    Her lovely eyes and sighed,—
"I'd rather be yours truly, sir!"
    She blushingly replied.

ONLY FIVE.

I AM a very litte girl,
    I'm only five years old;
I hope that none who hear me speak
    Will think I am too bold.

THE CHICKENS.

SAID the first little chicken,
　　With a queer little squirm,
"I wish I could find
　　A fat little worm."

Said the next little chicken,
　　With an odd little shrug,
"I wish I could find
　　A fat little slug,"

Said the third little chicken,
　　With a sharp little squeal,
"I wish I could find
　　Some nice yellow meal."

Said the fourth little chicken,
　　With a small sigh of grief,
"I wish I could find
　　A little green leaf."

Said the fifth little chicken,
　　With a faint little moan,
"I wish I could find
　　A wee gravel stone."

"Now, see here," said the mother,
　　From the green garden patch,
"If you want any breakfast,
　　Just come here and scratch."

THE LITTLE DREAMER.

A LITTLE boy was dreaming,
  Upon his mother's lap,
That the pins fell out of all the stars,
  And the stars fell in his cap!

So, when his dream was over,
  What should this little boy do?
Why, he went and looked inside his **cap**,
  And found it was'nt true!

SPEAK THE TRUTH.

S PEAK the truth!
  Speak it boldy, never fear;
Speak it so that all may hear;
In the end it shall appear
Truth is best in age and youth.
Speak the truth.

LITTLE MIDGET.

M Y papa sometimes scolds and **says**,
  I'm always in a fidget;
But mamma says, I keep quite still
  For such a little midget.

My teacher said to-day, she thought
  That it was very smart
For such a little thing as I
  To learn a speech "by heart."

HOW THE BABIES GROW.

BABY wee, baby wee!
  What does little baby see?
All among her pillows lying,
Never fretful, never crying;
    Caper and crow, caper and crow!
    That's the way that babies grow!

Baby fair, baby fair!
Rosy cheeks and curly hair,
All among her pillows playing,
Little chubby hands displaying;
    Caper and crow, caper and crow!
    That's the way that babies grow!

                    JENNIE CARROLL.

USEFUL LITTLE WORDS.

HEARTS, like doors, can ope with **ease**
  To very, very little keys;
And don't forget that they are these:
"*I thank you, sir,*" and, "*If you please.*"

Then let us watch these little things,
    And so respect each other;
That not a word, or look, or tone,
    May wound a friend or brother.

THE QUEEN IN HER CARRIAGE.

OH, the queen in her carriage is passing by;
　　Her cheeks are like roses, her eyes like the sky;
Her wonderful teeth are as white as new milk;
Her pretty blonde hair is softer than silk.

She's the loveliest monarch that ever was seen;
You ask of what country the darling is queen;
Her empire extends not to far-distant parts,
She is queen of our household, the mistress of hearts.

For scepter she lifts her soft, dimpled hands;
Her subjects all hasten to heed her commands;
Her smile is bewitching, and fearful her frown,
And all must obey when she puts her foot down.

May blessings descend on the bright little head,
From the time she awakes till she's safely in bed;
And now do you guess, when I speak of the queen,
'Tis only our six-months' baby I mean?

MY WEEK.

ON Monday I wash my dollie's clothes,
　　On Tuesday smoothly press 'em;
On Wednesday mend their little hose,
　　On Thursday neatly dress 'em.

On Friday I play they're taken ill,
　　On Saturday something or other,
But when Sunday comes, I say, "Lie still;
　　I'm going to church with mother."

THE MINUTES.

WE are but minutes—little things!
　　Each one furnished with sixty wings,
With which we fly on our unseen track,
And not a minute ever comes back.

We are but minutes, yet each one bears
A little burden of joy or cares;
Take patiently the minutes of pain—
The worst of minutes cannot remain.

We are but minutes; when we bring
A few of the drop's from pleasure's spring,
Taste their sweetness while yet we stray,
It takes but a minute to fly away.

We are but minutes—use us well,
For how we are used we must some day tell.
Who uses minutes, has hours to use;
Who loses minutes, whole years must lose.

THE BUSY BEE.

"BUSY bee! busy bee!
　　Where is your home?"
"In truth, pretty maiden,
　　I live in a comb."

"And you, little rabbit,
　　Where do you rush?"
"I rush to my home, dear,
　　Under the brush!"

I'M VERY YOUNG.

I'M very young! but what of that?
  You once were young as I;
And you don't know what I can do
  Until you see me try.

I cannot tell you all I know—
  I guess I won't tell half;
For if I should I'm very sure
  You'd only sit and laugh.

GIVE THE LITTLE BOYS A CHANCE.

LITTLE hands will soon be strong
  For the work that they must do;
Little lips will sing their song
  When these early days are through.
So, you big boys, if we're small,
  On our toes you needn't dance;
There is room enough for all—
  Give the little boys a chance.

THE STARS.

WE cannot count the stars on high,
  We only see them shine;
We only know the gracious hand
  That made them is divine.

LITTLE FOXES.

AMONG my tender vines I spy,
 A little fox named "By-and-By."

Then set upon him, quick, I say,
The swift young hunter "Right Away."

Around each tender vine I plant,
I find the little fox "I Can't!

Then fast as ever hunter ran,
Chase him with brave and bold "I Can."

"No Use in Trying!" lags and whines
This fox among my tender vines.

Then drive him low and drive him high,
With this good hunter named "I'll try."

Among the vines in my small lot,
Creeps in the fox "I Forgot."

Then hunt him out and to his den,
With "I-Will-Not-Forget-Again."

A little fox is hidden there
Among my vines, named "I Don't Care."

Then let "I'm sorry," hunter true
Chase him far from vines and you.

STOP, STOP, PRETTY WATER.

"STOP, stop, pretty water!"
    Said Mary, one day,
To a frolicsome brook
    That was running away.

"You run on so fast!
    I wish you would stay;
My boat and my flowers
    You will carry away.

"But I will run after
    Mother says that I may;
For I would know where
    You are running away."

So Mary ran on;
    But I have heard say
That she never could find
    Where the brook ran away.

MRS. FOLLEN.

BABY.

WHO is it coos just like a dove?
    Who is it that we dearly love—
The brightest blessing from above?
            Our baby.

While silent watch the angels keep,
Who smiles so sweetly in his sleep,
And oft displays his dimples deep?
            Our baby.

THE BABY SLEEPS.

BABY sleeps, so we must tread
  Softly round her little bed,
And be careful that our toys
  Do not fall and make a noise.

We must not talk, but whisper low;
  Mother wants to work, you know,
That when father comes to tea,
  All may eat and cheerful be.

FUNNY, ISN'T IT?

THE pipers are not made of pipes,
  And cowards are not made of cows;
And lyres are not made of lies,
  While bowers are not made of bows.
The wickets are not made of wicks,
  And candles are not made of cans;
And tickets are not made of ticks,
  While panels are not made of pans.
The cattle are not made of cats,
  While willows are not made of wills,
And battles are not made of bats,
  And pilgrims not made of grim pills,
The cornets are are not made of corns,
  A hotel is not made of a hoe;
And hornets are not made of horns,
  While all poets cannot be Poe.

TALE OF A DOG AND A BEE.

GREAT big dog,
   Head upon his toes;
Tiny little bee
   Settles on his nose.

Great big dog
   Thinks it is a fly,
Never says a word,
   Winks mighty sly.

Tiny little bee
   Tickles dog's nose—
Thinks like as not
   'Tis a blooming rose.

Dog smiles a smile,
   Winks his other eye,
Chuckles to himself
   How he'll catch a fly.

Then he makes a snap,
   Mighty quick and spry,
Gets the little bug,
   But doesn't catch the fly.

Tiny little bee,
   Alive and looking well,
Great big dog,
   Mostly gone to swell

MORAL.

Dear friends and brothers, all,
    Don't be too fast and free,
And when you catch a fly
    Be sure it ain't a bee.

THE RAIN.

DEAR rain, without your help, I know,
    The trees and flowers could not grow,
My roses all would fade and die,
If you staid up behind the sky!

But lonely little girls like me
Don't like to stay indoors, you see,
And through the long and lonesome day—
I'm tired of books, I'm tired of play.

I'm tired of listening to the sound
Of pattering drops upon the ground,
And watching through the misty pane
The clouded skies, O dreary rain!

And so I wish you'd tell me why,
Just to please me, you couldn't try
To let the bright sun shine all day,
And in the night, when he's away,

And all the world is dark and still.
And I'm asleep—*then*, if you will,
Come down and make my flowers grow,
Dear rain, and I will love you so.

WORK WHILE YOU WORK.

WORK while you work,
  And play while you play,
That is the way
To be cheerful and gay.
All that you do,
Do with your might,
Things done by halves
Are never done right;
One thing at once,
And that done well,
Is a very good rule,
As wise men tell.
Moments are useless,
Trifled away—
Work while you work,
And play while you play,

BEAUTY EVERYWHERE.

THERE is beauty in the forest,
  When the trees are green and fair
There is beauty in the meadow,
  Where wild flowers scent the air;
There is beauty in the sunlight,
  And the soft, blue sky above;
Oh, the world is full of beauty
  When the heart is full of love!
                    —W. L. SMITH.

WASHING DISHES.

LET boys have all the sport they will,
   In running, walking, riding—
The girls a surer pleasure have,
   And one that's more abiding.
The boys may hunt and fly their kites,
   Or try all day for fishes;
But, oh! there's nothing in the world
   So nice as washing dishes.

There's much to see and talk about
   Within this world of ours;
There's much to love and to admire
   In poetry and flowers;
But there cannot be a girl found
   Who asks, or hopes, or wishes
For any better picture than
   The fun of washing dishes.
        —CARRIE E. ELLIS.

"WHEN I AM BIG."

WHEN I am big I mean to buy
   A dozen platters of pumpkin pie,
A barrel of nuts, to have 'em handy,
And fifty pounds of sugar candy.

When I am big, I mean to wear
A long-tailed coat, and crop my hair;
I'll buy a paper, and read the news,
And sit up late whenever I choose.

THE LARK.

BIRD of the wilderness,
  Blithesome and cumberless,
Sweet be thy matin o'er moorland and lea!
  Emblem of happiness,
  Blest is thy dwelling-place—
Oh, to abide in the desert with thee!
  Wild is thy lay and loud,
  Far in the downy cloud;
Love gives it energy—love gave it birth:
  Where, on thy dewy wing—
  Where art thou journeying?
Thy lay is in heaven—thy love is on earth.

JAMES HOGG.

UPSIDE DOWN.

IF all the world were upside down,
  Our lilies would be stars so gay,
  Our brooks would make the milky **way,**
  And roses of the richest dye
  Would be the pretty sunset sky;
Instead of blue, the sky'd be brown—
If all the world were upside down.

If all the world were upside down,
  The moon would take the ocean's place,
  And stars the fields and gardens grace;

The ground, of course, would be sky blue;
  Another change would be quite new—
We'd wear our shoes upon our crown
If all the world were upside down.

GEORGE COOPER.

OLD SPECKLED HEN.

HAVE you e'er seen my speckled hen,
  That stole into a keg,
And after, cackled long and loud,
  Because she laid an egg?

This dear old cackling, speckled hen,
  Was quiet in her way,
And wisely cackled only when
  She laid an egg each day.

But soon she fluttered in and out,
  Her feathers all awry;
I wondered what 'twas all about,
  And thought she sure would die.

ow she would cluck and strut as fine,
  As any king or queen,
When she came off her nest to dine,
  Or getting drink was seen.

But silently she kept her house,
  And lay upon her bed,
As quiet as a churchyard mouse,
  And never raised her head.

And when three weeks had rolled around,
  A chirping sound I heard,
And, looking in the old keg, there
  I saw a yellow bird!

It's little eyes were black and bright,
  It cuddled in the nest;
And on its head were spots of brown,—
  In softest down 'twas dressed.

Chirp! Chirp! I searched and saw some more,
  The old hen looked knowing;
I counted them, one! two! three! four!
  The cockerel was crowing!

The hen flew out with cluck and clack,
  Her ten chicks followed slow;
The chicks were bright, the hen was proud
  As any hen I know.

LUCY S. RUGGLES.

THE BUMBLE BEE.

THE bumble-bee, the bumble-bee,
  He flew to the top of a tulip tree;
He flew to the top, but he could not stop,
  For he had to get home to his early tea.

The bumble-bee, the bumble-bee,
  He flew away from the tulip tree;
But he made a mistake and flew into the lake,
  And he never got home to his early tea.

MAMMA'S BOY.

I KNOW a house so full of noise
You'd think a regiment of boys,
From early morn till close of day,
Were busy with their romping play.
And yet I'm ready to declare,
There is but one small youngster there—
A little golden-headed chap,
Who used to think his mother's lap
The nicest place that e'er could be;
Until he grew so big that he
Was most a man, and learned what fun
It is to shout and jump and run.
This restless, noisy little elf,
Has learned, alas! to think himself
Too old in mother's arms to sleep,
Yet his blue eyes he cannot keep
From hiding 'neath their lids so white,
And climbing to the sofa's height,
He snuggles down, forgets his play,
And into dreamland sails away;
And then it is that mamma knows
Why the whole house so silent grows.

REMEMBER.

REMEMBER, though box in the plural makes
boxes,
The plural of ox should be oxen, not oxes;

And remember, though fleece in the plural is fleeces,
That the plural of goose isn't gooses nor geeses;
And remember, though house in the plural is houses,
The plural of mouse should be mice, not mouses.
Mouse, it is true, in the plural is mice,
But the plural of house should be houses, not hice;
And foot, it is true, in the plural is feet,
But the plural of root should be roots, and not reet.

PLAYING BARBER.

"I WISH I was a little fish,
　　Or else a little kitty,
Or something that don't have curls
　　Which grown folks think so pretty.

It hurts so when I have them brushed,
　　And Mary, ev'ry morning,
Says I am 'such a naughty girl'
　　She surely will 'give warning.'

"She jerks, and don't care how she pulls,
　　She says I'm 'very trying,'
But when they're tangled full of snarls,
　　How can I keep from crying?

"I'll play I am the barber-man
　　And cut them all to pieces.
I don't care if my papa does
　　Call them his 'golden fleeces.' "

THE LITTLE GIRL THAT WOULDN'T EAT CRUSTS.

THE awfulest times that ever could be
They had with a bad little girl of Dundee,
Who never would finish her crust.

In vain they besought her,
And patiently taught her
And told her she must.
Her grandma would coax,
And so would the folks,
And tell her the sinning
Of such a beginning.
But no, she wouldn't,
She couldn't, she shouldn't,
She'd have them to know—
So they might as well go.

And what do you think came soon to pass,
This little girl of Dundee, alas!
Who wouldn't take crusts in the regular way,
Sat down to a feast one summer's·day ;
And what did the people that little girl give?
Why, a dish of *bread pudding*—as sure as I live!

—MARY M. DODGE.

TWENTY FROGS AT SCHOOL.

TWENTY froggies went to school,
Down beside a rushy pool;

Twenty little coats of green,
Twenty vests all white and clean.
"We must be in time," said they;
"First we study then we play;
That is how we keep the rule
When we froggies go to school."

Master bullfrog, grave and stern,
Called the classes in their turn;
Taught them how to nobly strive
Likewise how to leap and dive;
From his seat upon the log
Showed them how to say "Ker-chog!"
Also, how to dodge a blow
From the sticks which bad boys throw

Twenty froggies grew up fast;
Bullfrogs they became at last;
Not one dunce among the lot,
Not one lesson they forgot.
Polished in a high degree,
As each froggie ought to be,
Now they sit on other logs,
Teaching other little frogs.

WHAT THE DAISY SAID.

I AM a little daisy
Right from the dewy earth;
I've come to add my sweetness,
To this bright scene of mirth.

THE WATERMILLION.

THERE were a watermillion
   Growing on a vine,
And there were a pickaninny
   A-watching it all the time.

And when that watermillion
   Were a-ripening in the sun,
And the stripes along its jacket
   Were coming one by one,

That pickaninny hooked it,
   And toting it away,
He ate that entire million
   Within a single day.

He ate the rind and pieces,
   And finished it with vim,
And then that watermillion
   Just up and finished him.

TWINKLE, TWINKLE.

TWINKLE, twinkle, little star,
   How I wonder what you are!
Up above the world so high,
Like a diamond in the sky.

When the glorious sun is set,
When the grass with dew is wet,
Then you show your little light;
Twinkle, twinkle all the night.

In the dark blue sky you keep,
Often thro' my curtain peep;
For you never shut your eye
Till the sun is in the sky.

As your bright and tiny spark
Lights the traveler in the dark;
Though I know not what you **are,**
Twinkle, twinkle little star.

SUPPOSE.

SUPPOSE, my little lady,
　　Your doll should break her head,
Could you make it whole by crying
　　Till your eyes and nose are red?
And wouldn't it be pleasanter
　　To treat it as a joke,
And say you're glad 'twas dolly's
　　And not your head that broke?

Suppose you're dressed for walking,
　　And the rain comes pouring down,
Will it clear off any sooner
　　Because you scold and frown?
And wouldn't it be nicer
　　For you to smile than pout,
And so make sunshine in the house
　　When there is none without?

Suppose your task, my little man,
    Is very hard to get,
Will it make it any easier
    For you to sit and fret?
And wouldn't it be nicer
    Than waiting like a dunce,
To go to work in earnest
    And learn the thing at once?

"I CAN'T" AND "I CAN."

"I CAN'T" is a sluggard, too lazy to work;
From duty he shrinks, every task he will shirk;
No bread on his board, and no meal in his bag,
His house is a ruin, his coat is a rag.

"I Can" is a worker; he tills the broad fields,
And digs from the earth all the wealth that it yields;
The hum of his spindles begins with the light,
And the fires of his forges are blazing all night.

                    W. A. BUTLER.

A BUTTERFLY ON BABY'S GRAVE.

A BUTTERFLY basked on a baby's grave,
    Where a lily had chanced to grow;
"Why art thou here with thy gaudy dye,
    When she of the blue and sparkling eye
Must sleep in the churchyard low?"
    Then it lightly soared through the sunny air,
And spoke from its shining track:
    "I was a worm till I won my wings,
And she whom thou mourn'st like a seraph sings;
    Would'st thou call the blessed one back?"

THE PIG AND THE HEN.

THE pig and the hen,
  They both got in one pen,
And the hen said she would't go out;
  "Mistress hen," says the pig,
  "Don't you be quite so big!"
And he gave her a push with his snout.

"You are rough, and you're fat,
  But who cares for all that;
I will stay if I choose," says the hen.
  "No, mistress, no longer!"
  Says pig: "I'm the stronger,
And mean to be boss of my pen!"

Then the hen cackled out
  Just as close to his snout
As she dare: "You're an ill-natured brute;
  And if I had the corn,
  Just as sure as I'm born,
I would send you to starve or to root!"

"But you don't own the cribs;
  So I think that my ribs
Will be never the leaner for you;
  This trough is my trough,
  And the sooner you're off,"
Says the pig, "why the better you'll do!"

"You're not a bit fair,
  And you're cross as a bear;

What harm do I do in your pen?
  But a pig is a pig,
  And I don't care a fig
For the worst you say," says the hen.

  Says the pig, "You will care
  If I *act* like a bear
And tear your two wings from your neck."
  "What a nice little pen
  You have got!" says the hen,
Beginning to scratch and to peck.

  Now the pig stood amazed,
  And the bristles, upraised
A moment past, fell down so sleek.
  "Neighbor Biddy," says he,
  "If you'll just allow me,
I will show you a nice place to pick!"

  So she followed him off,
  And they ate from one trough—
They had quarrelled for nothing, they saw;
  And when they had fed,   ·
  "Neighbor hen," the pig said,
"Wont you stay here and roost in my straw?"

  "No, I thank you; you see
  That I sleep in a tree,"
Says the hen; "but I *must* go away;
  So a grateful good-bye"—
  "Make your home in my sty,"
Says the pig, "and come in every day."

Now my child will not miss
The true moral of this
Little story of anger and strife;
For a word spoken soft
Will turn enemies oft
Into friends that will stay friends for life.

ALICE CARY.

BABY IS A SAILOR.

BABY is a sailor boy,
Swing, cradle, swing;
Sailing is the sailor's joy,
Swing, cradle, swing.

Snowy sails and precious freight,
Swing, cradle, swing;
Baby's captain, mother's mate,
Swing, cradle, swing.

HUNDREDS!

HUNDREDS of stars in the pretty sky,
Hundreds of shells on the shore together,
Hundreds of birds that go singing by,
Hundreds of bees in the sunny weather.
Hundreds of dew-drops to greet the dawn,
Hundreds of lambs in the purple clover,
Hundreds of butterflies on the lawn,
But only one mother the wide world over.

GOD SEES.

WHEN I run about all day,
  When I kneel at night to pray,
God sees.

When I'm dreaming in the dark,
When I lie awake and hark,
  God sees.

Need I ever know a fear,
Night and day my Father's near—
  God sees.

A LITTLE BOY'S LECTURE.

LADIES AND GENTLEMEN: Nearly four hundred years ago the mighty mind of Columbus, traversing unknown seas, clasped this new continent in its embrace.

A few centuries later arose one here who now lives in all our hearts as the Father of his Country. An able warrior, a sagacious statesman, a noble gentleman. Yes, Christopher Columbus was *great*. George Washington was *great*. But here, my friends, in this glorious nineteenth century is—a *grater!* [Exhibiting a large, bright tin grater. The large kind used for horseradish could be most easily distinguished by the audience.]

JULIA M. THAYER. .

"ISN'T GOD UPON THE OCEAN JUST THE SAME
AS ON THE LAND?"

WE were crowded in the cabin,
  Not a soul would dare to sleep,
It was midnight on the waters,
  And a storm was on the deep

'Tis a fearful thing in winter
  To be shattered by the blast,
And to hear the rattling trumpet
  Thunder, "Cut away the mast!"

As thus we sat in darkness,
  Each one busy with his prayers,
'We are lost!" the captain shouted,
  As he staggered down the stair

But his little daughter whispered
  As she took his icy hand,
Isn't God upon the ocean,
  Just the same as on the land

THE LONG SERMON.

OH, the sun is bright and the day is fair,
  And the sweet breeze wanders everywhere,
And the sweet birds sing as they lightly fly,
And I wish we could join them, Joe and I.

We were bidden to listen, and so we do,
Shut up in the narrow and stuffy pew;

Behaving just as well as we can,
We look over there at the preacher-man.

We can't understand, though we take such pains;
All sense seems gone from our little brains;
So we just sit quiet, as best we may,
And wait till the long hour wears away.

Oh, how can he have so much to say,
The preacher-man, such a lovely day?
And what in the world he is talking about
We do not know and we can't find out.

OUR JIM.

ONLY a boy, with his noise and fun,
    The veriest mystery under the sun;
As brimful of mischief, and wit and glee,
As ever a human frame can be,
And as hard to manage, as—ah! ah, me!
        'Tis hard to tell;
        Yet we love him well.

Only a boy, with his restless tread,
Who cannot be driven, but must be led;
Who troubles the neighbors' dogs and cats,
And tears more clothes, and spoils more hats,
Loses more tops, and kites and bats,
        Than would stock a store
        For a year or more.

SUNBEAMS.

MERRY little sunbeams,
  Flitting here and there;
Joyous little sunbeams,
  Dancing everywhere.
Come they with the morning light,
And chase away the gloomy night.

Kind words are little sunbeams,
  That sparkle as they fall;
And loving smiles are sunbeams
  A light of joy for all.
In sorrow's eye they dry the tear,
And bring the fainting heart good cheer.

LITTLE THINGS.

LITTLE moments make an hour;
  Little thoughts, a book;
Little seeds, a tree or flower;
  Water drops, a brook;
Little deeds of faith and love,
Make a home for you above.

WHAT THE SNOW-DROP SAYS.

I AM a little snow-drop,
  As pure as pure can be:
I come with bright-eyed Daisy
  The Queen of May to see.

THE ROBIN AND THE CHICKEN.

A PLUMP little robin flew down from a tree
To hunt for a worm which he happened to see:
A frisky young chicken came scampering by,
And gazed at the robin with wondering eye.

Said the chick: "What a queer-looking chicken is
that!
Its wings are so long and its body so fat!"
While the robin remarked, loud enough to be heard;
"Dear me! an exceedingly strange-looking bird!"

"Can you sing?" robin asked, and the chicken said,
"No";
But asked in its turn if the robin could crow.
So the bird sought a tree and the chicken a wall,
And each thought the other knew nothing at all.

NINE PARTS OF SPEECH.

T HREE little words you often see
Are ARTICLES—*a*, *an*, and *the*.

A NOUN'S the name of anything,
As *school*, or *garden*, *hoop*, or *swing*.

ADJECTIVES tell the kind of noun,
As *great*, *small*, *pretty*, *white*, or *brown*.

Instead of Nouns the PRONOUNS stand—
Her head, *his* face, *your* arm, *my* hand.

VERBS tell of something to be done—
To *read*, *count*, *sing*, *laugh*, *jump* or *run*.

How things are done the ADVERBS tell,
As *slowly*, *quickly*, *ill*, or *well*.

CONJUNCTIONS join the words together,
As man *and* woman, wind *or* weather.

The PREPOSITION stands before
A Noun, as *at* or *through* the door.

The INTERJECTION shows surprise,
As *Ah!* how pretty, *Oh!* how wise.

The whole are called Nine Parts of Speech,
Which reading, writing, speaking teach.

WHEN MAMMA WAS A LITTLE GIRL.

WHEN mamma was a little girl
　　(Or so they say to me)
She never used to romp and run,
Nor shout and scream with noisy fun,
　　Nor climb an apple tree.
She always kept her hair in curl,—
When mamma was a little girl.

When mamma was a little girl
　　(It seems to her, you see)
She never used to tumble down,
Nor break her doll, nor tear her gown,
　　Nor drink her papa's tea.

She learned to knit, "plain," "seam" and "purl,"—
When mamma was a little girl.

But grandma says—it must be true—
    "How fast the seasons o'er us whirl!
Your mamma, dear, was just like you,
    When she was grandma's little girl."

GRACE F. COOLIDGE.

GOOD-NIGHT.

GOOD-NIGHT! the sun is setting,
    "Good-night!" the robins sing,
And blue-eyed dolls and blue-eyed girls
    Should soon be following.
Come! lay the Lady Geraldine
    Among the pillows white;
'Tis time the little mother kissed
    Her sleepy doll good-night.

And, Willie, put the cart away,
    And drive into the shed
The pony and the muley cow—
    'Tis time to go to bed.
For, listen! in the lilac tree
    The robin does not sing;
"Good-night!" he sang, and tucked his head
    Beneath his weary wing.

Soon all the world will go to rest,
        And all the sky grow dim;
God "giveth His beloved sleep,"
        So we may trust in Him.
The Lord is in the shadow,
        And the Lord is in the light,
To guard His little ones from harm;
        Good-night, dear hearts, good-night!

WHAT IS MAN?

LIKE as the damask rose you see,
        Or like the blossoms on the tree,
Or like the dainty flower of May,
Or like the morning to the day,
Or like the sun, or like the shade,
Or like the gourd which Jonah had,
E'en such is man;—whose thread is spun,
Drawn out and cut, and so is done.

SMILES AND TEARS.

BOTH swords and guns are strong, no doubt,
        And so are tongue and pen,
And so are sheaves of good bank notes
        To sway the souls of men;
But guns and swords, and gold and thought,
        Though mighty in their sphere,
Are often poorer than a smile,
        And weaker than a tear.

MISS FRET AND MISS LAUGH.

CRIES little Miss Fret,
    In a very great pet,
"I hate this warm weather; it's horrid to tan
    It scorches my nose
    And it blisters my toes,
And wherever I go I must carry a fan."

    Chirps little Miss Laugh:
    "Why, I couldn't tell half
The fun I am having this bright summer day.
    I sing through the hours,
    I cull pretty flowers,
And ride like a queen on the sweet-smelling hay."

"I CAN'T" AND "I CAN."

"I CAN'T" met "I can" out a-walking one day:
    Said "I Can't" to "I Can," "What's the reason,
        I pray,
That your always in spirits and I'm always out?
That you always succeed in what you set about,
    While I can't do a thing that I wish?"

Said "I Can" to "I Can't," with a smile in his eye,
"In asking your question you hint the reply:
Instead of 'I wish' say in future 'I will:'
'I can' for 'I can't,' and you'll not take it ill
    If I say you'll be twice what you are."

TEN TRUE FRIENDS.

TEN true friends you have,
    Who, five in a row,
Upon each side of you
    Go where you go.

Suppose you are sleepy,
    They help you to bed;
Suppose you are hungry,
    They see that you are fed.

They wake up your dolly
    And put on your clothes,
And trundle her carriage
    Wherever she goes.

And these ten tiny fellows,
    They serve you with ease;
And they ask nothing from you,
    But work hard to please.

Now, with ten willing servants
    So trusty and true,
Pray who would be lazy
    Or idle—would you?

THE LOST DOLL.

TWICE up and down the garden-walks
    I've looked; but she's not there,
Oh, yes, I've hunted in the hay,
    I've hunted everywhere.

The dark is coming fast, oh dear!
I'm in an awful fright;
I don't know where I've left my doll,
And she'll be out all night!

[*Retires crying.*]

DICKIE-BIRD! DICKIE-BIRD!

YOUR feathers are ruffled, your beak's rather long,
But dickie-bird, dickie-bird, sing me a song,

Dickie-bird, sing of the sun and the breeze;
Dickie-bird, sing of the birds and the bees;
The summer is short and the winter is long,
So dickie-bird, dickie-bird, sing me a song.

The thrushes and linnets are singing so sweet,
But we are content to sit here at your feet,
For we would not leave you alone on the tree;
So sing, dickie, sing to my polly and me.

And we will be happy the whole summer day,
The dickie shall sing and the dolly shall play—
Oh, funniest dickie that ever I saw,
It is not a song if you only say "Caw."

IT'S GOOD TO HAVE A MOTHER.

BIRDIES with broken wings,
Hide from each other,
But babies in trouble,
Can run home to mother.

NEVER PUT OFF.

"NEVER put off till to-morrow,
     What should be done to-day;"
This is a motto for those who work,
Not more than for those who play!

THE LITTLE ARTIST.

LITTLE May is an artist, who draws very well,
     And of one of her pictures, just list while I tell:
Her good doggie Carlo was standing one day,
Very still, in a dignified sort of a way.
With a look that was solemn and earnest and wise,
In his beautiful, dark and intelligent eyes.
"O, you dear, good, old Carlo," cried sweet little
     May,
"I'll make a nice picture of you right away,
And when I am old I'll have it to say,
This looks just like Carlo that bright summer's day!"
So May found her pencil and big drawing book,
And gave Carlo a very wise sort of a look,
As if to say, "Quiet, now, nor one movement
     make,
Every one must keep still when his picture I
     take."
And Carlo was as still as if he well knew
What it was little May was trying to do.
So the picture was finished, and I'm sure you would
     say,
It was very well done for a small child like May."

CHUBBY FIST.

WITH a big piece of bread in her chubby fist,
Baby ran off and was not missed.
The geese came in from the orchard near
And said to each other "What have we here?"

But baby in terror cried out "Go 'way!"
I came out here by myself to play."
"We see," said the geese, "where's your mother?
We were goslings once, are you another?"

JACK AND THE RABBIT.

A GAY little rabbit,
Of frolicsome habit,
Went out for a cool midnight stroll;
And a strange fixture meeting,
Though it set his heart beating,
"Dear me!" said the rabbit, "How droll!"

He stopped for a minute,
To see what was in it,
And nibbled a bit at the bait;
Very tempting he found it,
He walked all around it,
And then he went in at the gate.

But quicker than winking,
And quicker than thinking,
Master Rabbit was swung on high,
And not a bit tardy,
Came little Jack Hardy
From where he'd been hiding close by.

The old moon was crying,
The pine-trees were sighing,
And I think that the stars were in tears,
As into his casket,
Jack's snug, covered basket,
Poor Bunny was dropped by his ears.

Then Jack fled the gate-way,
In order that straightway
Some other good game he might trap.
When Bunny kicked over
The basket and cover,
And scampered off to his home, and his wife!

QUEER LITTLE STITCHES.

OH, queer little stitches,
    You surely are witches,
        To bother me so!
I'm trying to plant you:
Do stay where I want you,
    All straight in a row.

Now keep close together!
I never knew whether
    You'll do as I say.
Why can't you be smaller?
You really grow taller,
    Try hard as I may!

There! now my thread's knotted,
My finger is dotted
    With sharp needle-pricks!

I mean to stop trying;
I cannot help crying;
    Oh, dear what a fix!

Yes, yes, little stitches,
I *know* you are witches—
    I'm sure of it now—
Because you don't bother
Grown people like mother
    When *they* try to sew.

You love to bewilder
Us poor little "childer"
    (As Bridget would say),
By jumping and dancing,
And leaping and prancing,
    And losing your way.

Hear the bees in the clover!
Sewing "over and over"
    They don't understand.
I wish I was out there,
And playing about there
    In that great heap of sand!

The afternoon's going;
I *must* do my sewing
    Before I can play.
Now behave, little stitches,
Like good-natured witches,
    The rest of the day.

I'd almost forgotten
About waxing my cotton,
  As good sewers do;
And—oh, what a memory!—
Here is my emery
  To help coax it through.

I'm so nicely provided,
I've really decided
  To finish the things.
There's nothing like trying;
My needle is flying
  As if it had wings.

There, good-bye, little stitches!
You obstinate witches,
  You're punished, you know.
You've been very ugly,
But now you sit snugly
  Along in a row.

DEEDS OF KINDNESS.

HOW many deeds of kindness
  A little child may do,
Although it has so little strength
  And little wisdom too!
It wants a loving spirit,
  Much more than strength, to prove
How many things a child can do
  For others by his love.

THE LITTLE THINGS.

LITTLE sands make up the shore;
Little drops cause rain to pour;
Little crimes great troubles bring;
Little slanders leave their sting;
Little words of love delight;
Little words of wrath cause fight;
Little shafts of malice pierce;
Little quarrels are a curse;
Little pigs do loudly squeak;
Little boys like me can speak.

ONE OF HIS NAMES.

NEVER a boy had so many names;
They called him Jimmy, and Jim, and James,
Jeems and Jamie; and well he knew
Who it was that wanted him, too.

The boys in the streets ran after him,
Shouting out loudly, "Jim! hey, J-i-m-m!"
Until the echoes, little and big,
Seemed to be dancing a Jim Crow jig.

And little Mable, out in the hall,
"Jim*my!* Jim*my!*" would sweetly call,
Until he answered and let her know
Where she might find him; she loved him so.

Grandpapa, who was dignified,
And held his head with an air of pride,

Didn't believe in abridging names,
And made the most he could of "J-a-m-e-s!"

But if papa ever wanted him,
Crisp and curt was the summons—"Jim!"
That would make the boy on his errands run
Much faster than if he had said "my son."

Biddy O'Flynn could never, it seems,
Call him anything else but "Jeems;"
And when the nurse, old Mrs. McVyse,
Called him "Jamie," it sounded nice.

But sweeter and dearer than all the rest,
Was the one pet name he liked the best;
"Darling!" he heard it whate'er he was at,
For none but his mother called him that.

JOSEPHINE POLLARD.

SOME OF THE CHILDREN.

A IS for Apt little Annie,
  Who lives down in Maine with her grannie,
  Such pies she can make!
  And such doughnuts and cake!
Oh, we like to make visits to grannie.

C is for Curious Charlie,
Who lives on rice, oatmeal and barley.
  He once wrote a sonnet
  On his mother's best bonnet,
And he lets his hair grow long and snarley.

D is for Dear little Dinah,
Whose manners grow finer and finer.
   She smiles and she bows
   To the pigs and the cows,
And she calls the old cat Angelina.

G is for Glad little Gustave,
Who says says that a monkey he *must* have;
   But his mother thinks not;
   And says that they've got
All the monkey they care for in Gustave.

I is for Ignorant Ida,
Who doesn't know rhubarb from cider,
   Once she drank up a quart
   Which was more than she ought,
And it gave her queer feelings inside her.

M is for Mournful Miss Molly,
Who likes to be thought melancholy.
   She's as limp as a rag
   When her sisters play tag,
For its vulgar, she says, to be jolly.

MOTHER GOOSE'S TEA PARTY.

ONCE on a time Old Mother Goose,
   Decided to give a tea party;
I'm sure you'll be glad to hear the news,
   The old lady's well and hearty.
So one cold blustering winter day,
   She sent young Jacky Horner

To carry the cards around to her guests,
   And he had to leave his corner!
And they all came in style,
   From Little Boy Blue
To that patient old lady,
   Who lived in a shoe.
There was Old Mother Hubbard,
   With no bone in her cupboard·
And Jack and Gill,
   Who fell down the hill;
And the funny old woman,
   Who went on the sly,
To sweep all the cobwebs
   Out of the sky.
There was little Miss Muffett,
   Who sat on her tuffet;
And wilful Miss Mary
   Who was so contrary;
While to furnish the music,
   The cat and the fiddle,
Played tunes while they balanced,
   And danced down the middle!
Oh, the sight was so funny,
   I'm sure you would laugh,
If I had but the space
   To tell you the half!

                     ELLEN DEAN.

LITTLE BROWN BUSHY-TAIL.

LITTLE brown Bushy-Tail lived up a tree,
  And mossy and snug was his nest;
Acorns and beechnuts in plenty had he,
  And he scarcely knew which he liked best.

He was cheery of temper, and agile of limb,
  And his own little will was his law;
For what was the world and its worries to him,
  When he held a plump nut in his claw?

As he cracked it he twinkled his knowing black
    eyes,
  The kernel picked out by and by;
Then he ate it and looking uncommonly wise,
  Said, "Folk may be worse off than I.

"For I'm sure I'm content with my portion in life,
  And of nuts I've a plentiful store;
With my little brown babies and little brown wife,
  What on earth could a squirrel want more?"

He had lots of near neighbors as merry as he,
  They were cheery and playful each one;
Don't they show us that happy 'tis easy to be,
  If good humor we give with our fun?

Content with the blessings our Father may give,
  How happy would all of us be,
If we tried with our friends and our neighbors' to
    live
  As the brown squirrel did in the tree!

                              A. H. BALDWIN.

WE LITTLE BOYS.

IF older boys can make a speech,
  We little boys can, too,
And though we may not say so much,
  Yet we've a word for you.
This world is large and full of room,
  There is a place for all;
The rich, the poor, the wise, the good,
  The large as well as small.
So give the little ones a chance
  To show off what they know,
And shun us not because we're small,
  For little boys will grow.

THE BUSY BEE AND MULE.

HOW doth the little busy bee
  Improve each shining hour,
And gather stores of honey by,
  To eat in winter's hours?

How doth the little busy mule
  Toil patiently all day,
And switch his tail, and elevate
  His lofty ears, and bray?

How doth his eye, with drowsy gleam,
  Let naught escape his ken,
But when he elevates his heels,
  Where is the driver then?

THE FIRST PAIR OF BREECHES.

I'VE got a pair of breeches now,
  And I'll have to be a man,
I know I can if just I try,
  My mamma says I can!

I'm going to school now very soon,
  And learn my A, B, C;
My mamma says I'm too young yet,
  But I am way past three.

And I've got pockets in my pants,
  To put my pencil in;
For mamma says that I must write
  In school when I begin,

I'll soon be tall as papa—now
  I'll grow fast as I can,
And don't you think that very soon
  I'll be a full-grown man?

THE COURAGEOUS BOY.

SOME of the boys in our school,
  Whose elbows I can't reach,
Are ten times more ashamed than I
  To rise and make a speech.

I guess they are afraid some girl
  Who is about their age,
May laugh and criticise their looks
  When they come on the stage.

TOMMY'S PLAN.

I LOVE my mamma very much,
  I love my papa, too;
And when I am a great big man,
  I'll tell you what I'll do!
I'll buy my papa a bicycle,
  And my mamma a rockaway,
And I'll let them ride just all they please
  If it's sixty miles a day!

OUR CHARLEY.

WELL, what do you think of our Charley?
  He's a splendid boy, you say;
But a noisy, troublesome mischief,
  And always in the way.
Now, that's unfair to Charley;
  Dear breezy, happy boy!
He sings, and shouts, and dances,
  Because he is full of joy.

Oh, yes, he is very curious,
  And goes where he shouldn't go;
And meddles with things forbidden,
  And breaks them too, I know.
But there's nothing bad in Charley—
  Nothing that's very wrong.
He's a beautiful human engine,
  But the pressure of steam is strong.

THE TWO SQUIRRELS.

THERE were two squirrels
   That lived in a wood;
The one was naughty,
   The other was good.

The naughty one's name was Dandy Jim;
His mother was very fond of him.
The good one's name was Johnny Black;
He had beautiful fur upon his back,
And he never went near the railroad track.

   But Dandy Jim,
   Alas for him!
   He ran away
   One summer day,
   Over the hills and far away;
And his mother sought for him far and near,
But never a word of Jim could she hear.

   He never came back;
   For, crossing the track,
   The railroad cars ran over him,
   And that was the end of Dandy Jim.

   But Johnny Black,
   He always came back,
Whenever he went from his home away;
He thought at home was the place to stay.
   He minded his mother,
     Where'er he might be;
   He thought that his mother
     Knew better than he.

VALEDICTORY.

IT now, kind friends, devolves on me
  To speak our Val-e-dic-to-ry;
You've seen our Exhibition through,
We've tried to please each one of you—
And if we've failed in any part,
Lay it to *head*, and not to *heart;*
For we have striven, night and day,
To study well both speech and play.
We hope, within another year,
Again before you to appear.
But ere we part—before you go—
We wish you, one and all, to know
We thank you for your presence here—
Such kindness does our bosoms cheer,
And causes every boy to feel
He ought to study with more zeal;
While all the girls it will inspire
With an ambition to rise higher.
We feel much more than words can tell—
Accept our heart-felt thanks—farewell!

VALEDICTORY.

OUR exercises for the day
  Will close without much more delay.
We thank you for the interest
Your kind attention has expressed.

We know we are but young and weak,
To stand before a crowd to speak;
But mighty *oaks* from *acorns* grow,
And some of us, for aught you know,
May climb the noble hill of Fame,
And make a great and lasting name;
While none of us, we hope, may live
To loving hearts one pain to give.
Again we tender thanks to you;
Till next we meet, kind friends, adieu!

AN ADDRESS TO A TEACHER.

DEAR TEACHER: The pleasant duty has been assigned me by my schoolmates of presenting you this token as an evidence of our lasting esteem, friendship and love. We could not consent to part with you without leaving in your hands some memorial, however trifling, of deep and abiding gratitude for your unceasing efforts to benefit us. When in future days you look upon this memento, let it be a pleasant token of the deepest love and reverence of our young hearts.

FOR VACATION.

VACATION is coming, and we are all glad. We have studied and read and sung for many weeks, and it will be pleasant to play all day, with no lessons to learn. I hope we can all go home to-night feeling sure we have done our best to learn and to be good boys and girls. If we cannot, let us try hard for it next term. We love each other, and we love our teacher, and we hope this will be the happiest vacation that any school ever had.

Good-by, teacher and scholars and friends. Good-by to you all.

AUNT TABITHA.

WHATEVER I do and whatever I say,
Aunt Tabitha tells me that isn't the way,
When she was a girl (forty summers ago),
Aunt Tabitha tells me they never did so.

Dear aunt! If I only would take her advice—
But I like my own way, and I find it so nice!
And besides I forget half the things I am told;
But they all will come back to me—when I am old.

If a youth passes by, it may happen no doubt,
He may chance to look in as I chance to look out;
She would never endure an impertinent stare,
It is horrid, she says, and I musn't sit there.

A walk in the moonlight has pleasure, I own,
But it isn't quite safe to be walking alone;
So I take a lad's arm—just for safety, you know—
But Aunt Tabitha tells me, *they* didn't do so.

How wicked we are, and how good they were then!
They kept at arm's length those detestable men;
What an era of virtue she lived in!—but stay—
Were the men such rogues in Aunt Tabitha's day?

If the men were so wicked—I'll ask my papa
How he dared to propose to my darling mamma?
Was he like the rest of them? goodness! who knows?
And what shall I say, if a wretch should propose?

I am thinking if aunt knew so little of sin,
What a wonder Aunt Tabitha's aunt must have been!
And her grand-aunt—it scares me—how schock-
     ingly sad
That we girls of to day are so frightfully bad!

A martyr will save us, and nothing else can;
Let us perish to rescue some wretched young man!
Though when to the altar a victim I go,
Aunt Tabitha 'll tell me—she never did so.

                    O. W. HOLMES.

THE MODERN BELLE.

THE daughter sits in the parlor,
     And rocks in her easy-chair;
She is dressed in silks and satins,
     And jewels are in her hair;
She winks, and giggles, and simpers,
     And simpers, and giggles, and winks;
And though she talks but little,
     It's vastly more than she thinks.

Her father goes clad in russet—
　　All brown and seedy at that;
His coat is out at the elbows.
　　And he wears a shocking bad hat.
He is hoarding and saving his dollars,
　　So carefully, day by day,
While she on her whims and fancies
　　Is squandering them all away.

She lies in bed of a morning
　　Until the hour of noon,
Then comes down, snapping and snarling
　　Because she's called too soon.
Her hair is still in papers,
　　Her cheeks still bedaubed with paint—
Remains of last night's blushes
　　Before she attempted to faint.

Her feet are so very little,
　　Her hands are so very white,
Her jewels so very heavy,
　　And her head so very light;
Her color is made of cosmetics—
　　Though this she'll never own;
Her body is mostly cotton,
　　And her heart is wholly stone.

She falls in love with a fellow
　　Who swells with a foreign air;
He marries her for her money,
　　She marries him for his hair—

One of the very best matches;
  Both are well mated in life;
She's got a fool for a husband,
  And he's got a fool for a wife.

———————

IT'S NOT WORTH WHILE TO HATE.

LIFE is not very long at best—
  We cannot alter fate;
And, for the few years we shall live,
  "It's not worth while to hate."

A few more meetings and farewells
  Each one of us await;
Why should we stop to wrangle, then?
  "It's not worth while to hate."

A few more smiles, a few more tears,
  For rich, and poor, and great;
And soon we'll all be called away—
  "It's not worth while to hate."

The old and young will find grim Death
  Ready on each to wait,
To let them down into the grave—
  "It's not worth while to hate."

Bright angels on "the other side"
  Stand at the GOLDEN GATE,
To welcome all that practice here—
  "It's not worth while to hate."

THE QUAIL'S SONG.

ONCE on a time a quail was known
  To fly into a pet,
Because it did not rain when he
    Called out aloud, "More wet!"
But quails as well as children,
    Must live to learn some day,
That everybody in this world,
    Can't always have their way.
Cut all along life's pathway,
    Some things for which we long,
Must now and often fail of truth;
    Just like that poor quail's song.

A VISIT FROM ST. NICHOLAS.

'TWAS the night before Christmas, when all
    through the house
Not a creature was stirring, not even a mouse;
The stockings were hung by the chimney with care,
In hopes that St Nicholas soon would be there
The children were nestled all snug in their beds,
While visions of sugar-plums danced through their
    heads;
And mamma in her kerchief, and I in my cap,
Had just settled our brains for a long winter's nap,
When out on the lawn there arose such a clatter,
I sprang from the bed to see what was the matter.

Away to the window I flew like a flash,
Tore open the shutters and threw up the sash.
The moon on the breast of the new-fallen snow
Gave the lustre of mid-day to objects below;
When, what to my wondering eyes should appear,
But a miniature sleigh, and eight tiny reindeer
With a little old driver, so lively and quick,
I knew in a moment it must be St. Nick.
More rapid than eagles his coursers they came,
And he whistled, and shouted, and called them by
    name:
"Now, Dasher! now, Dancer! now, Prancer! and
    Vixen!
On, Comet! on, Cupid! on, Donder and Blitzen!
To the top of the porch! to the top of the wall!
Now dash away! dash away! dash away all!"
As dry leaves that before the wild hurricane fly,
When they meet with an obstacle, mount to the sky,
So up to the house-top the coursers they flew,
With the sleighful of toys, and St. Nicholas too.
And then, in a twinkling, I heard on the roof
The prancing and pawing of each little hoof.
As I drew in my head, and was turning around,
Down the chimney St. Nicholas came with a bound.

SOMEBODY'S DARLING.

INTO a ward of whitewashed walls,
    Where the dead and dying lay,

Wounded by bayonets, shells, and balls,
　　Somebody's Darling was borne one day—
Somebody's Darling, so young and so brave,
　　Wearing yet on his pale sweet face,
Soon to be hid by the dust of the grave,
　　The lingering light of his boyhood's grace.

Matted and damp are the curls of gold,
　　Kissing the snow of that fair young brow;
Pale are the lips of delicate mould—
　　Somebody's Darling is dying now.
Back from his beautiful blue-veined brow
　　Brush all the wandering waves of gold,
Cross his hands on his bosom now,
　　Somebody's Darling is still and cold.

Kiss him once for somebody's sake
　　Murmur a prayer soft and low;
One bright curl from its fair mates take,
　　They were somebody's pride, you know;
Somebody's hand had rested there,—
　　Was it a mother's soft and white?
And have the lips of a sister fair
　　Been baptized in those waves of light?

God knows best; he has somebody's love;
　　Somebody's heart enshrined him there;
Somebody wafted his name above,
　　Night and morn on the wings of prayer.
Somebody wept when he marched away,
　　Looking so handsome, brave, and grand;

Somebody's kiss on his forehead lay,
   Somebody clung to his parting hand.

Somebody's waiting and watching for him——
   Yearning to hold him again to the heart;
And there he lies with his blue eyes dim,
   And the smiling childlike lips apart.
Tenderly bury the fair young dead,
   Pausing to drop on his grave a tear;
Carve on the wooden slab at his head,——
   "Somebody's Darling slumbers here."

MARIE R. LACOSTE.

TOTAL ANNIHILATION.

HE was a Bowery bootblack bold,
   And his years they numbered nine;
Rough and unpolished was he, albeit
   He constantly aimed to shine.

As proud as a king, on his box he sat,
   Munching an apple red;
While the boys of his set looked wistfully on,
   And "Give us a bite!" they said.

But the bootblack smiled a lordly smile;
   "No free bites here!" he cried.
Then the boys they sadly walked away,
   Save *one* who stood at his side.

"Bill, give us the core?" he whispered low,
   That bootblack smiled once more,
And a mischievous dimple grew in his cheek:
   "There *ain't goin' to be no core!*"

AFTON WATER.

FLOW gently, sweet Afton, among thy green
    braes,
Flow gently, I'll sing thee a song in thy praise;
My Mary's asleep by thy murmuring stream,
Flow gently, sweet Afton, disturb not her dream.

Thou stockdove whose echo resounds through the
    glen,
Ye wild whistling blackbirds in yon thorny den,
Thou green-crested lapwing, thy screaming forbear,
I charge you disturb not my slumbering fair.

How lofty, sweet Afton, thy neighboring hills,
Far marked with the courses of clear, winding rills;
There daily I wander as noon rises high,
My flocks and my Mary's sweet cot in my eye.

How pleasant thy banks and green valleys below,
Where wild in the woodland the primroses blow;
There oft as mild evening weeps over the lea
The sweet-scented birk shades my Mary and me

Thy crystal stream, Afton, how lovely it glides,
And winds by the cot where my Mary resides;
How wanton thy waters her snowy feet lave,
As gathering sweet flowerets she stems thy clear
    wave
Flow gently, sweet Afton, among thy green braes,
Flow gently, sweet river, the theme of my lays;
My Mary's asleep by thy murmuring stream,
Flow gently, sweet Afton, disturb not her dream.

                  ROBERT BURNS.

THE DUMB WIFE.

THERE was a jovial blade,
    Who wed a country maid,
And safely conducted her home, home, home,
    She was neat without art,
    And she pleased him to the heart;
But, alack and alas! she was dumb, dumb, dumb!

    She could brew and she could bake,
    She could sew and she could make,
And sweep out the house with a broom, broom,
        broom.
    But, alas! the silly swain
    Did nothing but complain,
Because his lovely wife was dumb, dumb, dumb.

    There lived a doctor nigh,
    To whom he did apply,
To cure his lovely wife of her mum, mum, mum,
    He cut the chattering string,
    And her tongue began to ring,
Till it rattled in his ears like a drum, drum, drum.

    To the doctor then he goes,
    With a heart full of woes,
Crying: "Doctor! oh, *doctor!* I'm undone, done,
        done!
    For my wife she's turned a scold,
    And her tongue she will not hold,
And it rattles in my ears like a drum, drum, drum."

Says the doctor, "Of my art,
It is far the better part
To make a woman speak that is dumb, dumb, dumb.
But 'tis past the art of man,
Let him do whate'er he can,
To make a scolding woman hold her tongue, tongue,
tongue!"

A LAWYER'S POEM TO SPRING.

WHEREAS, on certain boughs and sprays
    Now divers birds are heard to sing,
And sundry flowers their heads upraise,—
    Hail to the coming on of Spring!

The songs of those said birds arouse
    The memory of our youthful hours,
As green as those said sprays and boughs,
    As fresh and sweet as those said flowers.

The birds aforesaid—happy pairs—
    Love, 'mid the aforesaid boughs, enshrines
In freehold nests; themselves, their heirs,
    Administrators and assigns.

O, busiest term of Cupid's court,
    Where tender plaintiffs actions bring,
Season of frolic and of sport,
    Hail, as aforesaid, coming Spring!

                                H. H. BROWNELL.

RUNNING AWAY.

THE sky was clear, the stars were bright,
   The grass was wet with dew;
When Johnny rose, put on his clothes,
   And vowed what he would do.

"I'll leave my pa, I'll leave my ma;
   I'll go from here to stay;
My parents both have been unkind,
   And so I'll run away.

"I'll take my clothes, I'll take my all,
   A slave I will not be;
I'll go out west, and do my best—
   I'll strike for liberty!"

And Johnny started bravely out,
   And said he'd ne'er return;
He said he'd go where he could live
   And let his genius burn.

He traveled all that summer night,
   And bravely through the day;
And then he said: "I wish that I
   Had never run away.

"I'm tired and weak—I'm sick," said he,
   With sadness in his tone;
"It isn't best to go out west—
   At least to go *alone*.

(THE FARMER SAT IN HIS EASY CHAIR.)

THE farmer sat in his easy chair,
  Smoking his pipe of clay,
While his hale old wife, with busy care,
  Was clearing the dinner away;
A sweet, little girl, with fine blue eyes,
On her grandfather's knee was catching flies.

The old man laid his hand on her head,
  With a tear on his wrinkled face;
He thought how often her mother, dead,
  Had sat in that self-same place.
As the tear stole down from his half-shut eye,
"Don't smoke!" said the child; how it makes you
    cry!"

The house-dog lay stretched out on the floor,
  Where the shade after noon used to steal;
The busy old wife, by the open door;
  Was turning the spinning wheel;
And the old brass clock on the mantel-tree
Had plodded along to almost three.

Still the farmer sat in his easy-chair,
  While close to his heaving breast
The moistened brow and the cheek so fair
  Of his sweet grandchild were pressed;
His head, bent down, on her soft hair lay:
Fast asleep were they both, that summer day!

/ C. G. EASTMAN. \

THE GROVES.

THE groves were God's first temples, 'ere man
    learned
To hew the shaft and lay the architrave,
And spread the roof above them—ere he framed
The lofty vault, to gather and roll back
The sound of anthems, in the darkling wood,
Amid the cool and silence, he knelt down
And offered to the Mightiest solemn thanks
And supplication. Let me, then, at least,
Here in the shadow of this aged wood,
Offer one hymn—thrice happy if it find
Acceptance in His ear.

                   BRYANT.

FANNY'S MUD PIES.

UNDER the apple-trees, spreading and thick,
    Happy with only a pan and a stick,
On the soft grass in the meadow that lies,
Our little Fanny is making mud pies.

On her bright apron, and bright, drooping head,
Showers of pink and white blossoms are shed;
Tied to a branch, that seems just meant for that,
Dances and flutters her little straw hat.

Gravely she stirs, with a serious look,
Making believe she's a true pastry cook;
Sundry brown plashes on forehead and eyes
Show that our Fanny is making mud pies.

But all the soil of her innocent play
Clean soap and water will soon wash away;
Many a pleasure in daintier guise
Leaves darker traces than Fanny's mud pies.

Dash, full of joy in the bright summer day,
Zealously chases the robins away,
Barks at the squirrels, or snaps at the flies,
All the while Fanny is making mud pies.

Sunshine and soft summer breezes astir,
While she is busy, are busy with her,—
Cheeks rosy glowing, and bright, sparkling eyes,
Bring they to Fanny while making mud pies.

Dollies and playthings are all laid away,
Not to come out till the next rainy day;
Under the blue of those sweet summer skies
Nothing so pleasant as making mud pies.

ELIZABETH SILL.

A LIFE ON THE OCEAN WAVE.

A LIFE on the ocean wave,
    A home on the rolling deep;
Where the scattered waters rave,
    And the winds their revels keep;
Like an eagle caged I pine
    On this dull, unchanging shore;
Oh, give me the flashing brine,
    The spray and the tempests roar!

Once more on the deck I stand
    Of my own swift-gliding craft:
Set sail! farewell to the land;
    The gale follows fair abaft.
We shoot through the sparkling **foam,**
    Like an ocean bird set free,—
Like the ocean-bird, our home
    We'll find far out on the sea.

The land is no longer in view,
    The clouds have begun to frown;
But with a stout vessel and crew,
    We'll say, Let the storm come down!
And the song of our hearts shall be,
    While the wind and the waters rave,
A home on the rolling sea!
    A life on the ocean wave!

MY SWEETHEART.

"NOW, mamma, if only you'll promise me true
    That you never will tell, I will show it to you—
This beautiful picture—and then you will will see
How lovely the face of my sweetheart must be.
Her cheeks they are rosy, her eyes they are bright,
Her hair always shines when it catches the light,
Her voice is so soft when she speaks with a smile,
I know she is loving me well all the while.
And when I am hurt—and—well—cry (for you see,
They have to sometimes, even big boys like me),

She puts her arms round me and comforts me so,
I'm sure to forget it the first thing I know.
She sings about sunshine and fairies and flowers,
And the stories she tells—you could listen for hours.
"Who is she?   Well, tell me, what name do you
      guess?
When you get to the sweetest of all I'll say yes,—
No, no,—you are wrong.   I must give you a peep;
But you'll surely remember the secret to keep
And never let out who is fondest of me?
Ho, ho, mamma, look in this glass and you'll see!"
                                SYDNEY DAYRE.

THE BACHELOR SALE.

I DREAMED a dream in the midst of my slumbers,
And as fast as I dreamed it was coined into num-
      bers;
My thoughts ran along in such beautiful metre,
I'm sure I ne'er saw any poetry sweeter.

It seemed that a law had been recently made
That a tax on old bachelors' pates should be laid;
And, in order to make them all willing to marry,
The tax was as large as a man could well carry.

The bachelors grumbled, and said 'twas no use,
'Twas cruel injustice and horrid abuse—
And declared that to save their own hearts' blood
      from spilling,
Of such a vile tax they would ne'er pay a shilling.

But the rulers determined their scheme to pursue,
So they set all the bachelors up at vendue.
A crier was sent through the town to and fro,
To rattle his bell and his trumpet to blow,
And to bawl out to all he might meet on his way:
"Ho! forty old bachelors sold here to-day."

And presently all the old maids of the town—
Each one in her very best bonnet and gown—
From thirty to sixty, fair, plain, red, and pale,
Of every description, all flocked to the sale.

The auctioneer, then, in his labor began;
And called out aloud, as he held up a man:
"How much for a bachelor?   Who wants to buy?"
In a twink, every maiden responded, "I—I."

In short, at a hugely extravagant price,
The bachelors all were sold off in a trice,
And forty old maidens—some younger, some older—
Each lugged an old bachelor home on her shoulder.

THE COBBLER'S SECRET.

A WAGGISH cobbler once, in Rome,
    Put forth a proclamation
That he'd be willing to disclose,
    For a due consideration,
A secret which the cobbling world
    Could ill afford to lose—
The way to make, in one short day,
    A hundred pairs of shoes!

From every quarter, to the sight,
  There ran a thousand fellows—
Tanners, cobblers, boot-men, shoe-men,
  Jolly leather-sellers—
All redolent of beer and smoke,
  And cobbler's wax and hides;
Each fellow pays his thirty pence,
  And calls it cheap, besides.

Silence! the cobbler enters,
  And casts around his eyes—
Then curls his lip, the rogue! then frowns;
  And then looks wondrous wise.
"My friends," he says, " 'tis simple, quite,
  The plan that I propose;
And every one of you, I think,
  Might learn it, if he chose.

"A good, sharp knife is all you'll **need**,
  In carrying out my plan;
So easy is it, none can fail,
  Let him be child or man.
, To make a hundred pairs of shoes,
  Just go back to your shops,
And take a hundred pairs of boots,
  And cut off all the tops!"

-------•-------

POPPING CORN.

AND there they sat, a-popping corn,
  John Styles and Susan Cutter—

John Styles as fat as any ox,
  And Susan fat as butter.

And there they sat and shelled the corn,
  And raked and stirred the fire;
And talk.d of different kinds of corn,
  And hitched their chairs up nigher.

Then Susan she the popper shook,
  Then John he shook the popper,
Till both their faces grew as red
  As saucepans made of copper.

And then they shelled, and popped, and ate,
  All kinds of fun a-poking,
While he haw-hawed at her remarks,
  And she laughed at his joking.

And still they popped, and still they ate—
  John's mouth was like a hopper—
And stirred the fire, and sprinkled salt,
  And shook and shook the popper.

The clock struck nine—the clock struck ten—
  And still the corn kept popping;
It struck eleven, and then struck twelve,
  And still no signs of stopping.

And John he ate, and Sue she thought—
  The corn did pop and patter,
Till John cried out, "The corn's a-fire!
  Why, Susan, what's the matter?"

Said she, "John Styles, it's one o'clock;
   You'll die of indigestion;
I'm sick of all this popping corn—
   Why don't you pop the question?"

THE BOY AND THE BOOT.

"BOTHER!" was all that John Clatterby said;
  His breath came quick and his cheeks were red
He flourished his elbows and looked absurd
While, over and over, his "Bother!" I heard.

Harder and harder he tugged and worked;
Vainly and savagely still he jerked;
The boot, half on, would dawdle and flap,
"Bother!" and then he burst the strap.

Redder than ever his hot cheek flamed;
Louder than ever he fumed and blamed;
He wiggled his heel and he tugged at the leather
Till his knees and his chin came bumping together.

"My boy," said I, in a voice like a flute,
"Why not first try your troublesome boot
On the other foot?" "I'm a goose!" laughed John,
As he stood, in a flash, with his two boots on.

In half the affairs of this every-day life
(As that same day I said to my wife),
Our troubles come from trying to put
The *left-hand* boot on the *right-hand* foot.

THE EAGLE.

WHAT is that, mother?
                    The eagle, boy—
Proudly careering his course of joy,
Firm in his own mountain vigor relying,
Breasting the dark storm, the red bolt defying;
His wing on the wind, and his eye on the sun,
He swerves not a hair, but bears onward, right on.
Boy, may the eagle's flight ever be thine,
Onward and upward, true to the line.

BISHOP DONNE.

TRUTH IN PARENTHESIS.

I REALLY take it very kind,
    This visit, Mrs. Skinner;
I have not seen you such an age,
    (The wretch has come to dinner!)
Your daughters, too, what loves of girls!
    What heads for painters' easels!
Come here, and kiss the infant, dears!
    (And give it, p'raps, the measles!)

Your charming boys, I see, are home,
    From Reverend Mr. Russell's;
'Twas very kind to bring them both,
    (What boots for my new Brussels?)
What! little Clara left at home?
    Well now, I call that shabby!
I should have loved to kiss her so!
    (A flabby, dabby babby!)

And Mr. S., I hope he's well;
  But though he lives so handy,
He never once drops in to sup,
  (The better for our brandy!)
  ome, take a seat; I long to hear
  About Matilda's marriage;
You've come, of course, to spend the day,
  (Thank heaven! I hear the carriage!)

What! must you go?   Next time, I hope,
  You'll give me longer measure;
Nay, I shall see you down the stairs;
  (With most uncommon pleasure!)
Good bye! good bye! Remember, all,
  Next time you'll take your dinners;
(Now, David, mind I'm not at home,
  In future to the Skinners.)

                    THOMAS HOOD.

THE SMACK IN SCHOOL.

A DISTRICT school not far away,
    'Mid Berkshire hills one winter's day,
Was humming with its wonted noise
Of three-score mingled girls and boys.
Some few upon their tasks intent,
But more on furtive mischief bent.
The while the master's downward look
Was fastened on a copy-book;
When, suddenly, behind his back,

Rose sharp and clear a rousing smack!
As 'twere a battery of bliss
Let off in one tremendous kiss!
"What's that?" the startled master cries;
"That, thir," a little imp replies,
"Wath William Willith, if you pleathe—
I thaw him kith Thuthanna Peathe!"
With frown to make a statue thrill,
The master thundered, "Hither, Will!"
Like wretch o'ertaken in his track,
With stolen chattels on his back,
Will hung his head in fear and shame,
And to the awful presence came,—
A great, green, bashful simpleton,
The butt of all good-natured fun.
With smile suppressed, and birch upraised,
The threatener faltered—"I'm amazed
That you, my biggest pupil, should
Be guilty of an act so rude!
Before the whole set school to boot—
What evil genius put you to 't?"
" 'Twas she herself, sir," sobbed the lad,
"I did not mean to be so bad;
But when Susannah shook her curls,
And whispered I was 'fraid of girls,
And dursn't kiss a baby's doll,
I couldn't stand it, sir, at all,
But up and kissed her on the spot!

I know—boo-hoo—I ought to not,
But, somehow, from her looks—boo-hoo—
I thought she kind o'wished me to!"

W. P. PALMER.

KATYDID.

I LOVE to hear thy earnest voice,
　Wherever thou art hid;
Thou testy little dogmatist,
　Thou pretty Katydid!
Thou mindest me of gentlefolks—
　Old gentlefolks are they—
Thou say'st an undisputed thing
　In such a solemn way.

Thou art a female, Katydid,
　I know it by the trill
That quivers through thy piercing notes,
　So petulant and shrill.
I think there is a knot of you
　Beneath the hollow tree,
A knot of spinster Katydids—
　Do Katydids drink tea?

O, tell me where did Katy live,
　And what did Katy do?
And was she very fair and young,
　And yet so wicked, too?
Did Katy love a naughty man?

Or kiss more cheeks than one?
I warrant Katy did no more
Than many a Kate has done.
O. W. HOLMES.

THE BURIAL OF SIR JOHN MOORE.

NOT a drum was heard, not a funeral note,
As his corse to the rampart we hurried:
Not a soldier discharged his farewell shot
O'er the grave where our hero we buried.

We buried him darkly at dead of night,
The sods with our bayonets turning;
By the struggling moonbeam's misty light,
And the lantern dimly burning.

No useless coffin enclosed his breast,
Nor in sheet or in shroud we wound him;
But he lay like a warrior taking his rest,
With his martial cloak around him.

Few and short were the prayers we said,
And we spoke not a word of sorrow,
But we steadfastly gazed on the face of the dead,
And we bitterly thought of the morrow.

We thought, as we hollowed his narrow bed,
And smoothed down his lonely pillow,
That the foe and the stranger would tread o'er his
head,
And we far away on the billow.

Lightly they'll talk of the spirit that's gone,
  And o'er his cold ashes upbraid him;
But little he'll reck if they let him sleep on
  In the grave where a Briton has laid him.

But half of our heavy task was done,
  When the clock struck the hour for retiring;
And we heard the distant and random gun
  That the foe was sullenly firing.

Slowly and sadly we laid him down
  From the field of his fame fresh and gory;
We carved not a line, we raised not a stone
  But we left him alone with his glory.

                          ⸤ CHARLES WOLFE.

THE MISER.

INSIDE a squalid chamber,
    Upon the cold, bare floor,
The miser crouches softly,
    And counts his treasure o'er.
No warmth in his heart, no light in his eye,
Nor ear for the busy passers by;
For his heart is shut 'gainst love that's bright,
As he counts his gold in the silent night,
By the flick'ring taper's sickly light.

    At night in his squalid chamber
    The miser strives to rest;

With no refreshing slumber
  His weary eyes are blessed:
If only the wind his casement shakes,
With tremor and start the wretch awakes;
Into every nook and corner he pries,
Each lock and bar and bolt he tries
In terror, lest thieves should steal his prize.

  Again in the squalid chamber
    The miser doth appear;
  His clay-cold form is resting
    Upon a rough low bier.
No friend to sorrow, no eye to weep,
As he lies alone in his silent sleep;
For death is taking him far from earth,
Where soon he'll learn the senseless worth
Of the gold that makes of the soul a dearth.

  Once more in the squalid chamber
    Upon the miser's store,
  The heirs at law are making
    Of claims a perfect score.
For now he is gone, 'tis little they care
For the fate of him whose gold they share;
They seize the treasure and scatter it wide
In the folly and pomp of earthly pride,
Forgetting the miser e'er lived or died.

WE ALL LIKE SHEEP.

"WE all like sheep," the tenors shrill
  Begin, and then the church is still.

While back and forth across the aisle
Is seen to pass the "catching" smile.

"We all like sheep," the altos moan
In low, and rich, and mellow tone,
While broader grows the merry grin
And nose gets further off from chin.

"We all like sheep," sopranos sing
Till all the echoes wake and ring;
The young folks titter, and the rest
Suppress the laugh in bursting chest.

"We all like sheep," the bassos growl—
The titter grows into a howl,
And e'en the deacon's face is graced
With wonder at the singers' taste.

"We all like sheep," runs the refrain,
And then, to make their meaning plain,
The singers altogether say,
"We all, like sheep, have gone astray."

THE OYSTER MAN.

IT was a tall young oysterman lived by the river-
side,
His shop was just upon the bank, his boat was on
the tide;
The daughter of a fisherman, that was so straight
and slim,
Lived over on the other bank, right opposite to
him.

It was the pensive oysterman that saw a lovely maid,
Upon a moonlight evening, a sitting in the shade;
He saw her wave her handkerchief, as much as if
    to say,
"I'm wide awake, young oysterman, and all the
    folks away."

Then up arose the oysterman and to himself said he:
"I guess I 'll leave the skiff at home, for fear that
    folks should see;
I read it in the story-book, that, for to kiss his dear,
Leander swam the Hellespont,—and I will swim
    this here."

And he has leaped into the waves, and crossed the
    shining stream,
And he has clambered up the bank, all in the moon-
    light gleam;
O, there were kisses sweet as dew, and words as
    soft as rain,—
But they have heard her father's step, and in he
    leaps again!

Out spoke the ancient fisherman,—"O what was
    that, my daughter?"
"'T was nothing but a pebble, sir, I threw into the
    water."
"And what is that, pray tell me, love, that paddles
    off so fast?"
"It 's nothing but a porpoise, sir, that's been a
    swimming past."

Out spoke the ancient fisherman,—"Now bring me
    my harpoon!
I'll get into my fishing-boat, and fix the fellow
    soon."
Down fell that pretty innocent, as falls a snow-white
    lamb,
Her hair dropped round her pallid cheeks, like see-
    weed on a clam.

Alas for those two loving ones! she waked not from
    her swound,
And he was taken with the cramp, and in the waves
    was drowned;
But Fate has metamorphosed them, in pity of their
    woe,
And now they keep an oyster-shop for mermaids
    down below.

O. W. HOLMES.

THE REMORSEFUL CAKES.

A LITTLE boy named Thomas, ate
    Hot buckwheat cakes for tea—
A very rash proceeding, as
    We presently shall see.

He went to bed at eight o'clock,
    As all good children do,
But scarce had closed his little eyes,
    When he most restless grew.

He flopped on this side, then on that,
  Then keeled up on his head,
And covered, all at once, each spot
  Of his wee trundle-bed.

He wrapped one arm around his waist,
  And t'other 'round his ear,
While mamma wondered what on earth
  Could ail her little dear.

He fell asleep, and as he slept
  He dreamt an awful dream,
Of being spanked with hickory slabs,
  Without the power to scream.

He dreamt a great big lion came
  And ripped and raved and roared—
While on his breast two furious bulls
  In mortal combat gored.

He dreamt he heard the flop of wings
  Within the chimney flue—
And down there crawled, to gnaw his ears,
  An awful bugaboo!

When Thomas rose next morn, his face
  Was pallid as a sheet—
"I never more," he firmly said,
  "Will cakes for supper eat!"

EUGENE FIELD.

FAREWELL OLD SHOE.

(To be addressed to an old shoe which the speaker holds in his hand.)

ADIEU! adieu!
　　My poor old shoe!
What comfort I have had with you!
My *sole* companion day by day,
You've cheered and soothed my weary way!

　　A fond adieu,
　　My dear old shoe!
Most faithful friend I've found in you!
Alike, midst fair or wintry weather,
We've shared life's pilgrimage together.

　　Now rent and torn,
　　And sadly worn,
Of every trace of beauty shorn.
'Tis with an honest, heart-felt sigh
I feel that I must throw you by.

　　A sad adieu!
　　Poor worn-out shoe!
What sorry plights you've borne me through!
And, oh! it tears my tender heart
To think that you and I must part.

　　Once more, adieu!
　　My faithful shoe!
I ne'er shall find the likes o' you,
And I will bless your memory
For all the good you've been to me.

No other boot
Can ever suit
As you have done my crippled feet!
No other shoe can ever be
The tried, true friend you've been to me.

A last adieu,
Dear cast-off shoe!
Whatever may become of you,
Accept, dear, easiest, best of shoes,
This farewell offering of my muse.

HOHENLINDEN.

ON Linden, when the sun was low,
  All bloodless lay the untrodden snow,
And dark as winter was the flow
  Of Iser, rolling rapidly.

But Linden saw another sight,
When the drum beat, at dead of night,
Commanding fires of death to light
  The darkness of her scenery.

By torch and trumpet fast arrayed,
Each horseman drew his battle-blade,
And furious every charger neighed,
  To join the dreadful revelry.

Then shook the hills with thunder riven,
Then rushed the steed to battle driven,
And louder than the bolts of heaven
  Far flashed the red artillery.

But redder yet that light shall glow
On Linden's hills of stained snow,
And bloodier yet the torrent flow
    Of Iser, rolling rapidly.

'Tis morn, but scarce yon level sun
Can pierce the war-clouds rolling dun,
Where furious Frank and fiery Hun
    Shout in their sulphurous canopy.

The combat deepens.   On, ye brave,
Who rush to glory or the grave!
Wave, Munich! all thy banners wave,
    And charge with all thy chivalry.

Few, few shall part where many meet!
The snow shall be their winding-sheet,
And every turf beneath their feet
    Shall be a soldier's sepulchre.

THOMAS CAMPBELL.

WHIP-POOR-WILL.

"WHIP-POOR-WILL! whip-poor-will!"
    Heard little Rose in the gloaming:
The words came hurriedly and shrill,
    When she in the fields was roaming;
Then into the house she soon went skipping,
To ask why poor Will wanted a whipping.
"Has he been naughty?" she asked, with dread,
"That he must be whipped and sent to bed?"

"Whip-poor-will! whip-poor-will!"
Those words came again—those words only,
The wind was whispering softly and still,
And the world seemed dark and lonely,
"Whip-poor-will! whip-poor-will!" was still the cry
She heard from the tree-tops so tall and high
"What have you done?" called Rose, as shrill
As the voice that cried "Whip-poor-will!"

"Whip-poor-will! whip-poor-will!"
"What do you cry for?" said little Rose,
And this the thought that came to her still,
"Ah! cry for a whipping! I suppose,
What a strange, silly fool that thing must be,
To cry for a whipping up there in the tree."
Then she gravely said, with a sigh,
"Ah! you have been telling a lie!"

"Whip-poor-will! whip-poor-will!"
She heard till the sound grew weary!
The evening air was damp and chill,
The dim old wood was lone and dreary.
Ah! the notes were now so solemn and sad,
She thought the creature began to feel bad,
And in pity she softy said, .
"*Why don't you slyly steal to bed?*"

THE SHIP OF STATE.

THOU, too, sail on, O Ship of State!
Sail on, O Union, strong and great!

Humanity, with all all its fears,
With all the hopes of future years,
Is hanging breathless on thy fate!
We know what master laid thy keel,
What workmen wrought thy ribs of steel,
Who made each mast, and sail, and rope,
What anvils rang, what hammers beat,
In what a forge and what a heat
Were shaped the anchors of thy hope!

Fear not each sudden sound and shock,
'Tis of the wave, and not the rock;
'Tis but the flapping of the sail,
And not a rent made by the gale!
In spite of rock and tempest's roar—
In spite of false lights on the shore—
Sail on, nor fear to breast the sea!
Our hearts, our hopes, are all with thee;
Our hearts, our hopes, our prayers, our tears,
Our faith triumphant o'er our fears,
Are all with thee,—are all with thee!

H. W. LONGFELLOW.

THE LOVE OF COUNTRY.

WHENCE does this love of our country, this universal passion proceed? Why does the eye ever dwell with fondness upon the scenes of infant life? Why do we breathe with greater joy the breath of our youth? Why are not other soils as grateful, and other heavens as gay? Why does the soul of man ever cling to that earth where it first knew pleasure and pain, and, under the rough discipline of the passions, was roused to the dignity of moral life? Is it only that our country contains our kindred and our friends? And is it nothing but a name for our social affections? It cannot be this; the most friendless of human beings has a country which he admires and extols, and which he would, in the same circumstances, prefer to all others under heaven. Tempt him with the fairest face of nature, place him by living waters under shadowy trees of Lebanon, open to his view all the gorgeous allurements of the climates of the sun, he will love the rocks and deserts of his childhood better than all these, and thou canst not bribe his soul to forget the land of his nativity; he will sit down and weep by the waters of Babylon, when he remembers thee, O Sion!

SIDNEY SMITH.

ENGLISH HISTORY IN RHYME.

FIRST William the Norman,
Then William his son;
Henry, Stephen, and Henry,
Then Richard and John;
Next Henry the Third,
Edwards one, two and three;

And again, after Richard,
Three Henrys we see.
Two Edwards, third Richard,
If rightly I guess;
Two Henrys, sixth Edward,
Queen Mary, Queen Bess;
Then Jamie the Scotchman.
Then Charles, whom they slew,
Yet received, after Cromwell,
Another Charles, too.
Next Jamie the Second
Ascended the throne;
Then good William and Mary
Together came on;
Then Anne, Georges four,
And fourth William all passed
And Victoria came—
May she long be the last.

A BIT OF POTTERY.

THE potter stood at his daily work,
　　One patient foot on the ground;
The other with never-slacking speed,
　　Turning his swift wheel round.
Silent we stood beside him there;
　　Watching the restless knee,
Till my friend said low, in pitying voice,
　　"How tired his foot must be!"

The potter never paused in his work,
  Shaping the wondrous thing;
'Twas only a common flower-pot,
  But perfect in fashioning.
Siowly he raised his patient eyes,
  With homely truth inspired:
"No, marm, it isn't the foot that kicks—
  The one that stands gets tired."

THE SONG OF THE CORN POPPER.

PIP! pop! flipperty flop!
  Here am I, all ready to pop.
Girls and boys, the fire burns clear;
Gather about the chimney here.
Big ones, little ones, all in a row,
Hop away! pop away! here we go!

Pip! pop! flipperty flop!
Into the bowl the kernels drop.
Sharp, and hard, and yellow, and small,
Must say they don't look good at all;
But wait till they burst into warm white snow!
Hop away! pop away! here we go!

Pip! pop! flipperty flop!
Don't fill me too full; shut down the top!
Rake out the coals in an even bed,
Topaz yellow and ruby red;
Shade your eyes from the fiery glow.
Hop away! pop away! here we go!

Pip! pop! flipperty flop!
Shake me steadily; do not stop;
Backward and forward, not up and down;
Don't let me drop, or you'll burn it brown,
Never too high, and never too low.
Hop away! pop away! here we go!

Pip! pop! flipperty flop!
Now they are singing, and soon they'll hop.
Hi! the kernels begin to swell.
Ho! at last they are dancing well.
Puffs and fluffs of feathery snow.
Hop away! pop away! here we go!

Pip! pop! flipperty flop!
All full, little ones? Time to stop!
Pour out the snowy, feathery mass.
Here is a treat for lad and lass.
Open your mouths now, all in a row;
Munch away! crunch away! here we go!

LAURA E. RICHARDS.

THE CHARGE OF THE LIGHT BRIGADE.

HALF a league, half a league,
   Half a league onward,
All in the valley of Death
   Rode the six hundred.

"Forward, the Light Brigade!
Charge for the guns!" he said:
Into the valley of Death
 Rode the six hundred.

"Forward, the Light Brigade!"
Was there a man dismayed?
Not though the soldiers knew
 Some one had blundered:
Theirs not to make reply,
Theirs not to reason why,
Theirs but to do and die:
Into the valley of Death
 Rode the six hundred.

Cannon to right of them,
Cannon to left of them,
Cannon in front of them
 Volleyed and thundered;
Stormed at with shot and shell,
Boldly they rode and well,
Into the jaws of Death,
Into the mouth of Hell
 Rode the six hundred.

Flashed all their sabres bare,
Flashed as they turned in air,
Sabring the gunners there,
Charging an army, while
 All the world wondered:
Plunged in the battery smoke,

Right through the line they broke;
Cossack and Russian
Reeled from the sabre-stroke
  Shattered and sundered.
Then they rode back, but not,
  Not the six hundred.

Cannon to right of them,
Cannon to left of them,
Cannon behind them
  Volleyed and thundered:
Stormed at with shot and shell,
While horse and hero fell,
They that had fought so well
Came through the jaws of Death
Back from the mouth of Hell,
All that was left of them,
  Left of six hundred.

When can their glory fade?
O, the wild charge they made!
  All the world wondered.
Honor the charge they made!
Honor the Light Brigade,
  Noble six hundred!

TENNYSON.

HOSANNA.

WHEN His salvation bringing,
To Zion Jesus came,

The children all stood singing
    Hosanna to His name.
Nor did their zeal offend Him,
    But, as he rode along,
He bade them still attend Him,
    And smiled to hear their song.

And since the Lord retaineth
    His love for children still;
Though now, as King, He reigneth,
    On Zion's heavenly hill,
We'll flock around His banner,
    We'll bow before His throne,
And sing aloud, Hosanna
    To David's royal Son!

For should we fail proclaiming,
    Our great Redeemer's praise,
The stones, our silence shaming,
    Would their hosannas raise;
But shall we only render
    The tribute of our words?
No, while our hearts are tender,
    They, too, shall be the Lord's.
                JOSHUA KING.

BESSIE BO PEEP OF ENGLE STEEPE.

A DEAR little girl was Bessie Bo Peep,
   The pet and idol of Engle Steepe—
Her eyes were blue, she'd the sweetest smile
You'd see though you walked a hundred mile.

Not a cottage door in Engle Steepe,
But opened wide to Bessie Bo Peep—
As welcome as flowers that bloom in May,
She smiled, then passed like a sunbeam away,

But the little sick children of Engle Steepe,
Were most in love with Bessie Bo Peep—
Far better than medicine—powders or pills—
Her smile seemed to cure their many ills.

Whenever she sat by the sufferer's bed,
At least one half the suffering fled;
Her smile, and her kiss, and her little bouquet,
Would brighten the sick room all that day.

But a dark day came to Engle Steepe,
A cruel fever seized Bessie Bo Peep;
'Twas a sad day all through that country side,
When the pet and pride of the village died.

And now in the graveyard by Walter's Mill,
You may read on a stone these words if you will,
"The dearest child here lies asleep,
That ever breathed in Engle Steepe."

                              T. W. HANDFORD.

THE WIND IN A FROLIC.

THE Wind one morning sprang up from sleep,
  Saying, "Now for a frolic! now for a leap!
Now for a mad-cap galloping chase!
I'll make a commotion in every place!"

So it swept with a bustle right through a great town,
Creaking the signs, and scattering down
Shutters; and whisking, with merciless squalls,
Old women's bonnets and gingerbread stalls:
There never was heard a much lustier shout,
As the apples and oranges tumbled about;
And the urchins, that stand with their thievish eyes
Forever on watch, ran off each with a prize.
   Then away to the field it went blustering and hum-
        ming,
And the cattle all wondered whatever was coming;
It plucked by the tails the grave matronly cows,
And tossed the colts manes all over their brows,
'Till, offended at such a familiar salute,
They all turned their backs and stood sulkily mute.
   So on it went, capering, and playing its pranks,
Whistling with reeds on the broad river's banks,
Puffing the birds as they sat on the spray,
O'er the traveler grave on the king's highway
   It was not too nice to hustle the bags
Of the beggar, and flutter his dirty rags:
'T was so bold, that it fearned not to play its joke
With the doctor's wig or the gentleman's cloak.
Through the forest it roared, and cried, gayly, "Now,
You sturdy old oaks, I'll make you bow!"
And it made them bow without more ado,
Or cracked their great branches through and through.
   Then it rushed like a monster, on cottage and farm,
Striking their dwellers with sudden alarm,

So they ran out like bees when threatened with harm.
There were dames with their kerchiefs tied over their
    caps,
To see if their poultry were free from mishaps;
The turkeys they gobbled, the geese screamed aloud,
And the hens crept to roost in a terrified crowd;
There was rearing of ladders, and logs laying on,
Where the thatch from the roof threatened soon to be
    gone.
  But the wind had swept on, and met in a lane
With a school-boy, who panted and struggled in vain:
For it tossed him, and twirled him, then passed, and
    he stood
With his hat in a pool, and his shoe in the mud.
  Then away went the wind in its holiday glee!
And now it was far on the billowy sea;
And the lordly ships felt its staggering blow,
And the little boats darted to and fro:—
But lo! night came, and it sank to rest
On the sea-bird's rock in the gleaming west,
Laughing to think, in its fearful fun,
How little of mischief it had done!

WILLIAM HOWITT.

THE FROST.

THE frost looked forth one still, clear night,
    And whispered, "Now, I shall be out of sight,
So through the valley and over the height
    In silence I'll take my way;

I will not go on like that blustering train,
The wind and the snow, the hail and the rain,
Who make so much clatter and noise in vain,
 But I'll be busy as they."

So he flew to the mountain and powdered its crest,
He lit on the trees and their boughs he drest
In diamond beads, and over the breast
 Of the quivering lake he spread
A coat of mail, that it need not fear
The downward point of many a spear
That he hung on its margin, far and near,
 Where a rock might rear its head.

But he did one thing that was hardly fair;
He went to the cupboard, and finding there
That all had forgotten for him to prepare,
 "Now, just to set them a-thinking,
I'll bite this basket of fruit," said he;
"This costly pitcher I'll break in three,
And this glass of water they've left for me
 Shall tchick—to tell them I'm drinking!"

HANNAH F. GOULD.

LITTLE BROWN HANDS.

THEY drive home the cows from the pasture
 Up through the long shadowy lane,
Where the quail whistles loud in the wheatfield,
 That is yellow with ripening grain;

They find, in the thick waving grasses,
  Where the scarlet-lipped strawberry grows;
They gather the earliest snowdrops,
  And the first crimson buds of the rose.

They toss the hay in the meadow;
  They gather the elder-bloom white;
They find where the dusky grapes purple
  In the soft-tinted October light.
They know where the apples hang ripest,
  And are sweeter than Italy's wines;
They know where the fruit hangs the thickest,
  Oh the long, thorny blackberry vines.

They gather the delicate seaweeds,
  And build tiny castles of sand;
They pick up the beautiful seashells—
  Fairy barques that have drifted to land.
They wave from the tall, rocking treetops,
  Where the oriole's hammock-nest swings,
And at night-time are folded in slumber
  By a song that a fond mother sings.

Those who toil bravely are strongest;
  The humble and poor become great;
And from those brown-handed children
  Shall grow mighty rulers of state.
The pen of the author and statesman,
  The noble and wise of the land,
The sword, and chisel, and pallet,
  Shall be held in the little brown hand.

IT SNOWS.

"IT snows!" cries the School-boy, "Hurrah!" and
    his shout
Is ringing through parlor and hall,
While swift as the wing of a swallow, he's out.
    And his playmates have answered his call;
It makes the heart leap but to witness their joy;
    Proud wealth has no pleasure, I trow,
Like the rapture that throbs in the pulse of the boy,
    As he gathers his treasures of snow;
Then lay not the trappings of gold on thine heirs,
While health, and the riches of nature, are theirs.

"It snows!" sighs the Imbecile, "Ah!" and his breath
    Comes heavy, as clogged with a weight:
While, from the pale aspect of nature in death
    He turns to the blaze of his grate;
And nearer and nearer his soft-cushioned chair
    Is wheeled toward the life-giving flame;
He dreads a chill puff of the snow-burdened air,
    Lest it wither his delicate frame;
Oh! small is the pleasure existence can give,
When the fear we shall die only proves that we live!

"It snows!" cries the Traveler, "Ho!" and the word
    Has quickened his steed's lagging pace;
The wind rushes by, but its howl is unheard,
    Unfelt the sharp drift in his face;
For bright through the tempest his own home ap-
    peared,

Ay, through leagues intervened he can see;
There's the clear, glowing hearth, and the table
    prepared,
And his wife with her babes at her knee;
Blest thought! how it lightens the grief-laden hour,
That those we love dearest are safe from its power!

"It snows!" cries the Belle, "Dear, how lucky!" and
    turns
From her mirror to watch the flakes fall;
Like the first rose of summer, her dimpled cheek
    burns,
While musing on sleigh-ride and ball:
There are visions of conquests, of splendor, and
    mirth,
Floating over each drear winter's day;
But the tintings of Hope, on this storm-beaten earth,
Will melt like the snow-flakes away;
Turn, turn thee to Heaven, fair maiden, for bliss;
That world has a pure fount ne'er opened in this.

"It snows!" cries the Widow, "Oh God!" and her
    sighs
Have stifled the voice of her prayer;
It's burden you'll read in her tear-swollen eyes,
On her cheek sunk with fasting and care.
'Tis night, and her fatherless ask her for bread,
But "He gives the young ravens their food,"
And she trusts, till her dark hearth adds horror to
    dread,

And she lays on her last chip of wood.
Poor sufferer! that sorrow thy God only knows;
'Tis a most bitter lot to be poor, when it snows!

Mrs. S. J. Hale.

THE LITTLE GIRLS.

WHERE have they gone too—the little girls,
With natural manners and natural curls?
Who love their dollies and like their toys,
And talk of something beside the boys?

Little old women in plenty I find,
Mature in manners and old of mind:
Little old flirts who talk of their "beaux"
And vie with each other in stylish clothes.

Little old belles, who at nine and ten
Are sick of pleasure and tired of men,
Weary of travel, of balls, of fun—
And find no new thing under the sun.

Once, in the beautiful long ago,
Some dear little children I used to know;
Girls who were merry as lambs at play,
And laughed and rollicked the livelong day.

They thought not at all of the style of their clothes,
And never imagined that boys were "beaux"—
"Other girls' brothers" and "mates" were they·
Splendid fellows to help them at play.

Where have they gone to?   If you see
One of them anywhere, send her to me.
I would give a medal of purest gold
To one of those dear little girls of old,
With an innocent heart and an open smile,
Who knows not the meaning of "flirt" or "style."

ELLA WHEELER.

THE LITTLE BOYS.

WHERE have they gone to—the little boys,
   With natural manners and natural joys?
Who cherish their youth—at least till they're ten,
And wait for their manhood ere playing at men?

Little old men in plenty I find,
Boorish in manners and sensual in mind:
Who express great contempt for "only a girl,"
Spending hours on a mustache too honest to curl.

Little old beaux with gloves and a cane,
Aping their elders, their manners, their mien;
Little old fops, incipient dudes,
Who already suffer from "states" and from "moods."

Once, in the beautiful long ago,
There were little boys I used to know,
Kind in their manner, real boys in their play,
Who whistled and frolicked the livelong day.

Who liked the girls because they were "mates"—
Girls who ran races and climbed high gates—
Who never said, "Oh, only girls don't you know?"
Or "this is the fashion," or this is the "go."

Oh, where are these dear little gentlemen now?
Could I find one, I'd give him a bow:
I would place on his forehead a crown of pure gold,
And a gem-hilted sword in his right hand to hold.
.I would place him, then, on a beautiful throne,
And call all the children their king to own.

MATTIE E. MERRIAM.

DID NOT PASS.

(First verse to be recited by teacher.)

.(S O, John, I hear you did not pass;
    You were the lowest in your class,
    Got not a prize of merit,
But grumbling now is no avail;
Just tell me how you came to fail,
    With all your sense and spirit?"

"Well, sir, I missed 'mong other things,
The list of Egypt's shepherd kings
    (I wonder who does know it).
An error of three years I made
In dating England's first crusade;
    And, as I am no poet,

"I got Euripides all wrong,
And could not write a Latin song;
   And as for Roman History,
With Hun and Vandal, Goth and Gaul
And Gibbon's weary 'Rise and Fall,'
   'Twas all a hopeless mystery.

"But, father, do not fear or sigh
If Cram' does proudly pass me by,
   And pedagogues ignore me;
I've common sense, I've will and health,
I'll win my way to honest wealth;
   The world is all before me.

"And though I'll never be a Grecian,
Know Roman laws or art Phœnician,
   Or sing of love and beauty,
I'll plow, or build, or sail, or trade,
And you need never be afraid
   But that I'll do my duty."

Mary E. Burnett.

OLD-SCHOOL PUNISHMENT.

OLD Master Brown brought his ferrule down,
   And his face looked angry and red.
"Go, seat you there, now, Anthony Blair,
   Along with the girls," he said.
Then, Anthony Blair, with a mortified air,
   With his head down on his breast,

Took his penitent seat by the maiden sweet
  That he loved, of all, the best.
And Anthony Blair, seemed whimpering there,
  But the rogue only made believe;
For he peeped at the girls with the beautiful curls,
  And ogled them over his sleeve.

THAT GRUMBLING OLD WOMAN.

THERE was an old woman, and—what do you
    think?—
She lived upon nothing but victuals and drink!
But though victuals and drink were the chief of her
    diet,
Yet this grumbling old woman never was quiet.

She had a nice cottage a hen-house and barn,
And a sheep whose fine wool furnished blankets and
    yarn;
A cow that supplied her with butter and cheese,
A large flock of geese, and a hive full of bees.

Yet she grumbled and grumbled from morning till
    night,
For this foolish old woman thought nothing went
    right;
E'en the days of the week were all wrong, for on
    Sunday
She always declared that she wished it was Monday.

If cloudless and fair was the long summer day,
And the sun smiled down on the new-mown hay,
"There's a drouth," she said, "as sure as you're born!
If it doesn't rain soon, it will ruin the corn!"

But when descended the gentle rain,
Blessing the bountiful fields of grain,
And bringing new life to flower and bud,
She said there was coming a second flood.

She never gave aught to the needy and poor;
The outcast and hungry she turned from her door.
"Shall I work," she said, with a wag of the head,
"To provide for the idle and lazy their bread?"

But the rich she regarded with envy and spite;
She said 'twas a shame,—'twasn't decent nor right,—
That the haughty old squire, with his bow-legged son,
Should ride with two horses, while she rode with one.

And the crabbed old fellow—to spite her, no doubt,
Had built a new barn like a palace throughout,
With a cupola on it, as grand as you please,
And a rooster that whirled head and tail with the
    breeze.

"I wish, so I do," she said, cocking her eye,
"There'd come a great whirlwind, and blow it sky-
    high!"
And e'en as she spoke, a loud rushing was heard,
And the barn to its very foundations was stirred.

It stood the shock bravely, but—pitiful sight!—
The wind took the old woman up like a kite!
As she sailed up aloft over forest and hill,
Her tongue, so they say, it kept wagging on still.

And where she alighted, no mortal doth know,
Or whether she ever alighted below.

MORAL.

My moral, my dears, you will find if you try;
And if you don't find any, neither can I.

THE DEAD MOON.

THE moon is dead—defunct—played out,—
 So says a very learned doctor;
She looketh well, beyond a doubt;
 Perhaps she's in a trance, dear Proctor.

At any rate, she's most entrancing
 For one of such decrepit age;
And on her radiant beauties glancing,
 She charms the eyes of youth and sage.

And so the man upon her's perished!—
 He lived in doleful isolation;
Poor wretch! No wife his bosom cherished,
 No children squalled his consolation.

Yet she's adored by all the gypsies,
 Whose lovers sigh beneath her beams;
She aids the steps of staggering tipsies,
 And silvers o'er romantic streams.

And once she caught Endymion sleeping,
  And stooped to kiss him in a grove,
Upon him very slyly creeping;
  He was her first and early love.

But that's a very ancient story,
  And was a youthful indiscretion,
When she was in her primal glory,
  Ere scandal-schools had held a session.

Dear, darling moon: I dote upon her;
  I watch her nightly in the sky,
But, oh! upon my word of honor,
  I'd rather she were dead than I.

———————•◦•———————

MY MOTHER'S HYMN.

LIKE patient saint of olden time,
    With lovely face, almost divine,
So good, so beautiful and fair,
Her very attitude a prayer;
I heard her sing so low and sweet,
"His loving kindness—oh, how great!"
Turning, beheld the saintly face,
So full of trust and patient grace.
"He justly claims a song from me,
His loving kindness—oh, how free!"
Sweetly thus did run the song,
"His loving kindness," all day long;
Trusting, praising, day by day,

She sang the sweetest roundelay,
"He near my soul has always stood,
His loving kindness—oh, how good!
He safely leads my soul along,
His loving kindness—oh, how strong!"
So strong to lead her on the way
To that eternal, better day,
Where safe at last in that blest home
All care and weariness are gone,
She "sings with rapture and surprise
His loving kindness in the skies."

FARM-YARD SONG.

OVER the hills the farm-boy goes,
    His shadow lengthened along the land,
A giant staff in a giant hand;
In the poplar tree, above the spring,
The katydid begins to sing:
      The early dews are falling;—
Into the stone-heap darts the mink;
The swallows skim the river's brink;
And home to the woodland flies the crows,
When over the hill the farm-boy goes,
    Cheerily calling,—
    "Co', boss! co', boss! co'! co'! co'!"
Farther, farther, over the hill,
Faintly calling, calling still,—
    "Co', boss! co', boss! co'! co'!

Into the yard the farmer goes,
With grateful heart, at the close of day;
Harness and chain are hung away;
In the wagon-shed stand yoke and plow;
The straw's in the stack, the hay in the mow,
    The cooling dews are falling,—
The friendly sheep his welcome bleat,
The pigs come grunting to his feet,
The whinnying mare her master knows,
When into the yard the farmer goes,
    His cattle calling,—
    "Co,' boss! co', boss! co'! co'! co'!"
While still the cow-boy, far away,
Goes seeking those that have gone astray,—
    "Co', boss! co', boss! co'! co'!"

Now to her task the milkmaid goes,
The cattle come crowding through the gate,
Lowing, pushing, little and great;
About the trough, by the farm-yard pump,
The frolicsome yearlings frisk and jump,
    While the pleasant dews are falling;
The new-milch heifer is quick and shy,
But the old cow waits with tranquil eye;
And the white stream into the bright pail flows,
When to her task the milkmaid goes,
    Soothingly calling,—
    "So, boss! so, boss! so! so! so!"
The cheerful milkmaid takes her stool,

And sits and milks in the twilight cool,
 Saying, "So! so, boss! so! so!"

To supper at last the farmer goes,
The apples are pared, the paper read,
The stories are told, then all to bed.
Without, the cricket's ceaseless song
Makes shrill the silence all night long;
 The heavy dews are falling.
The housewife's hand has turned the lock;
Drowsily ticks the kitchen clock;
The household sinks to deep repose;
But still in sleep the farm-boy goes,
  Singing, calling,—
  "Co', boss! co', boss! co'! co'! co'!"
And oft the milkmaid in her dreams
Drums in the pail with the flashing streams,
  Murmuring, "So, boss! so!"

J. T. TROWBRIDGE.

WHAT A LITTLE LEAF SAID.

ONCE on a time a little leaf was heard to sigh and cry, as leaves often do when a gentle wind is about. And the twig said: "What is the matter, little leaf?"

"The wind," said the leaf, "just told me that one day it would pull me off, and throw me down on the ground to die."

The twig told it to the branch on which it grew, and the branch told it to the tree. When the tree heard it it rustled all over, and sent back word to the leaf: "Do not be afraid; hold on tightly and you shall not go till you want to."

So the leaf stopped sighing, and went on rustling and singing.

When the bright leaves of autumn came the little leaf saw the leaves around becoming very beautiful. Then it asked the tree what this meant, and the tree said: "All these leaves are getting ready to fly away, and they have put on those beautiful colors because of joy."

Then the little leaf began to want to go, and grew very beautiful in thinking of it. And when it was very gay in colors it saw that the branches of the tree had no color in them, so it said: "O, branch, why are you lead colored and we golden?"

"We must keep on our work clothes," said the tree, "for our life is not done yet, but your clothes are for a holiday, for your task is over."

GOOD-NIGHT AND GOOD-MORNING.

A FAIR little girl sat under a tree,
Sewing as long as her eyes could see;
Then smoothing her work and folding it right,
She said, "Dear work! Good-Night! Good-Night!"

Such a number of rooks came over her head,
Crying "Caw! Caw!" on their way to bed;

She said, as she watched their curious flight,
"Little black things! Good-Night! Good-Night!"

The horses neighed and the oxen lowed,
The sheep's "Bleat! Bleat!" came over the road;
All seeming to say with a quiet delight,
"Good little girl! Good-Night! Good-Night!"

She did not say to the Sun, "Good-Night!"
Though she saw him there like a ball of light;
For she knew that he had God's time to keep,
All over the world, and never could sleep.

The tall pink fox-glove bowed his head—
The violets curtsied and went to bed;
And good little Lucy tied up her hair,
And said, on her knees, her short, sweet prayer.

And while on her pillow she softly lay,
She knew nothing more till again it was day;
And all things said to the beautiful Sun,
"Good-Morning! Good-Morning! Our work is
    begun!"   LORD HOUGHTON.

RAIN ON THE ROOF.

WHEN the humid shadows hover
    Over all the starry spheres,
And the melancholy darkness
    Gently weeps in rainy tears,
What a bliss to press the pillow
    Of the cottage-chamber bed
And to listen to the patter
    Of the soft rain overhead!

Every tinkle on the shingles
   Has an echo in the heart;
And a thousand dreamy fancies
   Into busy being start,
And a thousand recollections
   Weave their air-threads into woof,
As I listen to the patter
   Of the rain upon the roof.

Now in memory comes my mother
   As she used long years agone,
To regard the darling dreamers
   Ere she left them till the dawn;
Oh, I see her leaning o'er me,
   As I list to this refrain
Which is played upon the shingles
   By the patter of the rain.

Then my little seraph sister,
   With her wings and waving hair,
And her star-eyed cherub brother,
   A serene angelic pair!—
Glide around my wakeful pillow,
   With their praise or mild reproof,
As I listen to the murmur
   Of the soft rain on the roof.

And another comes to thrill me
   With her eyes' delicious blue;
And I mind not, musing on her,
   That her heart was all untrue:

I remember but to love her
  With a passion kin to pain,
And my heart's quick pulses vibrate
  To the patter of the rain.

Art hath naught of tone or cadence
  That can work with such a spell,
In the soul's mysterious fountains,
  Whence the tears of rapture swell
As that melody of nature,
  That subdued, subduing strain
Which is played upon the shingles
  Bv the patter of the rain.

COATES KINNEY.

WARREN'S ADDRESS.

STAND! the ground's your own, my braves;
  Will ye give it up to slaves?
Will ye look for greener graves?
  Hope ye mercy still?
What's the mercy despots feel?
Hear it in that battle-peal!
Read it on yon bristling steel!
  Ask it—ye who will

Fear ye foes who kill for hire?
Will ye to your homes retire?
Look behind you!—they're afire!
  And, before you, see

Who have done it!   From the vale
On they come!—and will ye quail?
Leaden rain and iron hail
 Let their welcome be!

In the God of battles trust!
Die we may—and die we must!
But, O where can dust to dust
 Be consigned so well,
As where heaven its dew shall shed
On the martyred patriot's bed,
And the rocks shall raise their head,
 Of his deeds to tell?

JOHN PIERPONT.

OUR COUNTRY.

MY COUNTRYMEN! the moments are quickly passing, and we stand like some traveler upon a lofty crag that separates two boundless seas. The century that is closing is complete. "The past," said your great statesman, "is secure." It is finished and beyond our reach. The hand of detraction cannot dim its glories, nor the tears of repentance wipe away its stains. Its good and evil, its joy and sorrow, its truth and falsehood, its honor and its shame, we cannot touch. Sigh for them, blush for them, weep for them, if we will, we cannot change them now. The old century is dying and they are to be buried with him; his history is finished and they will stand upon its roll forever.

The century that is opening is all our own. The years that are before us are a virgin page. We can inscribe them as we will. The future of our country rests upon us. The happiness of posterity depends on us. The fate of humanity may be in our hands. That pleading voice, choked with the sob of ages, which has so often spoken to deaf ears, is lifted up to us. It asks us to be brave, benevolent, consistent, true to the teachings of our history, proving "divine descent by worth divine." It asks us to be virtuous, building up public virtue upon private worth; seeking that righteousness which exalteth nations. It asks us to be patriotic, loving our country before all other things; making her happiness our happiness, her honors ours, her fame our own. It asks us in the name of Charity, in the name of Freedom, in the name of God!

H. A. BROWN.

PRESENTATION SPEECH.

DEAR TEACHER:

I am commissioned by my schoolmates to ask your acceptance of this little token of their respect and affection. We wished in some way to show our appreciation of your ability as a preceptor, and of your patience and kindness in dealing with the faults to which that variety of the human species called the Boy is proverbially prone, and, after some debate as to the method of doing so, concluded that the most befitting exponent of our feelings would be a memento to which we could all contribute, and which, however insignificant its value might be when measured by the magnitude of our obligations, would agreeably remind you that we were not ungrateful. With our little gift, receive, dear sir, our warmest wishes for your health and prosperity. We hope to do credit to your tutelage. If we do not, it is our own fault, for you have done your part faithfully and zealously. You have taught us to look up to you not only as a wise instructor, but as a guardian and friend, and when we go into the world to turn the lessons you have taught to profitable account, we shall not forget to whom we owe our acquirements, but shall remember you ever with almost filial regard.

PRESENTATION SPEECH.

DEAR TEACHER:

I have been requested by the young ladies of this school (or institution) to offer you a slight token of our affection and regard. I cannot tell you how delighted I am to be the means of conveying to you the expression of our united love. What we offer you is but a poor symbol of our feelings, but we know you will receive it kindly, as a simple indication of the attachment which each one of us cherishes for you in her heart of hearts. You have made our lessons pleasant to us—so pleasant that it would be ungrateful to call them tasks. We know that we have often tried your temper and forbearance, but you have dealt gently with us in our waywardness, teaching us, by example as well as precept, the advantages of magnanimity and self-control. We will never forget you. We shall look back to this school (or institution) in after-life, not as a place of penance, but as a scene of mental enjoyment, where the paths of learning were strewn with flowers; and whenever memory recalls our school-days, our hearts will warm toward you as they do to-day. I have been requested by my school-mates not to address you formally, but as a beloved and respected friend. In that light, dear teacher, we all regard you. Please accept, with our little present, our earnest good wishes. May you always be as happy as you have endeavored to make your pupils, and may they— nothing better could be wished for them—be always as faithful to their duties to others as you have been in your duties to them.

SALLY IN OUR ALLEY.

OF all the girls that are so smart,
  There's none like Pretty Sally;
She is the darling of my heart,
  And lives in our alley

There's ne'er a lady in the land
  That's half so sweet as Sally;
She is the darling of my heart,
  And lives in our alley.

Her father he makes cabbage-nets,
  And through the streets does cry them;
Her mother she sells laces long
  To such as please to buy them;
But sure such folk can have no part
  In such a girl as Sally;
She is the darling of my heart,
  And lives in our alley.

When she is by, I leave my work,
  I love her so sincerely;
My master comes, like any Turk,
  And bangs me most severely;
But let him bang, long as he will,
  I'll bear it all for Sally;
She is the darling of my heart,
  And lives in our alley.

Of all the days are in the week,
  I dearly love but one day,
And that's the day that comes betwixt
  A Saturday and Monday;
For then I'm dressed, all in my best,
  To walk abroad with Sally;
She is the darling of my heart,
  And lives in our alley.

When Christmas comes about again,
    Oh, then I shall have money;
I'll hoard it up, and, box and all,
    I'll give it to my honey;
Oh, would it were ten thousand pounds,
    I'd give it all to Sally;
For she's the darling of my heart,
    And lives in our alley.

My master and the neighbors all
    Make game of me and Sally,
And but for her I'd better be
    A slave, and row a galley;
But when my seven long years are out,
    Oh, then I'll marry Sally,
And then how happily we'll live—
    But not in our alley.

                HENRY CAREY.

THE HOUSEKEEPER'S SOLILOQUY.

HERE'S a big washing to be done—
    One pair of hands to do it—
Sheets, shirts and stockings, coats and pants,
    How will I e'er get through it?

Dinner to get for six or more,
    No loaf left o'er from Sunday;
And baby cross as he can live—
    He's always so on Monday.

'Tis time the meat was in the pot,
  The bread was worked for baking,
The clothes were taken from the boil—
  Oh, dear! the baby's waking!

Hush, baby dear! there, hush–sh–sh,
  I wish he'd sleep a little,
Till I could run and get some wood,
  To hurry up the kettle.

Oh, dear! oh, dear! if P—— comes home,
  And finds things in this pother,
H'll just begin to tell me all
  About his tidy mother!

How nice her kitchen used to be,
  Her dinner always ready
Exactly when the noon-bell rang—
  Hush, hush, dear little Freddy!

And then will come some hasty words,
  Right out before I'm thinking—
They say that hasty words from wives
  Set sober men to drinking.

Now, is not that a great idea,
  That men should take to sinning,
Because a weary, half-sick wife
  Can't always smile so winning?

When I was young I used to earn
  My living without trouble,
Had clothes and pocket money, too,
  And hours of leisure double.

I never dreamed of such a fate
  When I, a-lass, was courted—
Wife, mother, nurse, seamstress, cook, housekeeper,
  chambermaid, laundress, dairy-woman, and scrub
  generally, doing the work of six,
    For the sake of being supported!

MRS. F. GAGE.

(THE MARINER'S DREAM.

IN slumbers of midnight the sailor boy lay;
  His hammock swung loose at the sport of the
      wind;
But watch-worn and weary, his cares flew away,
  And visions of happiness danced o'er his mind.

He dreamt of his home, of his dear native bowers,
  And pleasures that waited on life's merry morn;
While memory each scene gaily covered with flowers,
  And restored every rose, but secreted its thorn.

Then Fancy her magical pinions spread wide,
  And bade the young dreamer in ecstacy rise;
Now far, far behind him the green waters glide,
  And the cot of his forefathers blesses his eyes.

The jessamine clambers in flower o'er the thatch,
  And the swallow chirps sweet from her nest in the
      wall;
All trembling with transport, he raises the latch,
  And the voices of loved ones reply to his call.

A father bends o'er him with looks of delight;
   His cheek is bedewed with a mother's warm tear;
And the lips of the boy in a love-kiss unite
   With the lips of the maid whom his bosom holds
     dear.

The heart of the sleeper beats high in his breast;
   Joy quickens his pulses—his hardships seem o'er;
And a murmur of happiness steals through his rest—
   "O God! thou hast blest me—I ask for no more."

Ah! whence is that flame which now glares on his
    eye?
   Ah! what is that sound which now bursts on his
    ear?
'Tis the lightning's red gleam, painting hell on the
    sky!
   'Tis the crashing of thunders, the groan of the
    sphere!

He springs from his hammock—he flies to the deck;
   Amazement confronts him with images dire;
Wild winds and mad waves drive the vessel a wreck;
   The masts fly in splinters; the shrouds are on fire.

Like mountains the billows tremendously swell;
   In vain the lost wretch calls on Mercy to save;
Unseen hands of spirits are ringing his knell;   .
   And the death-angel flaps his broad wing o'er the
    wave!

O sailor boy, woe to thy dream of delight!
   In darkness dissolves the gay frost-work of bliss.

Where now is the picture that Fancy touched bright,
  Thy parents' fond pressure, and love's honeyed
    kiss?

O sailor boy! sailor boy! never again
  Shall home, love or kindred thy wishes repay;
Unblessed and unhonored, down deep in the main,
  Full many a fathom, thy frame shall decay.

No tomb shall e'er plead to remembrance for thee,
  Or redeem form or fame from the merciless surge;
But the white foam of waves shall thy winding-
    sheet be,
  And winds in the midnight of winter thy dirge!

On a bed of green sea-flowers thy limbs shall be
    laid—
  Around thy white bones the red coral shall grow;
Of thy fair yellow locks, threads of amber be made,
  And every part suit to thy mansion below.

Days, months, years and ages shall circle away,
  And still the vast waters above thee shall roll;
Frail, short-sighted mortals their doom mnst obey—
  O sailor boy! sailor boy! peace to thy soul!
              WILLIAM DIMOND.

OVER THE RIVER.

OVER the river they beckon to me—
  Loved ones who've passed to the further side;
The gleam of their snowy robes I see,
  But their voices are lost in the dashing tide.

There's one with ringlets of sunny gold,
  And eyes the reflection of heaven's own blue;
He crossed in the twilight gray and cold,
  And the pale mist him from mortal view;
We saw not the angels who met him there,
  The gates of the city we could not see—
Over the river, over the river,
  My brother stands waiting to welcome me!

Over the river the boatman pale
  Carried another, the household pet;
Her brown curls waved in the gentle gale—
  Darling Minnie! I see her yet.
She crossed on her bosom her dimpled hands,
  And fearlessly entered the phantom bark;
We felt it glide from the silver sands,
  And all our sunshine grew strangely dark;
We know she is safe on the further side,
  Where all the ransomed and angels be—
Over the river, the mystic river,
  My childhood's idol is waiting for me.

For none return from those quiet shores,
  Who cross with the boatman cold and pale;
We hear the dip of the golden oars,
  And catch a gleam of the snowy sail;
And lo! they have passed from our yearning heart,
  They cross the stream and are gone for aye;
We may not sunder the veil apart
  That hides from our vision the gates of day,

We only know that their barks no more
    May sail with us o'er life's stormy sea,
Yet, somewhere, I know, on the unseen shore,
    They watch, and beckon, and wait for me.

And I sit and think, when the sunset's gold
    Is flushing river and hill and shore,
I shall one day stand by the water cold
    And list for the sound of the boatman's oar;
I shall watch for a gleam of the flapping sail,
    I shall hear the boat as it gains the strand;
I shall pass from sight with the boatman pale,
    To the better shore of the spirit land.
I shall know the loved who have gone before,
    And joyfully sweet will the meeting be,
When over the river, the peaceful river,
    The Angel of Death shall carry me.

                Nancy P. Wakefield.

THE FOURTH OF JULY.

PATRICK an' Bridget, just shtep still the door;
  Faith! seed ye ever the loike soight before?
Flags all a-flyin' from windy an' roof,
Horses decked wid 'em from forelock to hoof;
All the small childer a-poppin' off cracks—
Troth, but they sound loike shillelahs' bould whacks!
Shpake up, swate Biddy, an' answer me, Pat;
Seed yez in Kerry the loike of all that?

"Phat is the row?" to a shpalpeen, sez I,
"Dade, thin," sez he, "its the Foorth uv July!"

Thin I drawed in from the windy me head,
Not wan word wiser for all that he said;
Long kem a leddy, so shmoilin' an' gay,
Troth, I spyakes oop till hersilf wid me say:
"Plaze, mem," I axed her, "what manes the parade?"
Whoy is the racket an' blatherin' made?
Who's been a foightin', an' what was the row?
Shtop a bit, leddy, an' tell me thrue, now."
Faith she looks oop, wid the shmoile in her eye,
" They're sillybratin' the Foorth uv July!"

What a gossoon wuz this Foorth uv July!
Who was the cratur', an' whin did he die?
Whist! Biddy, darlint, an' hear the band play!
See the lads steppin' so frisky an' gay!
Bould sojer laddies in all their galore,
Troth, but there's music an' dhrums to the fore!
Flags all a-flyin' an' powdher ablaze—
Thrue for yez, Biddy, these folk have quare ways.
Sure, thin, St. Pathrick was betther, sez I,
A *dale* betther mon, nor the Foorth uv July.

THE LAKE OF THE DISMAL SWAMP.

"THEY made her a grave, too cold and damp
    For a heart so warm and true;
And she's gone to the Lake of the Dismal Swamp
Where all night long, by a fire-fly lamp,
    She paddles her white canoe!"

"And her fire-fly lamp I soon shall see,
  And her paddle I soon shall hear;
Long and loving our life shall be,
And I'll hide the maid in a cypress, tree,
  When the footstep of death is near!"

Away to the Dismal Swamp he speeds—
  His path was rugged and sore,
Through tangled juniper, beds of reeds,
Through many a fen, where the serpent feeds,
  And man never trod before!

And, when on the earth he sunk to sleep,
  If slumber his eyelids knew,
He lay, where the deadly vine doth weep
Its venomous tear, and nightly steep
  The flesh with blistering dew!

And near him the she-wolf stirred the brake,
  And the copper-snake breathed in his ear,
Till he starting cried, from his dream awake,
"Oh, when shall I see the dusky lake,
  And the white canoe of my dear?"

He saw the lake, and a meteor bright
  Quick over its surface played—
"Welcome," he said, "my dear one's light"
And the dim shore echoed, for many a night,
  The name of the death-cold maid!

Till he hollowed a boat of the birchen bark,
  Which carried him off from shore;

Far, far he followed the meteor spark,
The wind was high and the clouds were dark,
    And the boat returned no more.

But oft from the Indian hunter's camp,
    This lover and maid so true
Are seen, at the hour of midnight damp,
To cross the lake by a fire-fly lamp,
    And paddle their white canoe!

THOMAS MOORE.

THE OLD SEXTON.

HIGH to a grave that was newly made,
    Leaned a sexton old on his earth-worn spade;
His work was done, and he paused to wait
The funeral train at the open gate.
A relic of bygone days was he,
And his locks were as white as the foamy sea;
And these words came from his lips so thin:
"I gather them in—I gather them in—
Gather—gather—I gather them in."

"I gather them in; for man and boy,
Year after year of grief and joy,
I've builded the houses that lie around
In every nook of this burial-ground.
Mother and daughter, father and son,
Come to my solitude one by one;
But come they stranger or come they kin,
I gather them in—I gather them in.

"Many are with me, yet I'm alone ;
I'm King of the Dead, and I make my throne
On a monument slab of marble cold—
My sceptre of rule is the spade I hold.
Come they from cottage, or come they from hall,
Mankind are my subjects, all, all, all!
May they loiter in pleasure, or toilfully spin,
I gather them in—I gather them in.

"I gather them in, and their final rest
Is here, down here, in the earth's dark breast!"
And the sexton ceased, as the funeral train
Wound mutely over that solemn plain;
And I said to myself: When time is told,
A mightier voice than that sexton's old
Will be heard o'er the last trump's dreadful din:
"I gather them in—I gather them in—
Gather—gather—gather them in!"

PARK BENJAMIN.

CHRISTMUS COMIN'.

CHRISTMUS comin,' Christmus comin',
   In de air it soun's a hummin';
I got Christmus in my bones,
Nigger fer de turkey hones.
Wish I was down at camp meetin',
Whar de righteous fokes is greetin',
Master tell me hoe de taters.
White fokes got sech cuyus naters.

Nebber mind, de sun is high,
Mornin' comin' by-an'-by.
In white shirt, an' lay-down collar,
Lazy nigger jump an' holler,
Crack his fingers, hoopin', dancin',
Yaller gals all come out prancing',
Mistiss giv' 'em plenty new
Dresses red 'an dresses blue.
Turn yo toes out, walk in line,
Satan see yo all de time,
Settin' watchin for de sinner,
Had six hundud for one dinner.
Glory, hallelujah high,
Jesus comin' by-an'-by.
Christmus comin' in de mornin',
Onct a year dat day be dawnin',
Sinner come an' git yo whippin',
Whisky jug yo dun been sippin,
Kan't yo wait till day is ober?
When yo ken lay down in clober,
Kick yo heels, an' walk in pride,
Eat an' drink an' swell yo side."

DOT MAID WID HAZEL HAIR.

DALK not to me 'boud maidens rare,
    Mit skin of bearly hue;
Dere vasn'd any kind combare
    Mit one I hafe in view.

She's gendle like der sofd gayzelle
 Her face vas awful fair—
She has dwo aupurn eyes of plue
 Und hazel vas her hair.

Her woice vas rich like anyding,
 Her moud was like der rose,
Her sheeks—dem plooms just like a beach
 Und dimpled vas her nose.

Her hands und feed vas shmall und need,
 Und von dot maiden sings,
Dem leedle birds dey glose deir eyes,
 Und flob deir leedle vings.

I'm going to dook dot leetle maid
 Some day to been my vife,
Und made her habby like I kin,
 Der balance of her life.

Und ven ve'm seddled down for goot,
 I'll show you someding rare,— .
Dwo shmiling aupurn eyes of plue,
 Und shblendid hazel hair.

———— •————

THE COUNTERSIGN.

ALAS! the weary hours pass slow,
 The night is very dark and still;
And in the marshes far below
 I hear the bearded whippoorwill;

I scarce can see a yard ahead,
  My ears are strained to catch each sound;
I hear the leaves about me shed,
  And the spring's bubbling through the ground.

Along the beaten path I pace,
  Where white rags mark my sentry's track;
In formless shrubs I seem to trace
  The foeman's form with bending back.
I think I see him crouching low:
  I stop and list—I stoop and peer,
Until the neighboring hillocks grow
  To groups of soldiers far and near.

With ready piece I wait and watch,
  Until my eyes, familiar grown,
Detect each harmless earthern notch,
  And turn guerillas into stone;
And then, amid the lonely gloom,
  Beneath the tall old chestnut trees,
My silent marches I resume,
  And think of other times than these.

"Halt! Who goes there?" my challenge cry,
  It rings along the watchful line;
"Relief!" I hear a voice reply;
  "Advance, and give the countersign!"
With bayonet at the charge I wait—
  The corporal gives the mystic spell;
With arms aport I charge my mate,
  Then onward pass, and all is well.

But in the tent that night awake,
   I ask, if in the fray I fall,
Can I the mystic answer make
   When the angelic sentries call?
And pray that Heaven may so ordain,
   Where'er I go, what fate be mine,
Whether in pleasure or in pain,
   I still may have the countersign.

WILLIAM TELL AMONG THE MOUNTAINS.

YE craigs and peaks, I'm with you once again!
   I hold to you the hands you first beheld,
To show they still are free.   Methinks I hear
A spirit in your echoes answer me,
And bid your tenant welcome to his home
Again!   O sacred forms, how proud ye look!
How high you lift your heads into the sky!
How huge you are! how mighty and how free!
Ye are the things that tower, that shine, whose smile
Makes glad, whose frown is terrible, whose forms,
Robed or unrobed, do all the impress wear
Of awe divine.   Ye guards of liberty!
I'm with you once again!—I call to you
With all my voice!   I hold my hands to you
To show they still are free.   I rush to you,
As though I could embrace you!
Scaling yonder peak,
I saw an eagle wheeling, near its brow,

O'er the abyss.   His broad, expanded wings
Lay calm and motionless upon the air,
As if he had floated there, without their aid,
By the sole act of his unlorded will,
That buoyed him proudly up!   Instinctively
I bent my bow; yet wheeled he, heeding not
The death that threatened him!   I could not shoot!
'T was liberty!   I turned my bow aside,
And let him soar away.
Once Switzerland was free!   Oh, with what pride
I used to walk these hills, look up to heaven,
And bless God that it was so!   It was free!
From end to end, from cliff to lake, 't was free!
Free as our torrents are, that leap our rocks,
And plough our valleys without asking leave;
Or as our peaks, that wear their caps of snow
In very presence of the regal sun!
How happy was I in it then!   I loved
Its very storms!   Ay, often have I sat
In my boat at night, when down the mountain gorge
The wind came roaring—sat in it, and eyed
The thunder breaking from his cloud, and smiled
To see him shake his lightnings o'er my head,
And think I had no master, save his own!
You know the jutting cliff, round which a track
Up hither winds, whose base is but the brow
To such another one, with scanty room
For two to pass abreast?   O'ertaken there
By the mountain-blast, I've laid me flat along,

And while gust followed gust more furiously,
As if 't would sweep me o'er the horrid brink,
And I have thought of other lands, whose storms
Are summer-flaws to those of mine, and just
Have wished me there—the thought that mine was
      free
Has checked that wish; and I have raised my head,
And cried, in thralldom, to that furious wind,
"Blow on!—This is the land of liberty!"

                J. S. KNOWLES.

THE LOVERS.

SALLY Salter, she was a young teacher who
    taught,
And her friend, Charley Church, was a preacher who
    praught,
Though his enemies called him a screecher who
    scraught.

His heart, when he saw her, kept sinking and sunk,
And his eye, meeting hers, began winking and wunk;
While she, in her turn, kept thinking and thunk.

He hastened to woo her, and sweetly he wooed,
For his love grew until to a mountain it grewed,
And what he was longing to do then he doed.

In secret he wanted to speak, and he spoke,
To seek with his lips what his heart long had soke;
So he managed to let the truth leak, and it loke.

He asked her to ride to the church, and they rode;
They so sweetly did glide that they both thought
  they glode,
And they came to the place to be tied, and were toed.

Then homeward, he said, let us drive, and they drove,
And as soon as they wished to arrive, they arrove,
For whatever he couldn't contrive, she controve.

The kiss he was dying to steal then he stole;
At the feet where he wanted to kneel, then he knole;
And he said, "I feel better than ever I fole."

So they to each other kept clinging, and clung,
While Time his swift circuit was winging and wung;
And this was the thing he was bringing and brung:

The man Sally wanted to catch, and had caught;
That she wanted from others to snatch, and had
  snaught;
Was the one that she now liked to scratch, and she
  scraught.

And Charley's warm love began freezing and froze,
While he took to teazing, and cruelly toze
The girl he had wished to be squeezing and squoze.

"Wretch!" he cried, when she threatenad to leave
  him, and left,
"How could you deceive me, as you have deceft?"
And she answered, "I promised to cleave, and I've
  cleft."   PHŒBE CARY.

LEEDLE YAWCOB STRAUSS.

I HAF von funny leedle poy
Vot gomes shust to my knee,—
Der queerest schap, der createst rogue
As efer you dit see.
He runs, und schumps, und smashes dings
In all barts off der house;
But vot off dat? He vas mine son,
Mine leedle Yawcob Strauss.

He get der measles und der mumbs,
Und eferyding dot's oudt:
He sbills mine glass off lager bier,
Poots snuff into mine kraut;
He fills mine pipe mit Limburg cheese—
Dot vos der roughest chouse;
I'd dake dot from no oder poy
But Leedle Yawcob Strauss.

He dakes der milk-ban for a dhrum,
Und cuts mine cane in dwo
To make der sticks to beat it mit—
Mine cracious, dot vas drue!
I dinks mine hed vas schplit abart,
He kicks oup sooch a touse;
But nefer mind, der poys vas few
Like dot young Yawcob Strauss.

He asks me questions sooch as dese:
Who baints mine nose so red?

Who vas it cuts der schmoodth blace oudt
Vrom der hair ubon mine hed?
Und vwhere der plaze goes vrom der lamp
Vene'er der glim I douse?
How gan I all dese dings eggsblain
To dot schmall Yawcob Strauss?

I somedimes dink I schall go vild
Mit sooch a grazy poy,
Und vish vonce more I gould haf rest
Und beaceful dimes enshoy.
But ven he vas ashleep in ped,
So quiet as a mouse,
I prays der Lord, "Dake anydings,
But leaf dot Yawcob Strauss."

C. F. ADAMS.

THE DESTRUCTION OF SENNACHERIB.

THE Assyrian came down like the wolf on the
    fold,
And his cohorts were gleaming in purple and gold.
And the sheen of their spears was like stars on the
    sea,
When the blue wave rolls nightly on deep Galilee.

Like the leaves of the forest when Summer is green,
That host with their banners at sunset were seen;
Like the leaves of the forest when Autumn hath
    flown,
That host on the morrow lay withered and strown.

For the angel of Death spread his wings on the blast,
And breathed in the face of the foe as he passed;
And the eyes of the sleepers waxed deadly and chill,
And their hearts but once heaved, and forever grew
    still!

And there lay the steed with his nostril all wide,
But through it there rolled not the breath of his
    pride;
And the foam of his gasping lay white on the turf,
And cold as the spray of the rock-beating surf.

And there lay the rider, distorted and pale,
With the dew on his brow and the rust on his mail;
And the tents were all silent, the banners alone,
The lances unlifted, the trumpet unblown.

And the widows of Ashur are loud in their wail,
And their idols are broke in the temple of Baal;
And the might of the Gentile, unsmote by the sword,
Hath melted like snow in the glance of the Lord!
                  BYRON.

BACHELOR'S HALL.

BACHELOR'S Hall, what a quare-lookin' place
    it is!
  Kape me from such all the days of my life!
Sure but I think what a burnin' disgrace it is,
    Niver at all to be gettin' a wife.

Pots, dishes, pans, an' such grasy commodities,
  Ashes and praty-skins, kiver the floor;
His cupboard's a storehouse of comical oddities,
  Things that had niver been neighbors before.

Say the old bachelor, gloomy an' sad enough,
  Placin' his tay-kettle over the fire;
Soon it tips over—Saint Patrick! he's mad enough,
  If he were prisent, to fight with the squire!

He looks for the platter—Grimalkin is scourin it!
  Sure, at a baste like that, swearin' 's no sin;
His dish-cloth is missing; the pigs are devourin' it—
  Thunder and turf! what a pickle he's in!

When his male's over, the table's left sittin' so;
  Dishes, take care of yourselves if you can;
Divil a drop of hot water will visit ye,—
  Och, let him alone for a baste of a man!

Now, like a pig in a mortar-bed wallowin',
  Say the old bachelor kneading his dough;
Troth, if his bread he could ate without swallowin',
  How it would favor his palate, ye know!

Late in the night, when he goes to bed shiverin',
  Niver a bit is the bed made at all;
He crapes like a terrapin under the kiverin';—
  Bad luck to the pictur of Bachelor's Hall!

JOHN FINLEY.

RORY O'MORE.

YOUNG Rory O'More courted Kathleen Bawn,—
He was bold as a hawk, she as soft as the dawn;
He wished in his heart pretty Kathleen to please,
And he thought the best way to do that was to tease.
"Now Rory, be aisy!" sweet Kathleen would cry,
Reproof on her lip, but a smile in her eye,—
"With your tricks, I don't know, in troth, what I'm
    about;
Faith! you've tazed till I've put on my cloak inside
    out."
"Och! jewel!" says Rory, "that same is the way
Ye've thrated my heart for this many a day;
And 'tis plazed that I am, and why not, to be sure?
For 'tis all for good luck," says bold Rory O'More.

"Indeed, then," says Kathleen, "don't think of the
    like,
For I half gave a promise to soothering Mike;
The ground that I walk on he loves, I'll be bound—"
"Faith!" says Rory, "I'd rather love you than the
    ground."
"Now, Rory, I'll cry if you don't let me go;
Sure I dream every night that I'm hating you so!"
"Och!" says Rory, "that same I'm delighted to hear,
For dhrames always go by conthraries, my dear,
So, jewel, kape dhraming that same till ye die,
And bright morning will give dirty night the black lie!
And 'tis plazed that I am' and why not, to be sure?
Since 'tis all for good luck," says bold Rory O'More.

"Arrah, Kathleen, my darlint, you've tazed me
    enough;
Sure I've thrashed, for your sake, Dinny Grimes and
    Jim Duff;
And I've made myself, drinking your health, quite a
    baste,
So I think, after that, I may talk to the praste."
Then Rory, the rogue, stole his arm round her neck,
So soft and so white, without freckle or speck;
And he looked in her eyes, that were beaming with
    light,
And he kissed her sweet lips,—don't you think he
    was right?
"Now, Rory, leave off, sir,—you'll hug me no more,
That's eight times to-day that you've kissed me be-
    fore."
"Then here goes another," says he, "to make sure!
For there's luck in odd numbers," says Rory O'More.

SAMUEL LOVER.

THE PHILOSOPHER'S SCALES.

A MONK, when his rites sacredotal were o'er,
    In the depths of his cell with its stone-covered
        floor,
Resigning to thought his chimerical brain,
Once formed the contrivance we now shall explain;
But whether by magic or alchemy's powers
We know ot; indeed 'tis no business of ours.

Perhaps it was only by patience and care,
At last that he brought his invention to bear,
In youth 'twas projected, but years stole away,
And ere 'twas complete he was wrinkled and gray;
But success is secure, unless energy fails,
And at length he produced THE PHILOSOPHER'S
    SCALES.

"What were they?" you ask. You shall presently
    see;
These scales were not made to weigh sugar and tea.
O no; for such properties wondrous had they,
That qualities, feelings, and thoughts they could
    weigh.
Together with articles small or immense
From mountains or planets to atoms of sense.

Naught was there so bulky but there it would lay,
And naught so ethereal but there it would stay,
And naught so reluctant but in it must go:
All which some examples more clearly will show.

The first thing he weighed was the head of Voltaire,
Which retained all the wit that had ever been there;
As a weight, he threw in the torn scrap of a leaf
Containing the prayer of the penitent thief;
When the skull rose aloft with so sudden a spell
That it bounced like a ball on the roof of the cell.

One time he put in Alexander the Great,
With the garment that Dorcas had made, for a
    weight;

And though clad in armor from sandals to crown,
The hero rose up and the garment went down.

A long row of almshouses, amply endowed
By a well-esteemed Pharisee, busy and proud,
Next loaded one scale; while the other was pressed
By those mites the poor widow dropped into the
    chest;
Up flew the endowment, not weighing an ounce,
And down, down the farthing-worth came with a
    bounce.

By further experiments (no matter how)
He found that ten chariots weighed less than one
    plough;
A sword with gilt trapping rose up in the scale,
Though balanced by only a ten-penny nail;
A shield and a helmet, a buckler and spear,
Weighed less than a widow's uncrystallized tear.

A lord and a lady went up at full sail,
When a bee chanced to light on the opposite scale;
Ten doctors, ten lawyers, two courtiers, one earl,
Ten counsellors' wigs, full of powder and curl,
All heaped in one balance and swinging from thence,
Weighed less than a few grains of candor and sense;
A first water diamond, with brilliants begirt,
Than one good potato just washed from the dirt;
Yet not mountains of silver and gold could suffice
One pearl to outweigh—'twas THE PEARL OF GREAT
    PRICE.

Last of all, the whole world was bowled in at the
    grate,
With the soul of a beggar to serve for a weight,
When the former sprang up with so strong a rebuff,
That it made a vast rent and escaped at the roof!
When balanced in air, it ascended on high,
And sailed up aloft, a balloon in the sky;
While the scale with the soul in 't so mightily fell
That it jerked the philosopher out of his cell.

JANE TAYLOR.

FLEA POWDER.

A FRENCHMAN once,—so runs a certain ditty,
Had crossed the straits to famous London city,
To get a living by the arts of France,
And teach his neighbor, rough John Bull, to dance.
But, lacking pupils, vain was all his skill,
His fortunes sank from low to lower still;
Until, at last, pathetic to relate,—
Poor Monsieur landed at starvation's gate.
Standing, one-day, beside a cook-shop door,
And gazing in, with aggravation sore,
He mused within himself what he should do
To fill his empty maw, and pocket too.
By nature shrewd, he soon contrived a plan,
And thus to execute it straight began:
A piece of common brick he quickly found,
And with a harder stone to powder ground,

Then wrapped the dust in many a dainty piece
Of paper, labeled "Poison for de Fleas,"
And sallied forth, his roguish trick to try,
To show his treasures, and to see who'd buy.
From street to street he cried, with lusty yell,
 'Here's grand and sovereign flea poudare to sell!"
And fickle fortune seemed to smile at last,
For soon a woman hailed him as he passed,
Struck a quick bargain with him for the lot,
And made him five crowns richer on the spot.
Our wight, encouraged by this ready sale,
Went into business on a larger scale;
And soon, throughout all London, scattered he
The "only genuine poudare for de flea."
Engaged, one morning, in his new vocation
Of mingled boasting and dissimulation,
He thought he heard himself in anger called;
And, sure enough, the self-same woman bawled,—
In not a mild or very tender mood,—
From the same window where before she stood,
"Hey, there," said she," you Monsher Powder-man!
Escape my clutches now, sir, if you can;
·I'll let you dirty, thieving Frenchmen know
That decent people won't be cheated so."
Then spoke Monsieur, and heaved a saintly sigh,
With humble attitude and tearful eye;—
"Ah, Madame! si'l vous plait, attendez-vous,—
I vill dis leetle ting explain to you:
My poudare gran! magnifique! why abuse him?

Aha! I show you how to use him;
First, you must wait until you catch de flea:
Den, tickle him on de petite rib, you see;
And when he laugh,—aha, he ope his throat;
Den poke de poudare down!—BEGAR, HE CHOKE.

WORDS AND THEIR USES.

RESPECTED WIFE: From these few lines my
      whereabouts thee'll learn—
Moreover, I impart to thee my serious concern:
The language of this people is a riddle unto me,
And words, with them, are figments of a reckless
      mockery!

For instance: As I left the cars, an imp with smutty
      face,
Said. "Shine?" "Nay, I'll not shine," I said, "except
      with inward grace!"
"Is 'inward grace' a liquid or a paste?" asked this
      young Turk;
"Hi, Daddy! What is inward grace '? How does
      the old thing work?"

"Friend," said I to Jehu, whose breath suggested gin,
"Can thee convey me straightway to a reputable
      inn?"
His answer's gross irrelevance I shall not soon forget;
Instead of simply yea or nay, he gruffly said You
      bet!"

"Nay, nay, I shall not bet," said I, "for that would
 be a sin—
Why don't thee answer plainly: Can thee take me
 to an inn?
Thy vehicle is doubtless meant to carry folk about
 in—
Then why prevaricate?" Said he, perversely, "Now
 yer shoutin'!"

"Nay, verily, I shouted not," quoth I, " my speech
 is mild:
But thine—I grieve to say it—with falsehood is de-
 filed.
Thee ought to be admonished to rid thy heart of
 guile."
"See here! my lively moke," said he, "You sling on
 too much style!"

"I've had these plain drab garments some twenty
 years and more," said I,
"And when thee says I 'sling on style,' thee tells a
 willful lie!"
At that he pranced around as if "a bee were in his
 bonnet,"
And, with hostile demonstrations, inquired if I was
 "on it!"

"On what? Till thee explains thyself, I cannot tell,"
 I said;
He swore that something was "too thin;" moreover,
 it was "played;"

But all his jargon was surpassed, in wild absurdity,
By threats, profanely emphasized, "to put a head on
    me!"

"No son of Belial," said I, "that miracle can do!"
Whereat he fell upon me with blows and curses, too,
But failed to work that miracle—if such was his
    design—
For instead of putting on a head, he strove to smite
    off mine!

Thee knows I cultivate the peaceful habit of our sect,
But this man's conduct wrought on me a singular
    effect ;
For when he slapped my broad-brim off, and asked,
    "How's that for high?"
It roused the Adam in me, and I smote him hip and
    thigh!

The throng then gave a specimen of calumny let
    loose,
And said I'd "snatched him bald-headed," and like-
    wise "cooked his goose!"
Although, I solemnly affirm, I did not pull his hair,
Nor did I cook his poultry—for he had no poultry
    there!

They called me "Bully boy," although I've seen nigh
    three-score year;
And said that I was "lightning" when I "got up on
    my ear!"

And when I asked if lightning climbed its ear, or
    dressed in drab,
"You know how 't is yourself!" said one inconse-
    quential blab!

Thee can conceive that by this time, I was somewhat
    perplexed ;
Yea, the placid spirit in me has seldom been so vexed;
I tarried there no longer, for plain-spoken men—like
    me—
With such perverters of our tongue, can have no unity.
                       FRANK CLIVE.

AUNT SILVA MEETS YOUNG MAS'R JOHN.

WHY, hi! young Mas'r John, dat you?
    Well, bless de goodness, so it is!
An' shake Aunt Silvy's han', you do?
    D' ole 'oman's mons'ous proud o' dis;
Dese ole eyes mighty dim, Mas' John,
An' streamin' tears don't help 'em none.

How is it wid me?   Well, you see,
    'T aint no time been so good but what
Ole mas'r's home befo' we's free
    Is nebber in de least fo'got—
Dese twenty years since I was dah,
An' you was fightin' in de wah.

I mind dem Sat'day a'ternoons,
    When, out befo' de cabins, all

De darkies sat—sich happy loons!—
  To rest an' talk, an' laugh an' bawl.
I likes my freedom, fust an' last,
But still I cries 'bout what's done past.

My ole man's in his grave, long 'go—
  Some chilluns dead, none lef' wid me;
I's gittin' mighty feeble, now,
  An' lonesome in dis world, you see.
Where does I lib? I's got no home,
So here an' dah I has to roam.

You's bought de ole place, you, Mas' John?
  An' takes me back to rest, you say?
De cabin's mine? Bless God, I'm done
  Wid troubles till my dyin' day!
Young mas'r, Silvy'll serve you still,
An' God will lub you, dat he will!

ED. P. THOMPSON.

UNCLE NEB'S DEFENSE.

MY breddren and sisters, I rises for to spiain
  Dis matter what ye's talk n' 'bout; I hopes to
    make it plain.
I'm berry sorry dat de ting hab come before de
    church,
For when I splains it you will see dat it am nuffin'
    much.

My friends, your humble speakah, while trabblin'
　　heah below,
Has nebber stopped to hoard up gold and silber for
　　to show,
He's only stoppin' heah a spell; we all hab got to die,
And so I always tried to lay my treasure up on high.

Da's just one ting dat pesters me, and dat am dis,
　　you see,
De rabens fed old Lijah, but de creturs won't feed me;
Da's got above dar business, and just go swoopin'
　　'round,
And nebber stop to look at me, awaitin' on de ground.

I waited mighty sartin like, my faith was powerful
　　strong,
I reckoned dat dem pesky birds would surely come
　　along;
But oh, my friendly hearers, my faith has kotched a
　　a fall,
Dem aggravatin' fowls went by, and never stopped
　　at all.

De meal and flour was almost gone, de pork-barrel
　　gettin' low,
And so one day I 'cluded dat I had better go
To Brudder Johnson's tater-patch to borrer just a
　　few.
'Twas evening 'fore I got a start—I had so much to do.

It happened dat de night was dark, but dat I didn't
    mind;
I knowed de way to dat dah patch—'twas easy nuff
    to find,
And den I didn't care to meet dat Johnson, for I
    knowed
Dat he would sass me 'bout de mess ob taters dat I
    owed.

I got de basket full at last, and tuck it on my back,
And den was goin' to tote it home, when somethin'
    went kerwhack.
I tot it was a cannon; but it just turned out to be
Dat Johnson's one-hoss pistol a-pointin' straight at
    me.

I tried to argufy wid him, I pologized a heap,
But he said dat stealin' taters was as mean as stealin'
    sheep;
Ob course, I could not take dat dar, it had an ugly
    sound,
So de only ting for me to do was just to knock him
    down.

And now, my friendly hearers, de story all am told;
Ob course, I pounded Johnson till he yelled for me
    to hold;
An' now I hopes you 'grees wid me, dat dis yer case
    and such
Am berry triflin' matters to fotch before de church.

MR. SOCRATES SNOOKS.

MR. SOCRATES SNOOKS, a lord of creation,
The second time entered the marriage relation,
Xantippy Caloric accepted his hand,
And thought him the jolliest man in the land.
But scarce had the honeymoon passed o'er his head,
When one morning, to Xantippy, Socrates said:
"I think, for a man in my standing in life,
This house is too small, as I now have a wife;
So as early as possible carpenter Cary
Shall be sent for to widen my house and my dairy."

"Now, Socrates, dearest," Xantippy replied,
"I hate to hear everything vulgarly *myed;*
So whenever you speak of our chattels again,
Say, *our* cow-house, *our* farm-house, and *our* pig-pen."
"By your leave, Mrs. Snooks, I will say as I please,
Of my houses, my lands, my gardens, my trees."
"SAY OUR!" Xantippy exclaimed, in a rage.
"I *won't*, Mrs. Snooks, tho' you ask it an age."

O woman! though only a part of man's rib,
(If the story of Genesis don't tell a fib,)
Should your naughty companion ere quarrel with you
You should certainly prove the best man of the two.
In the following case it was certainly true,
For the lovely Xantippy just pulled off her shoe,
And, laying about her on all sides at random,
The adage was verified, *Nil desperandum.*

Mr. Socrates Snooks, after trying in vain
To ward off the blows, which descended like rain,
Concluded that valor's part was discretion,
Crept under the bed like a terrified Hessian.
But the dauntless Xantippy, not one whit afraid,
Soon converted the siege into a blockade.

 r. Snooks, after reasoning the thing in his pate,
Concluded 'twas useless to strive against fate,
And so, like a tortoise, protruding his head,
Said "My dear, may we come out from under *our* bed?"
"Ha! ha!" she exclaimed, "Mr. Socrates Snooks,
I perceive you agree to my terms, by your looks.
Now, Socrates, hear me, from this happy hour,
If you'll only obey, I'll never look sour."

'Tis said the next Sabbath, ere going to church,
He chanced for a clean pair of trousers to search;
Having found them, he asked, with a few nervous
  twitches,
"My dear, may we put on *our* new Sunday breeches?"

NEVER GIVE UP.

NEVER give up!—it is wiser and better
 Always to hope than once to despair;
Fling off the load of doubt's cankering fetters,
 And break the dark spell of tyrannical care.
Never give up, or the burden may sink you,—
 Providence kindly has mingled the cup;

And in all trials and troubles bethink you,
  The watchword of life must be, "Never give up!"

Never give up; there are chances and changes,
  Helping the hopeful, a hundred to one,
And through the chaos, High Wisdom arranges
  Ever success, if you'll only hold on.
Never give up; for the wisest is boldest,
  Knowing that Providence mingles the cup,
And of all maxims, the best, as the oldest,
  Is the stern watchword of "Never give up!"

Never give up, though the grape-shot may rattle,
  Or the full thunder-cloud over you burst;
Stand like a rock, and the storm or the battle
  Little shall harm you, though doing their worst.
Never give up; if adversity presses,
  Providence wisely has mingled the cup ;
And the best counsel in all your distresses
  Is the brave watchword of " Never give up!"

THE MOUNTAINS OF LIFE.

THERE'S a land far away, 'mid the stars, we are
      told,
  Where they know not the sorrows of time,—
Where the pure waters wander through valleys of
      gold,
  And life is a treasure sublime;—

'Tis the land of our God, 'tis the home of the soul,
  Where the ages of splendor eternally roll;
Where the way-weary traveler reaches his goal,
  On the evergreen Mountains of Life.

Our gaze cannot soar to that beautiful land,
  But our visions have told of its bliss
And our souls by the gale of its gardens are fanned,
  When we faint in the desert of this :
And we sometimes have longed for its holy repose,
When our spirits were torn with temptations and
    woes,
And we've drank from the tide of the river that flows
  From the evergreen Mountains of Life.

Oh, the stars never tread the blue heavens at night,
  But we think where the ransomed have trod!
And the day never smiles from his palace of light,
  But we feel the bright smile of our God!
We are traveling homeward through changes and
    gloom,
To a kingdom where pleasures unceasingly bloom,
And our guide is the glory that shines through the
    tomb
  From the evergreen Mountains of Life.
               J. G. CLARK.

THE IVY GREEN.

OH, a dainty plant is the Ivy Green,
  That creepeth o'er ruins old;

Of right choice food are his meals, I ween,
  In his cell so lone and cold.
The wall must be crumbled, the stone decayed,
  To pleasure his dainty whim;
And the mouldering dust that years have made
  Is a merry meal for him.
      Creeping where no life is seen,
      A rare old plant is the Ivy Green.

Fast he stealeth on, though he wears no wings,
  And a staunch old heart has he;
How closely he twineth, how tight he clings
  To his friend the huge Oak-tree!
And slyly he traileth along the ground,
  And his leaves he gently waves,
As he joyously hugs and crawleth around
  The rich mould of dead men's graves.
      Creeping where grim death has been,
      A rare old plant is the Ivy Green.

Whole ages have fled, and their works decayed,
  And nations have scattered been;
But the stout old Ivy shall never fade
  From its hale and hearty green.
The brave old plant, in its lonely days,
  Shall fatten upon the past;
For the stateliest building man can raise
  Is the Ivy's food at last.
      Creeping on, where time has been,
      A rare old plant is the Ivy Green.
                              DICKENS.

THE O'LINCOLN FAMILY.

A FLOCK of merry singing-birds were sporting
       in the grove,
Some were warbling cheerily, and some were making
       love;
There were Bobolincon, Wadolincon, Winterseeble,
       Conquedle,
A livelier set was never led by tabor, pipe or fiddle,
Crying, "Phew, shew, Wadolincon, see, see, Bobo-
       lincon,
Down among the tickletops, hiding in the buttercups!
I know the saucy chap, I see his shining cap
Bobbing in the clover there,—see, see, see!"

Up flies Bobolincon, perching on an apple-tree,
Startled by his rival's song, quickened by his raillery;
Soon he spies the rogue afloat, curvetting in the air,
And merrily he turns about, and warns him to beware!
" 'Tis you that would a-wooing go, down among the
       rushes O!
But wait a week, till flowers are cheery,—wait a
       week, and, ere you marry,
Be sure of a house wherein to tarry,
Wadolink, Whiskodink, Tom Denny, wait, wait,
       wait!"

Every one's a funny fellow; every one's a little mel-
       low;
Follow, follow, follow, follow, o'er the hill and in the
       hollow!

Merrily, merrily, there they hie; now they rise and
  now they fly ;
They cross and turn, and in and out, and down in the
  middle, and wheel about,—
With a "Phew, shew, Wadolincon! listen to me,
  Bobolincon!—
Happy's the wooing that's speedily doing, that's
  speedily doing,
That's merry and over with the bloom of the clover!
Bobolincon, Wadolincon, Winterseeble, follow, fol-
  low me! "

WILSON FLAGG.

ROCK ME TO SLEEP.

BACKWARD, turn backward, O Time, in your
  flight,
Make me a child again, just for to-night;
Mother, come back from the echoless shore,
Take me again to your heart as of yore,
Kiss from my forehead the furrows of care,
Smooth the few silver threads out of my hair,
Over my slumbers your loving watch keep—
Rock me to sleep, mother,—rock me to sleep.

Backward, flow backward, O tide of the years!
I am so weary of toil and of tears,—
Toil without recompense, tears all in vain,—
Take them and give me my childhood again!

I have grown weary of dust and decay,—
Weary of flinging my soul-wealth away;
Weary of sowing for others to reap;—
Rock me to sleep, mother,—rock me to sleep!

Tired of the hollow, the base, the untrue,
Mother, O mother, my heart calls for you!
Many a summer the grass has grown green,
Blossomed, and faded our faces between,
Yet with strong yearning and passionate pain
Long I to-night for your presence again.
Come from the silence so long and so deep;—
Rock me to sleep, mother,—rock me to sleep!

Over my heart, in the days that are flown,
No love like mother-love ever has shone;
No other worship abides and endures,—
Faithful, unselfish, and patient, like yours:
None like a mother can charm away pain
From the sick soul and the world-weary brain.
Slumber's soft calms o'er my heavy lids creep;—
Rock me to sleep, mother,—rock me to sleep!

Come, let your brown hair, just lighted with gold,
Fall on your shoulders again as of old;
Let it drop over my forehead to-night,
Shading my faint eyes away from the light;
For with its sunny-edged shadows once more
Haply will throng the sweet visions of yore;
Lovingly, softly, its bright billows sweep;—
Rock me to sleep, mother,—rock me to sleep!

Mother, dear mother, the years have been long
Since I last listened your lullaby song:
Sing, then, and unto my soul it shall seem
Womanhood's years have been only a dream.
Clasped to your heart in a loving embrace,
With your light lashes just sweeping your face,
Never hereafter to wake or to weep;—
Rock me to sleep, mother,—rock me to sleep!

ELIZABETH A. ALLEN.

THE CONQUERED BANNER.

FURL that banner, for 'tis weary;
Round its staff 'tis drooping dreary;
Furl it, fold it, it is best;
For there's not a man to wave it,
And there's not a sword to save it,
And there's not one left to lave it
In the blood which heroes gave it;
And its foes now scorn and brave it:
Furl it, hide it—let it rest.

Take that banner down, 'tis tattered!
Broken is its shaft and shattered,
And the valiant host are scattered,
Over whom it floated high.
Oh, 'tis hard for us to fold it!
Hard to think there's none to hold it;
Hard that those that once unrolled it
Now must furl it with a sigh.

Furl that banner—furl it sadly—
Once ten thousands hailed it gladly
And ten thousands wildly, madly,
  Swore it should forever wave—
Swore that foeman's sword should never
Hearts like theirs entwined dissever,
'Till that flag should float forever
  O'er their freedom or their grave!

Furl it! for the hands that grasped it,
And the hearts that clasped it,
  Cold and dead are lying low;
And that banner—it is trailing!
While around it sounds the wailing
  Of its people in their woe.

For though conquered, they adore it!
Love the cold dead hands that bore it!
Weep for those who fell before it!
Pardon those who trailed and tore it,
But, Oh! wildly they deplore it,
  Now, who furl and fold it so.

Furl that banner! True 'tis gory,
Yet 'tis wreathed around with glory,
And 'twill live in song and story
  Though its folds are in the dust:
For its fame on brightest pages,
Penned by poets and by sages,
Shall go sounding down the ages—
  Furl its folds though now we must.

Furl that banner, softly, slowly;
Treat it gently—it is holy.
   For it droops above the dead.
Touch it not—unfold it never—
Let it droop there furled forever,
   For its people's hopes are dead!

ABRAM T. RYAN.

THE PICKET GUARD.

"ALL quiet along the Potomac," they say,
   "Except now and then a stray picket
Is shot, as he walks on his beat to and fro,
   By a rifleman hid in the thicket;
'Tis nothing—a private or two now and then
   Will not count in the news of the battle;
Not an officer lost—only one of the men,
   Moaning out, all alone, his death rattle."

All quiet along the Potomac to-night,
   Where the soldiers lie peacefully dreaming;
Their tents in the rays of the clear autumn moon
   Or the light of the watch-fires, are gleaming.
A tremulous sigh, as the gentle night-wind
   Through the forest-leaves softly is creeping;
While stars up above, with their glittering eyes,
   Keep guard—for the army is sleeping.

There's only the sound of the lone sentry's tread,
   As he tramps from the rock to the fountain,

And thinks of the two in the low trundle-bed
  Far away in the cot on the mountain.
His musket falls slack—his face, dark and grim,
  Grows gentle with memories tender,
As he mutters a prayer for the children asleep,
  For their mother—may Heaven defend her!

The moon seems to shine just as brightly as then,
  That night, when the love yet unspoken
Leaped up to his lips—when low-murmured vows
  Were pledged to be ever unbroken.
Then drawing his sleeve roughly over his eyes,
  He dashes off tears that are welling,
And gathers his gun closer up to its place,
  As if to keep down the heart-swelling.

He passes the fountain, the blasted pine-tree—
  The footstep is lagging and weary;
Yet onward he goes, through the broad belt of light,
  Toward the shades of the forest so dreary.
Hark! was it the night-wind that rustled the leaves?
  Was it moonlight so suddenly flashing?
It looked like a rifle——"Ah! Mary, good-bye!"
  And the life-blood is ebbing and plashing.

All quiet along the Potomac to-night;
  No sound save the rush of the river;
While soft falls the dew on the face of the dead—
  The picket is off duty forever.

ETHEL L. BEERS.

THE OLD OAKEN BUCKET.

HOW dear to my heart are the scenes of my
    childhood,
  When fond recollection presents them to view!--
The orchard, the meadow, the deep-tangled wild-
    wood,
  And every loved spot which my infancy knew!
The wide-spreading pond, and the mill that stood
    by it;
  The bridge, and the rock where the cataract fell;
The cot of my father, the dairy-house nigh it;
  And e'en the rude bucket that hung in the well—
The old oaken bucket, the iron-bound bucket,
  The moss-covered bucket which hung in the well.

That moss-covered vessel I hailed as a treasure;
  For often at noon, when returned from the field,
I found it the source of an exquisite pleasure—
  The purest and sweetest that nature can yield.
How ardent I seized it, with hands that were glow-
    ing,
  And quick to the white-pebbled bottom it fell!
Then soon, with the emblem of truth overflowing,
  And dripping with coolness, it rose from the
    well—
The old oaken bucket, the iron-bound bucket,
  The moss-covered bucket arose from the well.

How sweet from the green, mossy brim to receive it,
  As, poised on the curb, it inclined to my lips!
Not a full, blushing goblet could tempt me to leave it,
  The brightest that beauty or revelry sips
And now, far removed from the loved habitation,
  The tear of regret will intrusively swell,
As fancy reverts to my father's plantation,
  And sighs for the bucket that hangs in the well—
The old oaken bucket, the iron-bound bucket,
  The moss-covered bucket that hangs in the well!

SAMUEL WOODWORTH.

THE BLUE AND THE GRAY.

BY the flow of the inland river,
  Whence the fleets of iron have fled,
Where the blades of the grave-grass quiver,
  Asleep are the ranks of the dead;—
    Under the sod and the dew,
      Waiting the judgment-day;—
    Under the one, the Blue;
      Under the other, the Gray.

These in the robings of glory,
  Those in the gloom of defeat,
All with the battle-blood gory,
  In the dusk of eternity meet;—
    Under the sod and the dew,
      Waiting the judgment-day;—
    Under the laurel, the Blue;
      Under the willow, the Gray.

From the silence of sorrowful hours
  The desolate mourners go,
Lovingly laden with flowers
  Alike for the friend and the foe;—
    Under the sod and the dew,
      Waiting the judgment-day;—
    Under the roses, the Blue;
      Under the lillies, the Gray.

So with an equal splendor
  The morning sun-rays fall,
With a touch impartially tender,
  On the blossoms blooming for all;—
    Under the sod and the dew,
      Waiting the judgment-day;—
    'Broidered with gold, the Blue;
      Mellowed with gold, the Gray.

So, when the summer calleth,
  On forest and field of grain
With an equal murmur falleth
  The cooling drip of the rain;—
    Under the sod and the dew,
      Waiting the judgment day;—
    Wet with the rain, the Blue;
      Wet with the rain, the Gray.

Sadly, but not with upbraiding,
  The generous deed was done;
In the storm of the years that are fading,
  No braver battle was won;—

Under the sod and the dew,
    Waiting the judgment day;—
Under the blossoms, the Blue;
    Under the garlands, the Gray.

No more shall the war-cry sever,
    Or the winding rivers be red;
They banish our anger forever
    When they laurel the graves of our dead!
    Under the sod and the dew,
        Waiting the judgment-day;—
    Love and tears for the Blue;
        Tears and love for the Gray.
              FRANCIS M. FINCH.

WATERLOO.

THERE was a sound of revelry by night,
    And Belgium's capital had gathered then
Her beauty and her chivalry, and bright
The lamps shone o'er fair women and brave men;
A thousand hearts beat happily; and when
Music arose with its voluptuous swell,
Soft eyes looked love to eyes which spake again,
And all went merry as a marriage-bell;
But hush! hark! a deep sound strikes like a rising
    knell!

Did ye not hear it?   No; 't was but the wind
Or the car rattling o'er the stony street;
On with the dance! let joy be unconfined;
No sleep till morn, when youth and pleasure meet

To chase the glowing hours with flying feet;
But hark!—that heavy sound breaks in once more,
As if the clouds its echo would repeat;
And nearer, clearer, deadlier than before!
Arm! arm! it is—it is—the cannon's opening roar!

Ah! then and there was hurrying to and fro,
And gathering tears, and tremblings and distress,
And cheeks all pale, which but an hour ago
Blushed at the praise of their own loveliness;
And there were sudden partings, such as press
The life from out young hearts, and choking sighs
Which ne'er might be repeated; who could guess
If evermore should meet those mutual eyes,
Since upon night so .sweet such awful morn could
     rise!

And there was mounting in hot haste; the steed,
The mustering squadron, and the clattering car,
Went pouring forward with impetuous speed,
And swiftly forming in the ranks of war;
And the deep thunder, peal on peal afar;
And near, the beat of the alarming drum
Roused up the soldier ere the morning star;
While thronged the citizens with terror dumb,
Or whispering, with white lips,—"The foe! They
     come! they come!"

And wild and high the "The Cameron's gather-
     ing" rose!

The war-notes of Lochiel, which Albyn's hills
Have heard, and heard, too, have her Saxon foes;
How in the noon of night that pibroch thrills,
Savage and shrill!   But with the breath which fills
Their mountain-pipe, so fill the mountaineers
With the fierce native daring which instills
The stirring memory of a thousand years,
And Evan's, Donald's fame rings in each clansman's
    ears!

BYRON.

MARCO BOZZARIS.

AT midnight, in his guarded tent,
   The Turk was dreaming of the hour
When Greece her knee in suppliance bent,
   Should tremble at his power.
In dreams, through camp and court he bore
   The trophies of a conqueror;
In dreams his song of triumph heard;
Then wore his monarch's signet-ring,
Then pressed that monarch's throne—a king;
As wild his thoughts, and gay of wing,
   As Eden's garden bird.

At midnight, in the forest shades,
   Bozzaris ranged his Suliote band,—
True as the steel of their tried blades,
   Heroes in heart and hand.
There had the Persian's thousands stood,

There had the glad earth drunk their blood,
  On old Platæa's day ;
And now there breathed that haunted air
The sons of sires who conquered there,
With arm to strike, and soul to dare,
  As quick, as far, as they.

An hour passed on, the Turk awoke:
  That bright dream was his last;
He woke—to hear his sentries shriek,
  "To arms! they come! the Greek! the Greek!"
He woke—to die midst flame, and smoke,
And shout, and groan, and sabre-stroke,
  And death-shots falling thick and fast
As lightnings from the mountain-cloud ;
And heard, with voice as trumpet loud;
  Bozzaris cheer his band!
"Strike—till the last armed foe expires:
Strike—for your altars and your fires;
Strike—for the green graves of your sires
  God, and your native land! "

They fought, like brave men, long and well;
  They piled the ground with Moslem slain;
They conquered, but Bozzaris fell,
  Bleeding at every vein.
His few surviving comrades saw
His smile, when rang their proud hurrah,
  And the red field was won;
Then saw in death his eyelids close,

Calmly, as to a night's repose,
  Like flowers at set of sun.

Come to the bridal chamber, Death!
  Come to the mother when she feels
For the first time her first-born's breath;
  Come when the blessed seals
Which close the pestilence are broke,
And crowded cities wail its stroke;
Come in consumption's ghastly form,
The earthquake's shock, the ocean storm;
Come when the heart beats high and warm
  With banquet-song, and dance, and wine,
And thou art terrible: the tear,
The groan, the knell, the pall, the bier,
And all we know, or dream, or fear
  Of agony, are thine.

But to the hero, when his sword
  Has won the battle for the free,
Thy voice sounds like a prophet's word,
And in its hollow tones are heard
  The thanks of millions yet to be.

SOUTH CAROLINA AND MASSACHUSETTS.

[From a speech in defense of the Union and the Constitution, delivered in the Senate of the United States, January 26, 1830.

THE eulogium pronounced by the honorable gentleman on the character of the State of South
Carolina, for her Revolutionary and other merits,

meets my hearty concurrence.   I shall not acknowledge that the honorable member goes before me in
regard for whatever of distinguished talent or distinguished character South Carolina has produced.
I claim part of the honor; I partake in the pride of
her great names.   I claim them for countrymen, one
and all—the Laurenses, the Rutledges, the Pinck-
neys, the Sumters, the Marions—Americans all,
whose fame is no more to be hemmed in by State lines
than their talents and patriotism were capable of
being circumscribed within the same narrow limits.

In their day and generation they served and honored the country, and the whole country; and their
renown is of the treasures of the whole country.
Him whose honored name the gentleman himself
bears—does he esteem me less capable of gratitude
for his patriotism, or sympathy for his sufferings,
than if his eyes had first opened upon the light of
Massachusetts, instead of South Carolina? Sir, does
he suppose it in his power to exhibit a Carolina name
so bright as to produce envy in my bosom? No, sir;
increased gratification and delight, rather.   I thank
God that, if I am gifted with little of the spirit which
is able to raise mortals to the skies, I have yet none,
as I trust, of that other spirit, which would drag
angels down.

When I shall be found, sir, in my place here in
the Senate, or elsewhere, to sneer at public merit
because it happens to spring up beyond the limits of

my own State or neighborhood; when I refuse, for any such cause, or for any cause, the homage due to American talent, to elevated patriotism, to sincere devotion to liberty and the country; or if I see an uncommon endowment of heaven—if I see extraordinary capacity and virtue in any son of the South, and if, moved by local prejudice or gangrened by State jealousy, I get up here to abate the tithe of a hair from his just character and just fame—may my tongue cleave to the roof of my mouth.

Sir, let me recur to pleasing recollections; let me indulge in refreshing remembrances of the past; let me remind you that, in early times, no States cherished greater harmony, both of principle and feeling, than Massachusetts and South Carolina. Would to God that harmony might again return! Shoulder to shoulder they went through the Revolution; hand in hand they stood round the administration of Washington, and felt his own great arm lean on them for support. Unkind feeling, if it exist, alienation and distrust, are the growth, unnatural to such soils, of false principles since sown. They are weeds, the seeds of which that same great arm never scattered.

Mr. President, I shall enter on no encomium upon Massachusetts; she needs none. There she is. Behold her, and judge for yourselves. There is her history; the world knows it by heart. The past, at least, is secure. There is Boston, and Concord, and

Lexington, and Bunker Hill; and there they will remain forever. The bones of her sons, fallen in the great struggle for independence, now lie mingled with the soil of every State, from New England to Georgia; and there they will lie forever.

And, sir, where American liberty raised its first voice, and where its youth was nurtured and sustained, there it still lives, in the strength of its manhood, and full of its original spirit. If discord and disunion shall wound it; if party strife and blind ambition shall hawk at and tear it; if folly and madness, if uneasiness, under salutary and necessary restraint, shall succeed in separating it from that Union by which alone its existence is made sure—it will stand, in the end, by the side of that cradle in which its infancy was rocked; it will stretch forth its arm, with whatever of vigor it may still retain, over the friends who gathered round it; and it will fall at last, if fall it must, amid the proudest monuments of its own glory, and on the very spot of its origin.   DANIEL WEBSTER.

DEDICATION OF GETTYSBURG CEMETERY.

FOURSCORE and seven years ago our fathers brought forth upon this continent a new nation, conceived in liberty, and dedicated to the proposition that all men are created equal. Now we are engaged in a great civil war: testing whether that nation, or any nation, so conceived and so dedicated, can long endure. We are met on a great battle-field of that war. We are met to dedicate a portion of it as the final resting-place of those who here gave their lives that that nation might live.

It is altogether fitting and proper that we should do this. But in a larger sense we cannot dedicate, we cannot consecrate, we cannot hallow this ground. The brave men, living and dead, who struggled here, have consecrated it far above our power to add or detract. The world will little note, nor long remember what we say here, but it can never forget what they did here.

It is for us, the living, rather, to be dedicated here to the unfinished work they have thus far so nobly carried on. It is rather for us to be here dedicated to the great task remaining before us, that from these honored dead we take increased devotion to the cause for which they gave the last full measure of devotion; that we here highly resolve that these dead shall not have died in vain, that the nation shall, under God, have a new birth of freedom, and that the government of the people, by the people, and for the people, shall .not perish from the earth.   ABRAHAM LINCOLN.

VALLEY FORGE.

[Extract from an oration delivered upon the occasion of the first Centenary Anniversary of the Encampment at Valley Forge.]

MY COUNTRYMEN: The century that has gone by has changed the face of nature and wrought a revolution in the habits of mankind. We stand to-day at the dawn of an extraordinary age. Freed from the chains of ancient thought and superstition, man has begun to win the most extraordinary victories in the domain of science. One by one he has dispelled the doubts of the ancient world. Nothing is too difficult for his hand to attempt—no region too remote—no place too sacred for his daring eye to penetrate. He has robbed the earth of her secrets and sought to solve the mysteries of the heavens! He has secured and chained to his service the elemental forces of nature—he has made the fire his steed—the winds his ministers—the seas his pathway—the lightning his messenger. He has descended into the bowels of the earth, and walked in safety on the bottom of the sea. He has raised his head above the clouds, and made the impalpable air his resting-place. He has tried to analyze the stars, count the constellations, and weigh the sun. He has advanced with such astounding speed that, breathless we have reached a moment when it seems as if distance had been annihilated, time made as naught, the invisible seen, the inaudible heard, the unspeakable spoken, the intangible felt, the impossible accomplished. And already we knock at the door of a new century which promises to be infinitely brighter and more enlightened and happier than this. But in all this blaze of light which illuminates the present and casts its reflection into the distant recesses of the past, there is not a single ray that shoots into the future.   Not one step have we taken toward the solution of the mystery of life. That remains to-day as dark and unfathomable as it was ten thousand years ago.

We know that we are more fortunate than our fathers.   We believe that our children shall be happier than we.   We know that this century is more enlightened that the last.   We believe that the time to come will be better and more glorious than this.   We think, we believe, we hope, but we do not know.   Across that threshold we may not pass; behind that vail we may not penetrate.   Into that country it may not be for us to go.   It may be vouchsafed to us to behold it, wonderingly, from afar, but never to enter in.   It matters not.   The age in which we live is but a link in the endless and eternal chain.   Our lives are like the sands upon the shore; our voices like the breath of this summer breeze that stirs the leaf for a moment and is forgotten.   Whence we have come and whither we shall go, not one of us can tell.   And the last survivor of this mighty multitude shall stay but a little while.

But in the impenetrable To Be, the endless generations are advancing to take our places as we fall.   For them as for us shall the earth roll on and the seasons come and go, the snowflakes fall, the **flowers bloom, and the harvests be gathered in.**

For them as for us shall the sun, like the life of man, rise out of darkness in the morning and sink into darkness in the night. For them as for us shall the years march by in the sublime procession of the ages. And here, in this place of sacrifice, in this vale of humiliation, in this valley of the shadow of that Death out of which the life of America arose, regenerate and free, let us believe with an abiding faith that, to them, Union will seem as dear, and Liberty as sweet, and Progress as glorious, as they were to our fathers and are to you and me, and that the institutions which have made us happy, preserved by the virtue of our children, shall bless the remotest generations of the time to come. And unto Him who holds in the hollow of His hand the fate of nations, and yet marks the sparrow's fall, let us lift up our hearts this day, and into His eternal care commend ourselves, our children, and our country.   H. A. BROWN.

LIBERTY OR DEATH.

[From the speech delivered in March, 1775, in the second Virginia
Convention, in support of the resolution "that the colony
be immediately put in a state of defence."]

MR. PRESIDENT: It is natural to man to indulge in the illusions of hope. We are apt to shut our eyes against a painful truth, and listen to the song of that siren, till she transforms us into beasts. Is this the part of wise men, engaged in a great and arduous struggle for liberty? Are we disposed to be of the number of those who, having eyes, see not, and having ears, hear not, the things which so nearly concern their temporal salvation? For my part, whatever anguish of spirit it may cost, I am willing to know the whole truth—to know the worst, and to provide for it. I have but one lamp by which my feet are guided, and that is the lamp of experience. I know of no way of judging of the future but by the past; and, judging by the past, I wish to know what there has been in the conduct of the British ministry for the last ten years to justify those hopes with which gentlemen have been pleased to solace themselves and the House. Is it that insidious smile with which our petition has been lately received? Trust it not, sir; it will prove a snare to your feet! Suffer not yourselves to be betrayed with a kiss. Ask yourselves how this gracious reception of our petition comports with those warlike preparations which cover our waters and darken our land. Are fleets and armies necessary to a work of love and reconciliation? Have we shown ourselves so unwilling to be reconciled that force must be called in to win back our love?

Let us not deceive ourselves, sir. These are the implements of war and subjugation—the last arguments to which kings resort. I ask, sir, what means this martial array, if its purpose be not to force us to submission? Can gentlemen assign any other possible motive for it? Has Great Britian any enemy in this quarter of the world, to call for all this accumulation of navies and armies? No, sir, she has none; they are meant for us; they can be meant for no other.   They are sent over to bind and rivet upon us those chains which the British ministry have been so long forging.   And what have we to oppose to them? Shall we try argument? Sir, we have been trying that for the last ten years.   Have we anything new to offer upon the subject? Nothing.   We have held the subject up in every light of which it is capable, but it has been all in vain.   Shall we resort to entreaty and humble supplication? What terms shall we find which have not been already exhausted?   Let us not, I beseech you, sir, deceive ourselves longer. Sir, we have done everything that could be done to avert the storm that is now coming on.   We have petitioned; we have remonstrated; we have supplicated; we have prostrated ourselves before the throne, and have implored its interposition to arrest the tyrannical hands of the ministry and Parliament.

Our petitions have been slighted; our remonstrances have produced additional violence and insult; our applications have been disregarded; and we have been spurned with contempt from the foot of the throne! In vain, after these things, may we indulge the fond hope of peace and reconciliation. There is no longer any room for hope. If we wish to be free; if we mean to preserve inviolate those inestimable privileges for which we have been so long contending; if we mean not basely to abandon the noble struggle in which we have been so long engaged, and which we have pledged ourselves never to abandon until the glorious object of our contest shall be obtained, we must fight! I repeat it, sir: We must fight! An appeal to arms and to the God of Hosts is all that is left us!

They tell us, sir, that we are weak—unable to cope with so formidable an adversary; but when shall we be stronger? Will it be the next week, or the next year? Will it be when we are totally disarmed, and a British guard shall be stationed in every house? Shall we gather strength by irresolution and inaction? Shall we acquire the means of effectual resistance by lying supinely on our backs, and hugging the delusive phantom of hope, until our enemies shall have bound us hand and foot? Sir, we are not weak if we make a proper use of those means which the God of Nature hath placed in our power. Three millions of people armed in the holy cause of liberty, and in such a country as that which we possess, are invincible by any force which our enemy can send against us. Besides, sir, we shall not fight our battles alone: there is a just God who presides over the destinies of nations, and who will raise up friends to fight our battles for us. The battle is not to the strong alone: it is to the vigilant, the active, the brave. Besides, sir, we have no election. If we were base enough to desire it, it is now too late to retire from the contest. There is no retreat, but in submission or slavery! Our chains are forged! Their clanking may be heard on the plains of Boston! The war is inevitable, and let it come! I repeat it, sir: Let it come!

It is vain, sir, to extenuate the matter. Gentlemen may cry "Peace! peace!" but there is no peace. The war is actually begun! The next gale that sweeps from the north will bring to our ears the clash of resounding arms! Our brethren are already in the field! Why stand we here idle? What is it that gentleman wish? What would they have? Is life so dear, or peace so sweet, as to be purchased at the price of chains and slavery? Forbid it, Almighty God! I know not what course others may take, but, as for me, give me liberty, or give me death! PATRICK HENRY.

THE TWO ROADS.

IT was New Year's night. An aged man was standing at a window. He mournfully raised his eyes toward the deep blue sky, where the stars were floating like white lilies on the surface of a clear, calm lake. Then he cast them on the earth, where few more helpless beings than himself were moving towards their inevitable goal—the tomb. Already he had passed sixty of the stages which lead to it, and he had brought from his journey nothing but errors and remorse. His health was destroyed, his mind unfurnished, his heart sorrowful, and his old age devoid of comfort. The days of his youth rose up in a vision before him, and he recalled the solemn moment when his father had placed him at the entrance of two roads, one leading into a peaceful, sunny land, covered with a fertile harvest, and resounding with soft, sweet songs; while the other conducted the wanderer into a deep, dark cave, whence there was no issue, where poison flowed instead of water, and where serpents hissed and crawled.

He looked towards the sky, and cried out in his anguish: "O youth, return! O my father, place me once more at the crossway of life, that I may choose the better road!" But the days of his youth had passed away, and his parents were with the departed. He saw wandering lights float over dark marshes, and then disappear. "Such," he said, "were the days of my wasted life!" He saw a star shoot from heaven, and vanish in darkness athwart the churchyard. "Behold an emblem of myself!" he exclaimed; and the sharp arrows of unavailing remorse struck him to the heart.

Then he remembered his early companions, who had entered life with him, but who, having trod the paths of virtue and industry, were now happy and honored on this New Year's night. The clock in the high church-tower struck, and the sound, falling on his ear, recalled the many tokens of the love of his parents for him, their erring son; the lessons they had taught him; the prayers they had offered up in his behalf. Overwhelmed with shame and grief, he dared no longer look towards that heaven where they dwelt. His darkened eyes dropped tears, and, with one despairing effort, he cried aloud, "Come back, my early days! Come back!"

And his youth *did* return; for all this had been but a dream, visiting his slumbers on New Year's night. He was still young; his errors only were no dream. He thanked God fervently that time was still his own; that he had not yet entered the deep, dark cavern, but that he was free to tread the road leading to the peaceful land where sunny harvests wave.

Ye who still linger on the threshold of life, doubting which path to choose, remember that when years shall be passed, and your feet shall stumble on the dark mountain, you will cry bitterly, but cry in vain, "O youth, return! Oh, give me back my early days!" JEAN PAUL RICHTER.

THE POLISH BOY.

WHENCE came those shrieks so wild and shrill,
 That like an arrow cleave the air,
Causing the blood to creep and thrill
 With such sharp cadence of despair?
Once more they come! as if a heart
 Was cleft in twain by one quick blow
And every string had voice apart
 To utter its peculiar woe!

Whence came they? From yon temple, where
An altar raised for private prayer,
Now farms the warriors marble bed,
Who Warsaw's gallant armies led.
The dim funereal tapers threw,
A holy luster o'er his brow
And burnish with their rays of light
The mass of curls that gather bright
Above the haughty brow and eye
Of a young boy that's kneeling by.

What hand is that whose icy press
 Clings to the dead with death's own grasp,
But feels no answering caress—
 No thrilling fingers seek its clasp?
As is the hand of her whose cry
 Rang wildly late upon the air,
When the dead warrior met her eye,
 Outstretched upon the altar there.

Now with white lips and broken moan
She sinks beside the altar stone;
But, hark! the heavy tramp of feet
Is heard along the gloomy street;
Nearer and nearer yet they come
With clanking arms and noiseless drum.
They leave the pavement. Flowers that spread
Their beauties by the path they tread
Are crushed and broken. Crimson hands
Rend brutally their blooming bands.
Now whispered curses low and deep,
Around the holy temple creep.
The gate is burst   The ruffian band
Rush in and savagely demand
With brutal voice and oath profane,
The startled boy for exile's chain.

The mother sprang with gesture wild,
And to her bosom snatched her child;
Then with pale cheek and flashing eye,
Shouted with fearful energy—
    "Back, ruffians, back! nor dare to tread
Too near the body of my dead!
Nor touch the living boy —I stand
Between him and your lawless band!
No traitor he—but, listen, I
Have cursed your master's tyranny.
I cheered my lord to join the band
Of those who swore to free our land,

Or fighting, die; and when he pressed
Me for the last time to his breast,
I knew that soon his form would be
Low as it is, or Poland free."
He went and grappled with the foe,
Laid every haughty Russian low;
But he is dead—the good—the brave—
And I, his wife, am worse—a slave!
Take me, and bind these arms and hands
With Russia's heaviest iron bands,
And drag me to Siberia's wild
To perish, if 'twill save my child."

"Peace, woman, peace!" the leader cried,
Tearing the pale boy from her side;
And in his ruffian grasp he bore
His victim to the temple door.

"One moment," shrieked the mother, "one;
Can land or gold redeem my son? ·
If so, I bend my Polish knee,
And Russia, ask a boon of thee.
Take palaces, take lands, take all,
But leave him free from Russian thrall.
Take these," and her white arms and hands
She stripped of rings and diamond bands,
And tore from braids of long, black hair
The gems that gleamed like starlight there;
Unclasped the brilliant coronal

And carcanet of orient pearl;
Her cross of blazing rubies last,
Down at the Russian's feet she cast.

He stooped to seize the glittering store,
Upspringing from the marble floor,
The mother, with a cry of joy
Snatched to her leaping heart the boy!
But, no! the Russian's iron grasp
Again undid the mother's clasp;
Forward she fell, with one long cry,
Of more than mother's agony.

But the brave child is roused at length,
    And breaking from the Russian's hold,
He stands a giant in the strength
    Of his young spirit, fierce and bold.

Proudly he towers, his flashing eye
    So blue and fiercely bright,
Seems lighted from the eternal sky,
    So brilliant is its light.
His curling lips and crimson cheeks,
Foretell the thought before he speaks
With a full voice of proud command,
He turns upon his wondering band.

"Ye hold me not! no, no, nor can,
This hour has made the boy a man,
The world shall witness that one soul
Fears not to prove itself a Pole.

I knelt beside my slaughtered sire,
Nor felt one throb of vengeful ire;
I wept upon his marble brow—
Yes, wept—I was a child; but, now,
My noble mother, on her knee,
Has done the work of years for me.
Although in this small tenement
My soul is cramped, unbowed, unbent,
I've still within me ample power
To free myself this very hour.
This dagger in my heart! and then
Where is your boasting power, base men?"

He drew aside his broidered vest,
And there, like slumbering serpents crest,
The jeweled haft of a poniard bright,
Glittered a moment on the sight.
"Ha! start ye back! Fool! coward! knave!
Think you my noble father's glave,
Could drink the life-blood of a slave?
The pearls that on the handle flame
Would blush to rubies in their shame;
The blade would quiver in thy breast,
Ashamed of such ignoble rest;
No; thus I rend thy tyrant's chain
And fling him back a boy's disdain!"

A moment, and the funeral light
Flashed on the jeweled weapon bright ;
Another, and his young heart's blood

Leaped to the floor, a crimson flood;
Quick to the mother's side he sprang,
As on the ear his clear voice rang—
"Up! mother, up! look on my face
I only wait for thy embrace;
One last, last word—a blessing, one
To prove thou knowest what I have done
No look! no word! canst thou not feel
My warm blood o'er thy heart congeal?
Speak, mother, speak! lift up thy head,
What, silent still? then art thou dead!
Great God, I thank Thee! Mother I
Rejoice with thee, and thus to die.
Slowly he falls.   The clustering hair
Rolls back and leaves that forehead bare,
One long, deep breath, and his pale head
Lay on his mother's bosom, dead!

MRS. ANN S. STEPHENSON.

SMITING THE ROCK.

THE stern old judge, in relentless mood,
  Glanced at the two who before him stood;
She was bowed and haggard and old,
He was young and defiant and bold—
Mother and son; and to gaze at the pair,
Their different attitudes, look and air,
One would believe, ere the truth were known
The mother convicted, and not the son.

There was the mother; the boy stood nigh
With a shameless look, and his head held high.
Age had come over her, sorrow and care;
These mattered but little so he was there,
A prop to her years and a light to her eyes,
And prized as only a mother can prize;
But what for him could a mother say,
Waiting his doom on a sentence-day?

Her husband had died in his shame and sin,
And she, a widow, her living to win,
Had toiled and struggled from morn till night,
Making with want a wearisome fight,
Bent over her work with resolute zeal,
Till she felt her old frame totter and reel,
Her weak limbs tremble, her eyes grow dim;
But she had her boy, and she toiled for him.

And he—he stood in the criminal dock,
With a heart as hard as a flinty rock,
An impudent glance and a reckless air,
Braving the scorn of the gazers there;
Dipped in crime and encompassed round
With proof of his guilt by captors found,
Ready to stand, as he phrased it, "game,"
Holding not crime, but penitence, shame.

Poured in a flood o'er the mother's cheek
The moistened prayers where the tongue was weak,
And she saw through the mist of those bitter tears
Only the child in his innocent years;

She remembered him pure as a child might be,
The guilt of the present she could not see;
And. for mercy her wistful looks made prayer
To the stern old judge in his cushioned chair.

"Woman," the old judge crabbedly said,
"Your boy is the neighborhood's plague and dread;
Of a gang of reprobates chosen chief;
An idler and rioter, ruffian and thief.
The jury did right, for the facts were plain;
Denial is idle, excuses are vain.
The sentence the court imposes is one"—
"Your honor," she cried, "he's my only son."

The tipstaves grinned at the words she spoke,
And a ripple of fun through the court-room broke;
But over the face of the culprit came
An angry look and a shadow of shame.
"Don't laugh at my mother!" loud cries he;
"You've got me fast, and can deal with me;
But she's too good for your coward jeers,
And I'll—" then his utterance choked with tears

The judge for a moment bent his head,
And looked at him keenly, and then he said:
"We suspend the sentence—the boy can go;
"But say!"—and he raised his finger then,
And the words were tremulous, forced and low—
"Don't let them bring you hither again.
There is something good in you yet, I know;
I'll give you a chance—make the most of it—Go!"

The twain went forth, and the old judge said:
"I meant to have given him a year instead.
And perhaps 'tis a difficult thing to tell
If clemency here be ill or well.
But a rock was struck in that callous heart,
From which a fountain of good may start;
For one on the ocean of crime long tossed,
Who loves his mother, is not quite lost."

THE BURIAL OF THE DANE.

BLUE gulf all around us,
    Blue sky overhead;
Muster all on the quarter,
    We must bury the dead!

It is but a Danish sailor,
    Rugged of front and form—
A common son of the forecastle,
    Grizzled with son and storm.

His name and the strand he hailed from
    We know; and there's nothing more!
But perhaps his mother is waiting
    On the lonely Island of Fohr.

Still, as he lay there dying,
    Reason drifting awreck,
" 'Tis my watch," he would mutter
    "I must go upon deck!"

Ay, on deck—by the foremast!—
    But watch and look-out are done;

The Union-Jack laid o'er him,
  How quiet he lies in the sun!

Slow the ponderous engine,
  Stay the hurrying shaft!
Let the roll of the ocean
  Cradle our giant craft;
Gather around the grating,
  Carry your messmate aft!

Stand in order, and listen
  To the holiest pages of prayer;
Let every foot be quiet,
  Every head be bare;
The soft trade-wind is lifting
  A hundred locks of hair.

Our captain reads the service,
  (A little spray on his cheeks,)
The grand old words of burial,
  And the trust a true heart seeks—
"We therefore commit his body
  To the deep;" and, as he speaks,

Launched from the weather railing,
  Swift as the eye can mark,
The ghastly shotted hammock
  Plunges, away from the shark,
Down a thousand fathoms—
  Down into the dark.

A thousand summers and winters
   The stormy gulf shall roll
High o'er his canvas coffin;
   But silence to doubt and dole!
There's a quiet harbor somewhere
   For the poor a-weary soul.

Free the fettered engine,
   Speed the tireless shaft!
Loose to gallant and topsail,
   The breeze is fair abaft!

Blue are all around us,
   Blue sky bright overhead;
Every man to his duty!
   We have buried the dead.

H. H. BROWNELL.

CATILINE'S DEFIANCE.

CONSCRIPT FATHERS:

I DO not rise to waste the n ght in words:
   Let that Plebeian talk, 'tis not *my* trade;
But *here* I stand for right,—let him show *proofs*,—
For Roman right, though none, it seems, dare stand
To take their share with me. Ay, cluster there!
Cling to your master, judges, Romans, *slaves*!
His charge is false;—I *dare* him to his proofs,
You have my answer. Let my actions speak!

But this I will avow, that I *have* scorned
And still *do* scorn, to hide my sense of wrong

Who brands me on the forehead, breaks my sword,
Or lays the bloody scourge upon my back,
Wrongs me not half so much as he who shuts
The gates of honor on me,—turning out
The Roman from his birthright; and for what?

To fling your offices to every slave!
Vipers, that creep where man disdains to climb,
And having wound their loathsome track to the top
Of this huge, mouldering monument of Rome,
Hang hissing at the nobler man below.
　　Come, consecrated Lictors, from your thrones;
Fling down your sceptres; take the rod and axe,
And make the murder as you make the law.

Banished from Rome! What's banished, but set free
From daily contact of the things I loathe?
"Tried and convicted traitor!" Who says this?
Who'll prove it at his peril, on my head?
Banished! I thank you for't. It breaks my chain!
I held some slack allegiance till this hour ;
But *now* my sword's my own. Smile on, my Lords!
I scorn to count what feelings, withered hopes,
Strong provocations, bitter, burning wrongs,
I have within my heart's hot cells shut up;
To leave you in your lazy dignities.
But here I stand and scoff you! here I fling
Hatred and full defiance in your face!
Your Consul's merciful;—for this, all thanks.
He *dares* not touch a hair of Catiline!

"Traitor!" I go; but I *return!* This—trial!
Here I devote you Senate!   I've had wrongs
To stir a fever in the blood of age,
Or make the infant's sinews strong as steel.
This day's the birth of sorrow; this hour's work
Will breed proscriptions!   Look to your hearths,
     my Lords!
For there, henceforth, shall sit, for household gods,
Shapes hot from Tartarus; all shames and crimes;
Wan Treachery, with his thirsty dagger drawn;
Suspicion poisoning his brother's cup;
Naked Rebellion, with the torch and axe,
Making his wild sport of your blazing thrones;
Till Anarchy comes down on you like night,
And Massacre seals Rome's eternal grave.

  I go; but not to leap the gulf alone.
I go; but when I come, 'twill be the burst
Of ocean in the earthquake,—rolling back
In swift and mountainous ruin.   Fare you well!
You built my funeral-pile; but your best blood
Shall quench its flame!   Back slaves!
I will return.   GEORGE CROLY

RIENZI'S ADDRESS.

I COME not here to talk!   Ye know too well
  The story of our thraldom; we are slaves!
The bright sun rises to his course, and lights
A race of slaves!   He sets, and his last beam

Falls on a slave!—not such as, swept along
By the full tide of power, the conqueror leads
To crimson glory and undying fame;
But base, ignoble slaves—slaves to a horde
Of petty tyrants, feudal despots, lords,
Rich in some dozen paltry villages,
Strong in some hundred spearmen—only great
In that strange spell, a name! Each hour, dark
        fraud,
Or open rapine, or protected murder,
Cries out against them.   But this very day,
An honest man, my neighbor—there he stands—
Was struck—struck like a dog—by one who wore
The badge of Ursini! because, forsooth,
He tossed not high his ready cap in air
Nor lifted up his voice in servile shouts,
At sight of that great ruffian!   Be we men,
And suffer such dishonor? Men and wash not
The stains away in blood? Such shames are common.
I have known deeper wrongs, I that speak to you,
I had a brother once, a gracious boy,
Full of all gentleness, of calmest hope,
Of sweet and quiet joy; there was the look
Of heaven upon his face, which limners give
To the beloved disciple.   How I loved
That gracious boy!   Younger by fifteen years,
Brother at once and son!   He left my side,
A summer bloom on his fair cheeks, a smile
Parting his innocent lips.   In one short hour,

The pretty, harmless boy was slain! I saw
The corpse, the mangled corpse, and then I cried
For vengeance! Rouse, ye Romans! rouse, ye slaves!
Have ye brave sons? Look, in the next fierce brawl,
To see them die! Have ye fair daughters? Look
To see them live, torn from your arms, disdained,
Dishonored! and if ye dare call for justice,
Be answered by the lash! Yet this is Rome,
That sat on her seven hills, and from her throne
Of beauty, ruled the world! Yet we are Romans!
Why, in that elder day, to be a Roman
Was greater than a king!—and once again—
Hear me, ye walls, that echoed to the tread
Of either Brutus!—once again I swear,
The eternal city shall be free! her sons
Shall walk with princes!

M. B. MITFORD.

THE BLACK REGIMENT.

DARK as the clouds of even,
    Ranked in the western heaven,
Waiting the breath that lifts
All the dread mass, and drifts
Tempest and falling brand
Over a ruined land;—
So still and orderly,
Arm to arm, knee to knee,
Waiting the great event
Stands the black regiment.

Down the long dusky line
Teeth gleam and eye-balls shine;
And the bright bayonet,
Bristling, and firmly set,
Flashed with a purpose grand,
Long ere the sharp command
Of the fierce rolling drum
Told them their time had come—
Told them what work was sent
For the black regiment.

"Now," the flag-sergeant cried,
"Though death and hell betide,
Let the whole nation see
If we are fit to be free
In this land; or bound
Down, like the whining hound,—
Bound with red stripes of pain
In our cold chains again!"
Oh! what a shout there went
From the black regiment!

"Charge!" Trump and drum awoke;
Onward the bondmen broke ;
Bayonet and sabre stroke
Vainly opposed their rush.
Through the wild battle's crush,
With but one thought aflush.
Driving their lords like chaff,
In the guns' mouths they laugh;

Or at the slippery brands
Leaping with open hands,
Down they tear man and horse,
Down in their awful course;
Trampling with bloody heel
Over the crashing steel,—
All their eyes forward bent,
Rushed the black regiment. ·

"Freedom!" their battle-cry,—
"Freedom! or leave to die!"
Ah! and they meant the word,
Not as with us 'tis heard,
Not a mere party shout;
They gave their spirits out;
Trusted the end to God
And on the gory sod
Rolled in triumphant blood.
Glad to strike one free blow,
Whether for weal or woe;
Glad to breathe one free breath
Though on the lips of death,
Praying—alas! in vain!
That they might fall again,
So they could once more see
That burst to liberty!
This was what "freedom" lent
To the black regiment.

Hundreds on hundreds fell;
But they are resting well;
Scourges and shackles strong
Never shall do them wrong.
Oh, to the living few,
Soldiers, be just and true!
Hail them as comrades tried;
Fight with them side by side;
Never in field or tent,
Scorn the black regiment.

GEO. H. BAKER.

ONE NIGHT WITH GIN.

I'LL take some sugar and gin, if you please;
I've a hacking cough perhaps 'twill ease;
Exposed myself yesterday; caught a severe cold,—
And something warm—for it's good, I am told.

Some say it's injurious; and no doubt it is
To men who can't drink and attend to their biz;
I have my opinion of men who cannot
Drink now and then without being a sot.

Wasting their lives, stunting their brains,
Binding their families in poverty's chains
Seeking a bed in the gutter like swine
Forgetting they're human for whisky and wine.

But of course you don't sell to that class of men;
Don't blame you—correct—there's nothing in them;

They're a damage to trade; they injure your bar
More than their purses contribute, by far.

Another glass, if you please;—that's excellent gin.
My cough, I think, 's better than when I came in;
Import this yourself? From Holland, you say?
Like your taste for pure drinks. Here's a V; take
    your pay.

By the Good Templar's I'm annoyed and perplexed,
Coaxed to join their society until I am vexed.
A piece of absurdity too foreign to think
That one can't indulge in a good social drink.

Over myself I know I've control,
I can sip now and then from the rich flowing bowl,
Drink or not drink, do either with ease,—
What a pity all men can't do as they please!

Have a drink, did you say? Thank you, here's
    luck,—
That's the genuine article—no common truck.
When I start, prepare me a flask of that old,
For I'm certain it's helping my terrible cold.

So fill up the glasses, and now drink with me,
I've plenty of money, if you don't believe it, see:
Look at these fifties, these twenties, this ten.
Here's to you, drink hearty, and—(hic)—fill 'em
    again.

Stranger—(hic)—I'm getting tired on my feet,
So let's fill up and drink—(hic)—, then find a seat,
(Hic)—I like your appearance—(hic)—can see in
　　your face
That confidence in you is never misplaced.

With your permission I'll—(hic)—rest here a spell,
For, mister—(hic)—the fact is I'm not—(hic)—
　　feeling well,
Guess you may give me—(hic)—a glass of that best;
I think it's first-rate for a cold—(hic)—in the chest.

———

Heavy eyes, heavy heart, thirsty and mad;
The gin is all gone, the head's feeling bad;
The tongue's dry and parched; he calls for a drink
To waken his wits and to help him to think.

Then looks for his friend, the one of last night,
So winning and pleasant, so kind and polite;
But he's gone and a rough-looking man in his place,
With a dark, evil eye, and a coarse-bearded face.

He's told that his "*friend,*" so genial and witty,
Receiving a dispatch, has just left the city,
The wretched young man then feels for his purse,
Only to ejaculate "*Gone!*" with a curse.

He appeals to the bar, charges robbery, theft,
Calls for the man, he's informed has just left,
Then gently reminded they do not permit
Their establishment cursed in a mad drunken fit;

That he never lost money, had none to lose,—
Himself a thief, vagabond, thus to abuse
A respectable house, where gentlemen come
To socially quaff their ale, gin, and rum.

Then rudely cast in the cold, open street,
Moneyless, hungry, nothing to eat—
No food for thought, but reflection of shame,
And a head half-crazed with a sobering pain.

THE MISER'S WILL.

THIS tale is true, for so the records show;
'Twas in Germany, not many years ago:
Young Erfurth loved.   But ere the wedding-day
His dearest friend stole with his bride away.
The woman false that he had deemed so true,
The friend he trusted but an ingrate, too,
What wonder that his love to hatred grown,
His heart should seem to all mankind a stone?
All kindred ties he broke, himself he banned,
And sought a solitude in a stranger land.

Grief finds relief in something found to do,
The mind must find some object to pursue;
And so, ere long, his being was controlled
By sole, debasing, longing greed for gold.
How soon his little multiplied to much!
His hand seemed gifted with a Midas touch;
Yet still he kept himself unto himself,
None seeing but for increase of his pelf.

Death came at last; discovering ere he died,
His heart had yet one spot unpetrified;
For, on his bed, his hand upon it still,
There, open, lay the poor old miser's will.

The will was read; there to his brothers three
He left to each a thousand marks; and he.
The friend who caused him all his grief and shame,
Was, with his free forgiveness, left the same;
But none of these to whom such wealth he gave
Should follow his remains unto the grave,
On pain of *forfeit*.   'Neath his pillow pressed
Was found a letter, sealed, and thus addressed:
"To my dear native city of Berlin."

The brothers heard, and thought it was no sin
To stay away; besides, his absence long
Had quenched the love not ever over-strong.
What did the faithless friend?   He knelt in tears,
Looked back in angush o'er the vanished years,
Saw once again their happy boyhood's time,
Their manhood's friendship, his repented crime.
"Oh, my wronged Erfurth, now in death so cold,
I've your forgiveness, care I for your gold?"
And, at the funeral, striving to atone,
The single mourner there, he walked alone.

The letter, opened at the Mayor's will,
Was found to hold the miser's codicil,
Wherein he gave his hoarded gold and lands
To him that *disobeyed* the will's commands,

Should such there be—whose heart knew love or
   pity—
Or, failing, all went to his native city.

And so the friend who stole his bride away;
Who turned to night his joyous morn of day,
Humbly repentant, when his victim died,
Received his pardon and his wealth beside.

SAMPLE-ROOMS.

SAMPLES of wine, and samples of beer,
Samples of all kinds of liquor sold here;
Samples of whiskey, samples of gin,
Samples of all kinds of bitters.   Step in.
Samples of ale, and porter, and brandy;
Samples as large as you please, and quite handy;
Our samples are pure, and also you'll find
Our customers always genteel and refined;
For gentlemen know when they've taken enough,
And never partake of the common stuff.
Besides these samples within, you know,
There are samples without of what they can do;
Samples of headache, samples of gout;
Samples of coats with the elbows out;
Samples of boots without heels or toes;
Samples of men with a broken nose,
Samples of men in the gutter lying,
Samples of men with delirium dying,
Samples of men carousing and swearing,

Samples of men all evil daring;
Samples of lonely, tired men,
Who long in vain for their freedom again;
Samples of old men worn in the strife,
Samples of young men tired of life;
Samples of ruined hopes and lives,
Samples of desolate homes and wives;
Samples of aching hearts.grown cold
With anguish and misery untold;
Samples of noble youth in disgrace,
Who meet you with averted face;
Samples of hungry little ones,
Starving to death in their dreary homes.
In fact, there is scarcely a woe on earth
But these "samples" have nurtured or given birth!
Oh! all ye helpers to sorrow and crime,
Who deal out death for a single dime,
Know ye that the Lord, though he may delay,
Has in reserve for the last great day
The terrible "woe," of whose solemn weight
No mortal can know till the pearly gate
Is closed, and all with one accord
Acknowledge the justice of their reward.

THE BRAVE AT HOME.

THE maid who binds her warrior's sash,
    With smile that well her pain dissembles,
The while beneath her drooping lash

One starry tear-drop hangs and trembles,
Though Heaven alone records the tear,
  And fame shall never know the story,
Her heart has shed a drop as dear
  As e'er bedew'd the field of glory.

The wife who girds her husband's sword,
  Mid little ones who weep or wonder,
And bravely speaks the cheering word,
  What though her heart be rent asunder,
Doom'd nightly in her dreams to hear
  The bolts of death around him rattle,
Hath shed as sacred blood as e'er
  Was pour'd upon a field of battle!

The mother who conceals her grief,
  While to her breast her son she presses,
Then breathes a few brave words and brief,
  Kissing the patriot brow she blesses,
With no one but her secret God
  To know the pain that weighs upon her,
Sheds holy blood as e'er the sod
  Received on Freedom's field of honor.

T. B. READ.

THE CUMBERLAND.

AT anchor in Hampton Roads we lay,
  On board of the Cumberland sloop-of-war;
And at times from the fortress across the bay

The alarum of drums swept past,
  Or a bugle-blast
From the camp on the shore.

Then, far away to the South, uprose
  A little feather of snow-white smoke,
And we knew that the iron ship of our foes
    Was steadily steering its course
    To try the force
  Of our ribs of oak.

Down upon us heavily runs,
  Silent and sullen, the floating fort;
Then comes a puff of smoke from her guns,
    And leaps the terrible death,
    With fiery breath,
  From each open port.

We are not idle, but send her straight
  Defiance back in full broadside!
As hail rebounds from a roof of slate,
    Rebounds our heavier hail
    From each iron scale
  Of the monster's hide.

"Strike your flag!" the Rebel cries,
  In his arrogant old plantation strain.
"Never!" our gallant Morris replies;
    "It is better to sink than to yield!"
    And the whole air pealed
  With the cheers of our men.

Then, like a kraken huge and black,
 She crushed our ribs in her iron grasp!
Down went the Cumberland all a wrack,
  With a sudden shudder of death,
  And the cannon's breath
 For her dying gasp.

Next morn as the sun rose over the bay,
 Still floated our flag at the main mast-head,
Lord, how beautiful was Thy day!
  Every waft of the air
  Was a whisper of prayer,
 Or a dirge for the dead.

Ho! brave hearts that went down in the seas!
 Ye are at peace in the troubled stream.
Ho! brave land! with hearts like these,
  Thy flag, that is rent in twain,
  Shall be one again,
 And without a seam!   LONGFELLOW.

BILL AND I.

THE moon had just gone down, sir,
 But the stars lit up the sky;
All was still in tent and town, sir,
 Not a foeman could we spy.
It was our turn at picket,
So we marched into the thicket,
To the music of the cricket
  Chirping nigh.

Oh, we kept a sharp lookout, sir,
  But no danger could we spy,
And no foeman being about, sir,
  We sat down there, by-and-by;
And we watched to brook a-brawlin',
And counted the stars a-fallin',
Old memories overhaulin',
    Bill and I.

And says he, "Won't it be glorious
  When we throw our muskets by,
And home again, victorious,—
  We hear our sweethearts cry,
'Welcome back!' " A step! Who goes there?
A shot—by heaven, the foe's there!
Bill sat there, all composure,
    But not I.

By the red light of his gun, sir,
  I marked the enemy:
In an instant it was done, sir—
  I had fired and heard a cry.
I sprang across a stream, sir—
Oh, it seems just like a dream, sir,
The dizzy, dying gleam, sir.
    Of that eye!

A youth, a very boy, sir,
  I saw before me lie;
Some pretty school-girl's toy, sir,
  Had ventured here to die.

We had hated one another,
But I heard him murmur, "*Mother!*"
So I stooped and whispered, "*Brother!*"
　　No reply.

crossed the stream once more, sir,
　　To see why Bill warn't by;
He was sittin' as before, sir,
　　But a film was o'er his eye.
I scarce knew what it meant, sir,
Till a wail broke from our tent, sir,
As into camp we went, sir,
　　Bill and I.
　　　　　　　　G. H. MILES.

A HOUSEKEEPER'S TRAGEDY.

ONE day, as I wandered, I heard a complaining,
　　And saw a poor woman, the picture of gloom;
She glared at the mud on her doorsteps ('twas raining),
　　And this was her wail as she wielded the broom:

"Oh, life is a toil, and love is a trouble,
　　And beauty will fade, and riches will flee;
And pleasures they dwindle, and prices they double,
　　And nothing is what I could wish it to be.

"There's too much of worriment goes to a bonnet;
　　There's too much of ironing goes to a shirt;
There's nothing that pays for the time you waste
　　　　on it;
　　There's nothing that lasts but trouble and dirt.

"In March it is mud; it is slush in December;
  The midsummer breezes are loaded with dust;
In fall, the leaves litter; in muggy September,
  The wall-paper rots, and the candlesticks rust.

"There are worms in the cherries, and slugs in the
    roses,
  And ants in the sugar, and mice in the pies;
The rubbish of spiders no mortal supposes,
  And ravaging roaches and damaging flies.

"It's sweeping at six, and dusting at seven;
  It's victuals at eight, and dishes at nine;
It's potting and panning from ten to eleven;
  We scarce break our fast ere we plan how to dine.

"With grease and with grime, from corner to center,
  Forever at war, and forever alert,
No rest for a day, lest the enemy enter—
  I spend my whole life in a struggle with dirt.

"Last night, in my dreams, I was stationed forever
  On a bare little isle in the midst of the sea;
My one chance of life was a ceaseless endeavor
  To sweep off the waves ere they swept over me.

"Alas, 't was no dream!   Again I behold it!
  I yield; I am helpless my fate to avert!"
She rolled down her sleeves, her apron she folded,
  Then laid down and died, and was buried in dirt.

MILL RIVER RIDE.

OVER the hills through the valley away,
Spreading confusion and dreadful dismay,
Spurring his horse to his uttermost speed,
Halting a moment and changing his steed—

Crying aloud in a voice of command:
"Run! run! for your lives, high up on the land!
Away, men and children! up, quick, and be gone!
The water's broke loose; it is chasing me on!"

Away down the river like a spirit he runs,
While the roar of the torrent, like the roaring of guns,
Wakes the air with the echo of trembling might,
Till the flood from the reservoir rushes in sight.

Bear away! bear away in confusion and haste—
What of value remains will be swallowed in waste;
The torrent rolls onward in terrible force,
Dealing death and destruction to all in its course!

But bold Collins Graves has reached Williamsburg
            hills,
Spreading terror and fright throughout all the mills;
While the flood follows faster, increasing its speed,
New horsemen set forth on lightning-limbed steed.

In the valley of death, swept away like a flower,
Six scores of brave workmen destroyed in an hour!
With the rough, rugged rubbish that swept down the
            river,
'Mid groanings for help, they have perished forever!

O God! what a sight for mortals to see!
Whole households engulfed in the stream like a tree!
The day breaks in terror—in sorrow it ends,
For hundreds bewail the sad loss of their friends.

All night, through the darkness, loud groans may be
          heard,
Yet hundreds are dumb, who can utter no word!
The flood has gone down, and the ruins along
The course of the rapids have passed into song.

Of all that gave aid, or that battled those waves,
No name will shine brighter than bold *Collins Graves*
'Twas he that first rose at the sound of alarm,
And rode through the valley, foretelling of harm—
Forgetting his danger, in haste to do right;
Let us honor the gateman, and keep his name bright.

J. W. DONOVAN.

THE NEW CHURCH-ORGAN.

THEY'VE got a bran new organ, Sue,
     For all their fuss and search;
They've done just as they said they'd do,
     And fetched it into church.
They're bound the critter shall be seen,
     And on the preacher's right
They've hoisted up their new machine,
     In everybody's sight.
They've got a chorister and choir,
     Ag'in my voice and vote;

For it was never my desire
  To praise the Lord by note!

I've been a sister good and true,
  For five an' thirty year;
I've done what seemed my part to do,
  And prayed my duty clear;
I've sung the hymns both slow and quick,
  Just as the preacher read;
And twice, when Deacon Tubbs was sick,
  I took the fork an' led!
An' now their bold,. new-fangled ways
  Is comin' all about;
And I, right in my latter days,
  Am fairly crowded out!

To-day the preacher, good old dear,
  With tears all in his eyes,
Read—"I can read my title clear
  To mansions in the skies."
I al'ays liked that blessed hymn—
  I s'pose I al'ays will;
It somehow gratifies my whim,
  In good old Ortonville;
But when that choir got up to sing,
  I couldn't catch a word;
They sung the most dog-gondest thing
  A body ever heard!

Some worldly chaps was standin' near,
  An' when I see them grin,

I bid farewell to every fear,
  And boldly waded in.
I thought I'd chase the tune along,
  An' tried with all my might;
But, though my voice is good an' strong,
  I couldn't steer it right.
When they was high, then I was low,
  An' also contra'wise;
And I too fast, or they too slow,
  To "mansions in the skies."

An' after every verse, you know,
  They played a little tune;
I didn't understand, and so
  I started in too soon.
I pitched it purty middlin' high,
  And fetched a lusty tone;
But oh, alas! I found that I
  Was singin' there alone!
They laughed a little, I am told;
  But I had done my best;
And not a wave of trouble rolled
  Across my peaceful breast.

And Sister Brown—I could but look,
  She sits right front of me—
She never was no singin'-book,
  An' never went to be;
But then she al'ays tried to do

The best she could, she said;
She understood the time right through,
   An' kep' it with her head;
An' when she tried this mornin'. O,
   I had to laugh, or cough!
It kep' her head a bobbin' so,
   It e'n a'most come off!

An' Deacon Tubbs, he all broke down,
   As one might well suppose;
He took one look at Sister Brown,
   And meekly scratched his nose.
He looked his hymn-book through and through,
   And laid it on the seat,
And then a pensive sigh he drew,
   And looked completely beat.
An' when they took another bout,
   He didn't even rise;
But drawed his red bandanner out,
   An' wiped his weeping eyes.

I've been a sister, good an' true,
   For five an' thirty year;
I've done what seemed my part to do,
   An' prayed by duty clear;
But death will stop my voice, I know,
   For he is on my track;
And some day I'll to meetin' go,
   And nevermore come back.

And when the folks get up to sing—
  Whene'er that time shall be,
I do not want no *patent* thing
  A squealin' over me!

WILL M. CARLETON.

THE FAITHFUL LOVERS.

I'D been away from her three years—about that
  And I returned to find my Mary true;
And though I'd question her, I do not doubt that
  It was unnecessary so to do.

'Twas by the chimney corner we were sitting:
  "Mary," said I, "have you been always true?"
"Frankly," says she,—just pausing in her knitting—
  "I don't think I've unfaithful been to you;
But for the three years past I'll tell you what
I've done: then say if I've been true or not.

"When first you left, my grief was uncontrollable,
  Alone I mourned my miserable lot,
And all who saw me thought me inconsolable,
  Till Captain Clifford come from Aldershott;
To flirt with him amused me while 'twas new;
I don't count that unfaithfulness. Do you?

"The next—oh! let me see—was Frankie Phipps,
  I met him at my uncle's Christmas-tide;
And 'neath the mistletoe, where lips meet lips,
  He gave me his first kiss"—and here she sighed;

"We stayed six weeks at uncle's—how time flew!
I don't count that unfaithfulness.   Do you?

"Lord Cecil Fossmore, only twenty-one,
　　Lent me his horse.   Oh, how we rode and raced!
We scoured the downs—we rode to hounds—such
　　fun!
And often was his arm around my waist—
That was to lift me up or down.   But who
Would count that unfaithfulness? Do you?

"Do you know Reggy Vere? Ah, how he sings!
　　We met—'twas at a picnic.   Ah, such weather!
He gave me, look, the first of these two rings,
　　When we were lost in Cliefden woods together.
Ah, what happy times we spent, we two!
I don't count that unfaithfulness to you.

"I've got another ring from him.   D'you see
　　The plain gold circle that is shining here?"
I took her hand: "Oh, Mary!.can it be
　　That you"—quoth she, "that I am Mrs. Vere.
I don't count that unfaithfulness? Do you?"
"No," I replied, "FOR I AM MARRIED, TOO."

------------ · ------------

DER BABY.

SO help me gracious, efery day
　　I laugh me wild to see der vay
My small young baby drie to play—
　　Dot funny leetle baby.

Vhen I look on dhem leetle toes,
Und saw dot funny leetle nose,
Und heard der vay dot rooster crows,
　　I schmile like I was grazy.

Und when I heard der real nice vay
Dhem beoples to my wife dhey say,
" More like his fater every day,"
　　I vas so proud like blazes.

Sometimes dhere comes a leetle schquall,
Dot's vhen der vindy vind vill crawl
Righd in its leetle schtomach schmall,—
　　Dot's too bad for der baby

Dot makes him sing at night so schveet,
Und gorrybarric he must eat,
Und I must chumb shbry on my feet,
　　To help dot leetle baby.

He bulls my nose and kicks my hair,
Und grawls me ofer everywhere,
Und shlobbers me—but vat I care ?
　　Dot vas my schmall young baby.

Around my neck dot leetle arm
Vas sqveezing me so nice und varm ;
Mine Gott ! may never come some harm
　　To dot schmall leetle baby.

THE CHINESE EXCELSIOR.

THAT nightee teem he come chop-chop
One young man walkee, no can stop ;

Maskee snow, maskee ice ;
He colly flag wit'h chop so nice—
　　　　Top-side Galah !

He muchee solly : one piecee eye
Lookee sharp —so fashion—my ;
He talkee large, he talkee stlong,
Too muchee culio ; allee same gong.—
　　　　Top-side Galah !

Insidee house he can see light,
And evly loom got fire all light,
He lookee plenty ice more high,
Insidee mout'h he plenty cly—
　　　　Top-side Galah !

Ole man talkee, " No can walk,
Bimeby lain come, velly dark ;
Have got water, velly wide ! "
Maskee, my must go top-side,—
　　　　Top-side Galah !

" Man-man " one girlee talkee he :
" What for you go top-side look—see ? "
And one teem more he plenty cly,
But allee teem walk plenty high—
　　　　Top-side Galah !

" Take care t'hat spilum tlee, young man.
Take care t'hat ice, must go man-man."
One coolie chin-chin he good night ;
He talkee, " My can go all light "—
　　　　Top-side Galah !

That young man die : one large dog see
Too muchee bobbly findee he,
He hand b'long coldee, all same like ice,
He holdee flag, wit'h chop so nice—
     Top-side Galah !

THE DYING CONFESSION OF PADDY M'CABE.

PADDY McCabe was dying one day,
  And Father Molloy he came to confess him,
Paddy prayed hard he would make no delay,
  But forgive him his sins and make haste for to
    bless him.
" First tell me your sins," says Father Molloy,
" For I'm thinking you've not been a very good
    boy."

" Oh," says Paddy, " so late in the evenin' I fear
'Twould trouble you such a long story to hear,
For you've ten long miles o'er the mountain to go,
While the road *I've* to travel 's much longer, you
    know :
So give us your blessin' and get in the saddle ;
To tell all my sins my poor brain would addle ;
And the docthor gave orthers to keep me so quiet—
'Twould disturb me to tell all my sins, if I'd thry it—
And your Reverence has towld us unless we tell *all*
'Tis worse than not makin' confession at all :
So I'll say, in a word, I'm no very good boy,
And therefore your blessin', sweet Father Molloy."

" Well, I'll read from a book," says Father Molloy,
  " The manifold sins that humanity 's heir to ;
And when you hear those that your conscience
    annoy,
  You'll just squeeze my hand, as acknowledging
    thereto. "
Then the Father began the dark roll of iniquity,
And Paddy, thereat, felt his conscience grow rickety,
And he gave such a squeeze that the priest gave a
    roar—
" Oh, murther," says Paddy, " don't read any more ;
For if you keep readin', by all that is thrue,
Your Reverence's fist will be soon black and blue ;
Besides, to be troubled my conscience begins,
That your Reverence should have any hand in *my*
    sins.
So you'd better suppose I committed them all—
For whether they're great ones, or whether they're
    small,
Or if they're a dozen, or if they're four-score,
'Tis your Reverence knows how to absolve them,
    asthore :
So I'll say, in a word, I'm no very good boy,
And therefore, your blessin', sweet Father Molloy."
" Well," says Father Molloy, " your sins I forgive,
  So you must forgive all your enemies truly,
And promise me also that, if you should live,
  You'll leave off your old tricks, and begin to live
    newly. "

" I forgive ev'rybody," says Pat, with a groan,
" Except that big vagabone, Micky Malone ;
And him I will murdher if ever I can—"
" Tut, tut ! " says the priest, " you're a very bad
   man ;
For without your forgiveness, and also repentance,
You'll ne'er go to heaven, and that is my sentence."
" Pooh ! " says Paddy McCabe, " that's a very hard
   case.
With your Reverence and heaven I'm content to
   make pace ;
But with heaven and your Reverence I wonder—
   och hone,
You would think of comparin' that blackguard,
   Malone.
But since I'm hard pressed and that I *must* forgive,
I forgive—if I die ; but as sure as I live
That ugly blackguard I will surely desthroy !—
So *now* for your blessin', sweet Father Molloy ! "

     SAMUEL LOVER.

SONG OF THE CAMP.

"GIVE us a song!" the soldiers cried,
 The outer trenches guarding,
When the heated guns of the camps allied
 Grew weary of bombarding.

The dark Redan, in silent scoff,
 Lay grim and threatening under ;
And the tawny mound of the Malakoff
 No longer belched its thunder.

There was a pause.   A guardsman said :
  "We storm the forts to-morrow ;
Sing while we may, another day
  Will bring enough of sorrow."

They lay along the battery's side,
  Below the smoking cannon :
Brave hearts from Severn and from Clyde,
  And from the banks of Shannon.

They sang of love, and not of fame ;
  Forgot was Britain's glory :
Each heart recalled a different name,
  But all sang "Annie Laurie."

Voice after voice caught up the song,
  Until its tender passion
Rose like an anthem, rich and strong,—
  Their battle-eve confession.

Dear girl, her name he dared not speak,
  But as the song grew louder,
Something upon the soldier's cheek
  Washed off the stains of powder.

Beyond the darkening ocean burned
  The bloody sunset's embers,
While the Crimean valleys learned
  How English love remembers.

And once again a fire of hell
  Rained on the Russian quarters,

With scream of shot, and burst of shell,
   And bellowing of the mortars.

And Irish Norah's eyes are dim
   For a singer dumb and gory;
And English Mary mourns for him
   Who sang of "Annie Laurie."

Sleep, soldiers! still in honored rest
   Your truth and valor wearing;
The bravest are the tenderest—
   The loving are the daring.

BAYARD TAYLOR.

DOT BABY OFF MINE.

MINE cracious! Mine cracious! shust look here
   und see
A Deutscher so habby as habby can pe.
Der beoples all dink dat no prains I haf got,
Vas grazy mit trinking, or someding like dot;
Id vasn't pecause I trinks lager und vine,
Id vas all on aggount off dot baby off mine.

Dot schmall leedle vellow I dells you vas qveer;
Not mooch pigger roundt as a goot glass off beer,
Mit a bare-footed hed, and nose but a schpeck,
A mout dot goes most to der pack off his neck,
Und his leedle pink toes mit der rest all combine.
To gife sooch a charm to dot baby off mine.

I dells you dot baby vas von off der poys,
Und beats leedle Yawcop for making a noise;

He shusts has pecun to shbeak goot English, too,
Says " mama," und "bapa," und somedimes "ah—
            goo! "
You don't find a baby den dimes out off nine
Dot vos qvite so schmart as dot baby off mine.

He grawls der vloor ofer, und drows dings aboudt,
Und poots efryding he can find in his mout ;
He dumbles der shtairs down, and falls vrom his
            chair,
Und gifes mine Katrina von derrible sckare ;
Mine hair shtands like shquills on a mat borcubine
Ven I dinks off dose pranks off dot baby off mine.

Dere vos someding, you pet, I don'd likes pooty vell;
To hear in der nighdt-dimes dot young Deutscher
            yell,
Und dravel der ped room midout many clo'es
Vhile der chills down der shpine off mine back
            quickly goes ;
Dose leedle shimnasdic dricks vasn't so fine,
Dot I cuts oop at nighdt mit dot baby off mine.

Vell, deese leedle schafers vas goin' to pe men,
Und all off dess droubles vill peen ofer den ;
Dey vill vare a vhite shirt vront inshted off a bib,
Und vouldn't got tucked oop at nighds in deir crib—
Vell! Vell! ven I'm feeple und in life's decline,
May mine oldt age pe cheered py dot baby off mine.

                    CHARLES F. ADAMS.

THE MANIAC.

STAY, jailer, stay, and hear my woe !
　　She is not mad who kneels to thee ;
For what I'm now too well I know,
　　And what I was, and what I should be.
I'll rave no more in proud despair ;
　　My language shall be mild, though sad ;
But yet I firmly, truly swear,
　　I am not mad, I am not mad !

My tyrant husband forged the tale
　　Which chains me in this dismal cell ;
My fate unknown my friends bewail,—
　　O jailer, haste that fate to tell !
Oh, haste my father's heart to cheer !
　　His heart at once 'twill grieve and glad
To know, though kept a captive here,
　　I am not mad, I am not mad !

He smiles in scorn, and turns the key ;
　　He quits the grate ; I knelt in vain ;
His glimmering lamp still, still I see,—
　　'Tis gone ! and all is gloom again.
Cold, bitter cold !—No warmth ! no light.
　　Life, all thy comforts once I had ;
Yet here I'm chained this freezing night,
　　Although not *mad ! no, no,—not mad !*

'Tis sure some dream, some vision vain,
　　What ! *I,* the child of rank and wealth,—

Am *I* the wretch who clanks this chain,
   Bereft of freedom, friends and health ?
Ah ! while I dwell on blessings fled,
   Which nevermore my heart must glad,
How aches my heart, how burns my head ;
   But 'tis not *mad ; no, 'tis not mad !*

Hast thou, my child, forgot, ere this,
   A mother's face, a mother's tongue ?
She'll ne'er forget your parting kiss,
   Nor round her neck how fast you clung ;
Nor how with her you sued to stay ;
   Nor how that suit your sire forbade ;
Nor how—I'll drive such thoughts away ;
   They'll *make* me mad ; they'll *make* me mad !

His rosy lips, how sweet they smiled !
   His mild blue eyes, how bright they shone !
None ever bore a lovelier child,
   And art thou now forever gone ?
And must I never see thee more,
   My pretty, pretty, pretty lad ?
I *will* be free ! unbar the door !
   I am not mad ; I am not mad !

O, hark ! what mean those yells and cries ?
   His chain some furious madman breaks ;
He comes,—I see his glaring eyes ;
   Now, now, my dungeon-grate he shakes.
Help ! Help !—He's gone !—Oh, fearful woe,
   Such screams to hear, such sights to see !

My brain, my brain,—I know, I know
   I am *not* mad, but soon *shall* be.

Yes, soon ;—for, lo you !—while I speak,—
   Mark how yon demon's eyeballs glare !
He sees me ; now, with dreadful shriek,
   He whirls a serpent high in air.
Horror !—the reptile strikes his tooth
   Deep in my heart, so crushed and sad ;
Ay, laugh, ye fiends ;—I feel the truth ;
   Your task is done,—I'M MAD ! I'M MAD !
              M. G. LEWIS.

TOM.

YES, Tom's the best fellow that ever you knew.
       Just listen to this :
When old mill took fire and the flooring fell througn
And I with it, helpless, there, full in my view,
What do you think my eyes saw through the fire,
That crept along, crept along, nigher and nigher,
But Robin, my baby-boy, laughing to see
The shining ! He must have come there after me,
Toddled alone from the cottage without
Anyone's missing him. Then, what a shout—
Oh, how I shouted, " For heaven's sake men,
Save little Robin ! " Again and again
They tried, but the fire held them back like a wall.
I could hear them go at it, and at it, and call,
" Never mind, baby, sit still like a man,

We're coming to get you as fast as we can."
They could not see him, but I could ; he sat
Still on the beam, his little straw hat
Carefully placed by his side, and his eyes
Stared at the flame with a baby's surprise,
Calm and unconscious as nearer it crept.
The roar of the fire up above must have kept
The sound of his mother's voice shrieking his name
From reaching the child.   But *I* heard it.   It came
Again and again—O God, what a cry !
The axes went faster, I saw the sparks fly
Where the men worked like tigers, nor minded the
       heat
That scorched them—when, suddenly, there at their
       feet
The great beems leaned in — they saw him — then,
       crash,
Down came the wall !   The men made a dash—
Jumped to get out of the way—and I thought
" All's up with poor Robin," and brought
Slowly the arm that was least hurt to hide
The sight of the child there, when swift, at my side,
Some one rushed by, and went right through the
       flame
Straight as a dart—caught the child—and then came
Back with him—choking and crying, but—saved !
Saved safe and sound !
              Oh, how the men raved,
Shouted, and cried, and hurrahed !   Then they all

Rushed at the work again, lest the back wall
Where I was lying, away from the fire
Should fall in and bury me.

                Oh, you'd admire
To see Robin now ; he's as bright as a dime,
Deep in some mischief, too, most of the time ;
Tom it was, saved him.   Now isn't it true,
Tom's the best fellow that ever you knew ?
There's Robin now—see, he's strong as a log—
And there comes Tom too—

              Yes, Tom was our dog.
        CONSTANCE F. WOOLSON.

SOLILOQUY OF KING RICHARD III.

GIVE me another horse—bind up my wounds—
Have mercy, Jesu!—soft: I did but dream.
O coward conscience, how dost thou afflict me!
The lights burn blue.   It is now dead midnight.
Cold, fearful drops stand on my trembling flesh.
What do I *fear?* Myself! there's none else by.
Richard loves *Richard:* that is, I am I.
Is there a murderer here!   No: yes, I am.
Then fly.   What!   From myself?   Great reason:
    why?
Lest I revenge.   *What?*   Myself on myself?
I love myself.   Wherefore?   For any good
That I myself have done unto myself?
Oh, no: alas! I rather *hate* myself,
For hateful deeds committed by myself,

I am a villain: yet I *lie:* I am not.
Fool, of thyself speak well—fool, do not flatter—
My conscience hath a thousand several tongues·
And every tongue brings in a several tale;
And every tale condemns me for a *villain.*
Perjury, perjury in the highest degree;
Murder, stern murder in the direst degree,
All several sins, all used in each degree,
Throng to the bar, crying all, *guilty! guilty!*
I shall despair.   There is no creature *loves* me,
And, if I die, no soul will *pity* me ;
Nay; wherefore should they; since that I myself
Find in myself no pity to myself?—
Methought the souls of all that I had murdered
Came to my tent, and every one did threat
To-morrow's vengeance on the head of Richard.

SHAKSPEARE.

A GEORGIA VOLUNTEER.

FAR up the lonely mountain side
   My wandering footsteps led,
The moss lay thick beneath my feet,
   The pine sighed overhead;
The trace of a dismantled fort
   Lay in the forest nave,
And in the shadow near my path
   I saw a soldier's grave.

The bramble wrestled with the weed
   Upon the lowly mound;

The simple headboard, rudely writ,
  Had rotted to the ground.
I raised it with a reverent hand,
  From dust its words to clear,
But time had blotted all but these:
  "A Georgia Volunteer."

I heard the Shenandoah roll
  Along the vale below,
I saw the Alleghanies rise
  Toward the realms of snow ;
The valley campaign rose to mind,
  Its leader's name, and then
I knew the sleeper had been one
  Of Stonewall Jackson's men.

He sleeps; what need to question now
  If he were wrong or right?
He knows ere this whose cause is just
  In God the Father's sight;
He wields no warlike weapons now,
  Returns no foeman's thrust;
Who but a coward would revile
  An honored soldier's dust?

Roll, Shenandoah, proudly roll
  Adown thy rocky glen,
Above thee lies the grave of one
  Of Stonewall Jackson's men.

Beneath the cedar and the pine
 In solitude austere,
Unknown, unnamed, forgotten lies
 A Georgia volunteer.

CIVIL WAR.

"RIFLEMAN, shoot me a fancy shot
 Straight at the heart of yon prowling vidette;
Ring me a ball in the glittering spot
 That shines on his breast like an amulet!"

"Ah, Captain! here goes for a fine-drawn bead
 There's music around when my barrel 's in tune!"
Crack! went the rifle, the messenger sped,
 And dead from his horse fell the ringing dragoon.

"Now, Rifleman, steal through the bushes, and
  snatch
 From your victim some trinket to handsel first
  blood—
A button, a loop, or that luminous patch
 That gleams in the moon like a diamond stud."

"O Captain! I staggered, and sunk on my track,
 When I gazed on the face of that fallen vidette;
For he looked so like you as he lay on his back,
 That my heart rose upon me, and masters me yet.

"But I snatched off the trinket—this locket of gold;
 An inch from the centre my lead broke its way,
Scarce glazing the picture, so fair to behold,
 Of a beautiful lady in bridal array."

"Ha! Rifleman, fling me the locket!—'t she,
  My brother's young bride, and the fallen dragoon
Was her husband—Hush! soldier, 't was Heaven's
        decree ;
  We must bury him here, by the light of the moon!

"But, hark! the far bugles their warnings unite;
  War is a virtue—weakness a sin;
There 's lurking and loping around us to-night;
  Load again, Rifleman. keep your hand in!"

                        C. D. SHANLY

SHERIDAN'S RIDE.

UP from the South at break of day
  Bringing to Winchester fresh dismay,
The affrighted air with a shudder bore,
Like a herald in haste, to the chieftain's door,
The terrible grumble, and rumble, and roar,
Telling the battle was on once more,
And Sheridan twenty miles away.

And wider still those billows of war
Thundered along the horizon's bar;
And louder yet into Winchester rolled
The roar of that red sea uncontrolled,
Making the blood of the listener cold,
As he thought of the stake in that fiery fray,
And Sheridan twenty miles away.

But there is a road from Winchester town,
A good, broad highway leading down;

And there through the flush of the morning light,
A steed as black as the steeds of night
Was seen to pass, as with eagle flight.
As if he knew the terrible need,
He stretched away with his utmost speed;
Hills rose and fell; but his heart was gay,
With Sheridan fifteen miles away.

Still sprung from those swift hoofs, thundering South
The dust, like smoke from the cannon's mouth,
Or the trail of a comet, sweeping faster and faster,
Foreboding to traitors the doom of disaster.
The heart of the steed and the heart of the master
Were beating like prisoners assaulting their walls,
Impatient to be where the battlefield calls;
Every nerve of the charger was strained to full play,
With Sheridan only ten miles away.

Under his spurning feet, the road
Like an arrowy Alpine river flowed,
And the landscape sped away behind
Like an ocean flying before the wind,
And the steed, like a bark fed with furnace ire,
Swept on, with his wild eye full of fire.
But lo! he is nearing his heart's desire;
He is snuffing the smoke of the roaring fray,
With Sheridan only five miles away.

The first that the General saw were the groups
Of stragglers, and then the retreating troops;

What was done,—what to do,—a glance told him
    both.
And striking his spurs, with a terrible oath,
He dashed down the line, 'mid a storm of huzzas,
And the wave of retreat checked its course there
    because
The sight of the master compelled it to pause.
With foam and with dust the black charger was gray;
By the flash of his eye, and his red nostril's play,
He seemed to the whole great army to say,
" I have brought you Sheridan all the way
From Winchester down to save the day."

Hurrah, hurrah for Sheridan!
Hurrah, hurrah for horse and man!
And when their statues are placed on high,
Under the dome of the Union sky,—
The American soldiers' Temple of Fame,—
There with the glorious General's name
Be it said in letters both bold and bright :
"Here is the steed that saved the day
By carrying Sheridan into the fight,
From Winchester,—twenty miles away!"

                    T. B. READ.

THE BURNING PRAIRIE.

THE prairie stretched as smooth as a floor,
    As far as the eye could see,
And the settler sat at his cabin door,

With his little girl on his knee ;
Striving her letters to repeat,
And pulling her apron over her feet.

His face was wrinkled but not old,
  For he bore an upright form,
And his shirt sleeves back to the elbow rolled,
  They showed a brawny arm;
And near in the grass with toes upturned,
Was a pair of old shoes, cracked and burned.

A dog with his head betwixt his paws,
  Lay lazily dozing near,
Now and then snapping his tar black jaws
  At the fly that buzzed in his ear;
And near was the cow-pen, made of rails,
And a bench that held two milking-pails.

In the open door an ox-yoke lay,
  The mother's odd redoubt,
To keep the little one, at her play
  On the floor, from falling out;
While she swept the hearth with a turkey wing,
And filled her tea-kettle at the spring.

The little girl on her father's knee,
  With eyes so bright and blue,
From A, B, C, to X, Y, Z,
  Had said her lesson through,
When a wind came over the prairie land,
And caught the primer out of her hand.

The watch-dog whined, the cattle lowed
   And tossed their horns about;
The air grew gray as if it snowed;
   " There will be a storm, no doubt."
So to himself the settler said.
" But, father, why is the sky so red? "

The little girl slid off his knee,
   And all of a tremble stood;
" Good wife," he cried, " come out and see,
   The skies are as red as blood."
" God save us! " cried the settler's wife,
" The prairie's a-fire; we must run for life! "

She caught the baby up; " Come, come,
   Are ye mad? to your heels, my man."
He followed, terror-stricken, dumb;
   And so they ran and ran.
Close upon them was the snort and swing
Of buffaloes madly galloping.

The wild wind, like a sower, sows
   The ground with sparkles red;
And the flapping wings of the bats and crows,
   And the ashes overhead,
And the bellowing deer, and the hissing snake,
What a swirl of terrible sounds they make.

No gleam of the river water yet,
   And the flames leap on and on;
A crash and a fiercer whirl and jet,

And the settler's house is gone.
The air grows hot; " This fluttering curl
Would burn like flax," said the little girl.

And as the smoke against her drifts,
   And the lizard slips close by her,
She tells how the little cow uplifts
   Her speckled face from the fire;
For she cannot be hindered from looking back
At the fiery dragon on their track.

They hear the crackling grass and sedge,
   The flames as they whir and rave;
On, on! they are close to the water's edge—
   They are breast deep in the wave:
And lifting their little one high o'er the tide,
" We are saved, thank God, we are saved! "
     they cried.
              ALICE CAREY.

THE SEMINOLE'S REPLY.

BLAZE, with your serried columns!
   I will not bend the knee!
The shackles ne'er again shall bind
   The arm which now is free.
I've mailed it with the thunder,
   When the tempest muttered low;
And where it falls, ye well may dread
   The lightning of his blow!

I've scared ye in the city,
  I've scalped ye on the plain;
Go, count your chosen where they fell
  Beneath my leaden rain!
I scorn your proffered treaty!
  The pale-face I defy!
Revenge is stamped upon my spear,
  And blood my battle-cry!

Some strike for hope of booty,
  Some to defend their all,—
I battle for the joy I have
  To see the white man fall!
I love, among the wounded,
  To hear his dying moan,
And catch, while chanting at his side,
  The music of his groan.

Ye've trailed me through the forest,
  Ye've tracked me o'er the stream;
And struggling through the everglade
  Your bristling bayonets gleam;
But I stand as should the warrior,
  With his rifle and his spear;
The scalp of vengeance still is red,
  And warns ye—Come not here!

I loathe ye in my bosom,
  I scorn ye with mine eye;
And I'll taunt ye with my latest breath,
  And fight ye till I die!

I ne'er will ask ye quarter,
    And I ne'er will be your slave;
But I'll swim the sea of slaughter
    Till I sink beneath its wave.

PATTEN.

THE MAIN TRUCK, OR A LEAP FOR LIFE.

OLD Ironsides at anchor lay,
    In the harbor of Mahon ;
A dead calm rested on the bay,—
    The waves to sleep had gone ;
When little Hal the Captain's son,
    A lad both brave and good,
In sport, up shroud and rigging ran,
    And on the main truck stood !

A shudder shot through every vain,—
    All eyes were turned on high !
There stood the boy, with dizzy brain,
    Between the sea and sky,
No hold had he above, below :
    Alone he stood in air :
To that fair height none dared to go,—
    No aid could reach him there.

We gazed, but not a man could speak,–
    With horror all aghast,—
In groups, with pallid brow and cheek,
    We watched the quivering mast.

The atmosphere grew thick and hot,
  And of a lurid hue ;—
As riveted unto the spot,
  Stood officers and crew.

The father came on deck :—he gasped,
  " Oh, God ; thy will be done ! "
Then suddenly a rifle grasped,
  And aimed it at his son.
" Jump, far out, boy, into the wave,
  Jump, or I fire ! " he said ;
" That only chance your life can save ;
  Jump, jump, boy ! " He obeyed.

He sunk,—he rose,—he lived,—he moved,—
  And for the ship struck out.
On board we hailed the lad beloved,
  With many a manly shout,
His father drew, in silent joy,
  Those wet arms around his neck,
And folded to his heart his boy,—
  Then fainted on the deck.   COLTON.

SHYLOCK TO ANTONIO.

SIGNOR Antonio, many a time and oft
  In the Rialto you have rated me
About my moneys and my usances ;
Still have I borne it with a patient shrug,
For sufferance is the badge of all our tribe ;
You call me,—misbeliever, cut-throat, dog,

And spit upon my Jewish gaberdine,
And all for use of that which is mine own.
Well, then, it now appears, you need my help;
Go to, then ; you come to me, and you say,
Shylock, we would have moneys ; you say so ;
You that did void your rheum upon my beard,
And foot me, as you spurn a stranger cur
Over your threshold ; moneys is your suit.
What should I say to you?   Should I not say,
Has a *dog* money? is it possible
A *cur* can lend *three thousand ducats?* or
Shall I bend low, and in a bondman's key,
With 'bated breath, and whispering humbleness,
Say this ?
Fair sir, you *spit on me* on Wednesday last :
You *spurned* me such a day ; another time
You called me—*dog;* and for these *courtesies*
I'll *lend you* thus much *moneys.*

SHAKSPEARE.

THE GLADIATOR.

THEY led a lion from his den,
   The lord of Afric's sun-scorched plain ;
And there he stood, stern foe of men,
   And shook his flowing mane.
There's not of all Rome's heroes ten
   That dare abide this game.
His bright eye nought of lightning lacked ;
His voice was like the cataract.

They brought a dark-haired man along,
  Whose limbs with gyves of brass were bound ;
Youthful he seemed, and bold, and strong,
  And yet unscathed of wound.
Blithely he stepped among the throng,
  And carelessly threw around
A dark eye, such as courts the path
Of him who braves a Dacian's wrath.

Then shouted the plebeian crowd,—
  Rung the glad galleries with the sound ;
And from the throne there spake aloud
  A voice,—" Be the bold man unbound !
And by Rome's sceptre, yet unbowed,
  By Rome, earth's monarch crowned,
Who dares the bold, the unequal strife,
Though doomed to death, shall save his life."

Joy was upon the dark man's face ;
  And thus, with laughing eye, spake he :
" Loose ye the Lord of Zaara's waste,
  And let my arms be free ;
' He has a martial heart,' thou sayest ;
  But oh ! who will not be
A hero when he fights for life,
For home and country, babes and wife ?

" And thus I for the strife prepare :
  The Thracian falchion to me bring,
But ask th' imperial leave to spare
  The shield,—a useless thing.

Were I a Samnite's rage to dare,
   Then o'er me would I fling
The broad orb ; but to lion's wrath
The shield were but a sword of lath."

And he has bared his shining blade,
   And springs he on the shaggy foe ;
Dreadful the strife, but briefly played ;—
   The desert-king lies low :
His long and loud death-howl is made ;
   And there must end the show.
And when the multitude were calm,
The favored freed man took the palm.

" Kneel down, Rome's emperor beside ? "
   He knelt, that dark man ;—o'er his brow
Was thrown a wreath in crimson dyed ·
   And fair words gild it now :
" Thou art the bravest youth that ever tried
   To lay a lion low ;
And from our presence forth thou·go'st
To lead the Dacians of our host. "

Then flushed his cheek, but not with pride
   And grieved and gloomily spake he :
" My cabin stands where blithely glide
   Proud Danube's waters to the sea :
I have a young and blooming bride,
   And I have children three : —
No Roman wealth or rank can give
Such joy as in their arms to live.

" My wife sits at the cabin door,
  With throbbing heart and swollen eyes ;—
While tears her cheek are coursing o'er,
  She speaks of sundered ties ;
She bids my tender babes deplore
  The death their father dies ;
She tells these jewels of my home,
I bleed to please the rout of Rome.

" I cannot let those cherubs stray
  Without their sire's protecting care ;
And I would chase the griefs away
  Which·cloud my wedded fair."
The monarch spoke ; the guards obey ;
  And gates unclosed are :
He's gone !—No golden bribes divide
The Dacian from his babes and bride.

J. A. JONES.

THE GREAT ATTRACTION.

OH, charming Kitty, fair art thou,
    Fair as a rose in June ;
Thy hair like braided sunshine is,
  Thy voice a pleasant tune.
But 'tis not for thy Beauty, sweet,
I lay my heart beneath thy feet—
  Not for thy Beauty, sweet.

But thou art wise and witty too ;
  Thy little tongue can say

The shrewdest and the sweetest things
  In such a pleasant way.
But 'tis not for thy Wisdom, sweet,
I lay my heart beneath thy feet—
  Not for thy Wisdom, sweet.

And thou canst sing and dance and paint,
  And chatter French and Greek,
And to the poet, priest and sage,
  In his own way canst speak.
But 'tis not for thy Learning, sweet,
I lay my heart beneath thy feet—
  Not for thy Learning, sweet.

Thou art so amiable and true,
  Thy temper is so mild,
So humble and obedient, too,
  Love guides thee like a child.
But not for thy good Temper, sweet,
I lay my heart beneath thy feet—
  Not for thy Temper, sweet.

Not for thy Beauty or thy Youth,
  Not for thy Heart's rich store,
Not for thy sunny Temper's truth,
  Thy Wisdom, Wit, or Lore,
I love thee, sweet: such things are trash,
I love thy hundred thousand Cash—
  Thy $100,000 Cash !

BUSTIN' THE TEMPERANCE MAN.

HOARSELY demanding "Gimme a drink!"
    He sidled up to the bar,
And he handled his glass with the air of one
    Who had often before "been thar."
And a terrible glance shot out of his eyes,
    And over his hearers ran
As he muttered, " I'm hangin' around the town
    Fer to bust that temp'rance man!

" I've heerd he's a comin' with singin' and sich,
    And prayin' and heaps of talk ;
And allows he'll make all fellers what drink
    Toe square to the temp'rance chalk.
I reckon "—and here he pulled out a knife
    That was two feet long or more,
And he handled his pistols familiarly,
    While the crowd made a break for the door.

The good man came and his voice was kind,
    And his ways were meek and mild ;
" But I'm goin' to bust him," the roarer said—
    " Jess wait till he gits me riled."
Then he playfully felt of his pistol belt,
    And took up his place on the stage,
And waited in wrath for the temperance man
    To further excite his rage.

But the orator didn't ; he wasn't that sort,
    For he talked right straight to the heart,
And somehow or other the roarer felt

The trembling tear-drops start.
And he thought of the wife who had loved him well,
    And the children that climbed his knee,
And he said, as the terrible pictures were drawn,
    " He's got it kerrect—that's me!"

Then his thoughts went back to the years gone by,
    When his mother had kissed his brow,
As she tearfully told of the evils of drink,
    And he made her a solemn vow,
That he never should touch the poisonous cup
    Which had ruined so many before ;
And the tears fell fast as he lowly said :
    "He's ketchin' me more and more!"

He loosened his hold on his pistols and knife,
    And covered his streaming eyes.
And though it was homely, his prayer went up—
    Straight to the starlit skies.
Then he signed his name to the temperance pledge,
    And holding it high, said he,
" I came here to bust that temp'rance chap,
    But I reckon he's busted me."

                    A. L. HARVEY.

AUTOGRAPH-ALBUM VERSES.

CONTENTS.

AUTOGRAPH-ALBUM VERSES.

DEDICATORY.

Go, little book.   Bring the best wishes of happiness to the fair owner of this memorial of friendship; and gather the brightest gems of Virtue, Esteem and Love from the fairy fields of a bright future.

———:o:———

WHILE journeying through life's troubled sea
May this fair book a solace be !
Whene'er you turn its pages o'er,
Then think of those—perhaps no more–
Who, with their hearts so full of love,
Invoked the Muses from above
To aid them as they gladly penned
A tribute to their valued friend.
In leisure moments cast a look
Upon the pages of this book ;
When absent friends thy thoughts engage,
Think of the one who fills this page.

———:o:———

Go, album ! range the gay parterre;
From gem to gem, from flower to flower.
Select with taste and cull with care,
And bring your offering fresh and rare,
To this sweet maiden's bower !

319

MAY no presuming pen
  Write aught but faultless truth
Upon a page of this fair book,
  Sacred to Innocence and Truth.

———:o:———

To earnest words and eloquent,
To humor, wit and sentiment,
To language where ideas throng
To show the writer's friendship strong,
To chastened thought and cultured sense,
To simple lays without pretense,
To brief quotations chosen apt,
To hidden meanings quaintly wrapped,
To all the efforts meant to please
That come to pages such as these,
To show how much friends hold you dear,
I dedicate your album here.

———:o:———

——————— to thee are consecrate
  These leaves of smooth, unspotted white ;
Emblems most fitting of thy state,—
  So good—so fair—so pure—so bright.

———:o:———

HERE WIT will sparkling stanzas strew,—
  Here WISDOM solemn maxims store,—
Here FRIENDSHIP write its counsels true,—

Here LOVE may gently love implore.
When the sere Autumn leaves shall come—
    As come to all they surely will—
Your eyes may o'er these leaflets roam,
    And friends recall who love you still.

————:o:————

MY album is a garden spot
    Where all my friends may sow,
Where thorns and thistles flourish not,
    But flowers alone may grow.
With smiles for sunshine, tears for showers,
    I'll water, watch and guard these flowers.

————:o:————

DEAR friend, please take your facile pen in hand,
And—as if with a fairy's magic wand—
Record a page, a verse, or e'en a line ;
'Twill have a value for this heart of mine.
Not for its beauty only, but its truth ;
As bringing back the days of pleasant youth.

————:o:————

KIND friends, I beg that you will fill
This book with tokens of good-will.
If on my mission I'd succeed,
A word from every friend I'll need.
Here all may bow at friendship's shrine—
Here all that will may write a line.
Give me mementos that will tell
The names of those who wish me well.

My album's open !   Come and see !
What !   Don't you waste a line on me ?
Write but a thought, a word or two,
That memory may revert to you.

———:o:———

In this fair garden plants shall grow
And in their freshness bud and blow—
Plants to which love has beauty lent,
And blossoms sweet of sentiment.

———:o:———

I trust that ev'ry one that calls me friend
Will to this little book some trifle lend,
Whether some fancy flowers wildly sweet,
Or some wise proverb, or some couplet neat,
Or sentence from some writer, grave or funny :
From ev'ry hive the wise can take some honey,
Whether the bees have roam'd in wealth's rich
          bowers,
Or painful glean'd amid wild wayside flowers.

———:o:———

No carping critic's eye need scan
    For venial faults this little book ;
'Tis meant for Friendship's eye alone,
    Which seeks not pebbles in each brook.

SENTIMENT.

Fair girl, by whose simplicity
   My spirit has been won
From the stern earthliness of life,
   As shadows flee the sun,—
I turn again to think of thee,
   And half deplore the thought,
That for one instant, o'er my soul,
   Forgetfulness hath wrought !
I turn to that charmed hour of hope,
   When first upon my view
Came the pure sunshine of thine heart,
   Borne from thine eyes of blue.
'Twas thy high purity of soul—
   Thy thought-revealing eye—
That placed me spellbound at thy feet,
   Sweet wanderer from the sky.

———:o:———

Oh, lady ! there be many things
   That seem right fair above ;
But sure not one among them all
   Is half so sweet as love :
Let us not pay our vows alone,
But join two altars into one.

———:o:———

Speak of me kindly when life's dreams are o'er ;
Speak of me gently when I am no more.

323

'TIS not the fairest form that holds
The mildest, purest soul, within ;
'Tis not the richest plant that folds
The sweetest breath of fragrance in.

———:o:———

OUR grandsire, ere of Eve possess'd,
Alone, and e'en in Paradise unblest,
With mournful looks the blissful scene surveyed,
And wandered in the solitary shade ;
The Maker saw, took pity, and bestowed
Woman, the last, the best reserved of God.

———:o:———

A LOVELIER nymph the pencil never drew ;
For the fond graces formed her easy mien,
And heaven's soft azure in her eye was seen.

———:o:———

SOME little token of regard
You wish from me to claim ;
But as time is pressing hard,
I will but write my name.

———:o:———

SAVE thy toiling, spare thy treasure,
All I ask is friendship's pleasure ;
Let the shining orb lie darkling,
Bring no gem in lustre sparkling.
Gifts and gold are naught to me ;
I would only look on thee !

" I WILL not say I'd give the world
   To win those charms divine ;
I will not say I'd give the world—
   The world it is not mine.
The vow that's made thy love to win
   In simple truth shall be ;
My heart is all I have to give,
   And give that all to thee."

But while I knelt at beauty's shrine,
   And love's devotion paid,
I felt 'twas but an empty vow
   That passion's pilgrim made ;
For while, in raptur'd gazing lost,
   To give my heart I swore
One glance from her soon made me feel
   My heart was mine no more.

———:o:———

NEVER wedding, ever wooing,
Still a lovelorn heart pursuing,
Read you not the wrong you're doing,
   In my cheek's pale hue ?
All my life with sorrow strewing,—
   Wed, or cease to woo.

———:o:———

THE wildest ills that darken life
Are rapture to the bosom's strife;
The tempest, in its blackest form,
Is beauty to the bosom's storm.

A PEPPER-CORN is very small, but seasons every
 dinner
More than all other condiments, although 'tis
 sprinkled thinner ;
Just so a little Woman is, if Love will let you win
 her—
There's not a joy in all the world you will not find
 within her.

And as within the little rose you find the richest
 dyes,
And in a little grain of gold much price and value
 lies,
As from a little balsam much ordor doth arise,
So in a little Woman there's a taste of paradise.

————:o:————

 As O'VER the cold sepulchral stone
  Some name arrests the passer-by,
 Thus, when thou view'st this page alone,
  May mine attract thy pensive eye !

 And when by thee that name is read,
  Perchance in some succeeding year,
 Reflect on me as on the dead,   .
  And think my heart is buried here.

————:o:————

ON you, most loved, with anxious fear I wait,
And from your judgment must expect my fate.

————:o:————

 TAKE my esteem, if you on that can live,
 For frankly, sir, 'tis all I have to give.

LIVES there the man too cold to prove
The joys of Friendship and of Love?
Then let him die; when these are fled,
Scarce do we differ from the dead,

———:o:———

OH, still my fervent prayer will be—
"Heaven's choicest blessings rest on thee!"

———:o:———

SOME friends may wish thee happiness,
. Some others wish thee wealth ;
My wish for thee is better far—
Contentment, blest with health.

———:o:———

THOU sleep'st while the eyes of the planets are
watching,
Regardless of love and of me.
I sleep: but my dreams, at thy lineaments catching,
Present me with nothing but thee.

Thou are chang'd, while the color of night changes
not
Like the fading allurements of day;
I am changed, for all beauty to me seems a blot
While the joy of my heart is away.

———:o:———

WHEN thou art with me every sense is dull,
And all I am, or know, or feel, is thee:
My soul grows faint, my veins run liquid flame,
And my bewilder'd spirit seems to swim
In eddying whirls of passion dizzily.

I'VE gazed on many a brighter face,
    But ne'er on one, for years,
Where beauty left so soft a trace
    As it had left on hers;
But who can paint the spell that wove
    A brightness round the whole!
'Twould take an angel from the skies
    To paint the immortal soul,—
To trace the light, the inborn grace,
The spirit sparkling o'er her face.

——:o:——

WRITE your name in Love, Kindness and Charity, on the hearts of the people you come in contact with, and you will be loved by all.

——:o:——

OH, Woman! Woman! thou art form'd to bless
    The heart of restless man, to chase his care,
And charm existence by thy loveliness;
    Bright as the sunbeam, as the morning fair,
If but thy foot fall on a wilderness
    Flowers spring and shed their roseate blossoms
        there,
Shrouding the thorns that in thy pathway rise,
    And scattering o'er it hues of Paradise.

——:o:——

WELL, peace to thy heart, though another's it be,
And health to thy cheek, though it bloom not for
    me.

NOT purple violets in the early spring
Such graceful sweets, such tender beauties bring ;
The orient blush which does thy cheeks adorn,
Makes coral pale—vies with the rosy morn.

———:o:———

OH, fairest of creation! last and best
Of all God's works! creature in whom excelled
Whatever can to sight or thought be form'd
Holy, divine, good, amiable, or sweet!

———:o:———

THOU art beautiful, young lady—
But I need not tell you this ;
For few have borne, unconsciously
The spell of loveliness.

———:o:———

WOMAN's truth and woman's love
Trusting ever,
Faithless never, .
Blest on earth, is blest above.

Ministering oft in sorrow's hour,
Loving truly,
Fondly, duly
Proving e'er affection's power.

Ne'er forgetting, ne'er forgot ;
Richest treasures,
Joyful pleasures
Ever be her happy lot.

PASSIONS are likened best to floods and streams—
   The shallow murmur, but the deep are dumb :
So when affections yield discourse, it seems
   The bottom is but shallow whence they come.
They that are rich in words must needs discover
They are but poor in that which makes a lover.

———:o:———

OH ! how the passions, insolent and strong,
Bear our weak minds their rapid course along ;
Make us the madness of their will obey ;
Then die, and leave us to our griefs a prey.

———:o:———

I HAVE seen the wild flowers springing,
   In wood, and field, and glen,
Where a thousand birds were singing,
   And my thoughts were of thee then ;
For there's nothing gladsome round me,
   Or beautiful to see.
Since thy beauty's spell has bound me,
   But is eloquent of thee.

———:o:———

MAY'ST thou live in joy forever,
Naught from thee true pleasure sever ;
From thy heart arise no sigh,
And no tear bedew thine eye :
Joys be many, cares be few,
Smoothe the path thou shalt pursue,
And heaven's richest blessings shine
Ever on both thee and thine.

THE changeful sand doth only know
    The shallow tide and latest ;
The rocks have marked its highest flow,
    The deepest and the greatest :
And deeper still the flood-marks grow ;—
    So, since the hour I met thee,
The more the tide of time doth flow,
    The less can I forget thee !

———:o:———

MY heart is like a lonely bird
    That sadly sings,
Brooding upon its nest unheard,
    With folded wings.

———:o:———

THERE comes
For ever something between us and what
We deem our happiness.

———:o:———

SHE'S beautiful!—Her raven curls
Have broken hearts in envious girls;—
And then they sleep in contrast so,
Like raven feathers upon snow,
And bathe her neck,—and shade the bright
Dark eye from which they catch the light,
As if their graceful loops were made
To keep that glorious eye in shade,
And holier make its tranquil spell,
Like waters in a shaded well.

PURE as the snow the summer sun
Never at noon hath looked upon;
Deep as is the diamond wave,
Hidden in the desert cave,—
Changeless as the greenest leaves
Of the wreath the cypress weaves,—
Hopeless, often, when most fond,—
Without hope or fear beyond
Its own pale fidelity;—
And this woman's love can be.

———:o:———

WHEN the name that I write here is dim on the page,
And the leaves of your album are yellow with age,
Still think of me kindly, and do not forget
That, wherever I am, I remember you yet.

———:o:———

I LOOK upon the fair blue skies,
    And naught but empty air I see ;
But when I turn me to thine eyes,
    It seemeth unto me
Ten thousand angels spread their wings
Within those little azure rings.

———:o:———

FROM her lone path she never turns aside,
    Though passionate worshipers before her fall ;
Like some pure planet in her lonely pride,
    She seems to soar and beam above them all !

IF recollections of friends brighten moments of sad-
ness,
What a fund of delight is here treasured for thee!
If advice and kind wishes bring goodness and glad-
ness.
How perfect and happy thy future must be.

———:o:———

METHINKS long years have flown,
And, sitting in her old arm-chair,
——— has older grown.
With silver sprinkled in her hair,
Her album thus she holds,
And turns its many pages o'er,
And wonders if it still contains
The memories of yore.
As o'er these pages thus she runs,
With many a sigh and kiss,
Then suddenly she stops and says,
"Who could have written this?"

———:o:———

"TRUST in thee?" Ay, dearest, there's no one but
must,
Unless truth be a fable, in such as thee trust!
For who can see heaven's own hue in those eyes,
And doubt that truth with it came down from the
skies ;   [young light,
While each thought of thy bosom, like morning's
Almost ere 'tis born, flashes there on his sight!

WHAT thing so good which not some harm may
 bring ?
E'en to be happy is a dangerous thing.

——:o:——

WE meet and part—the world is wide;
We journey onward side by side
A little while, and then again
Our paths diverge.   A little pain—
A silent yearning of the heart
For what has grown of life a part,
A shadow passing o'er the sun,
Then gone, and light again has come.
We meet and part, and then forget ;
And life holds blessings for us yet.

——:o:——

OH, never can we know how dear
 Each loved one is, till we have known
The deep regret, the bitter tear,
 That comes when those loved ones are gone.

——:o:——

I ASK not what change
 Has come over thy heart ;
I seek not what chances
 Have doomed us to part ;
I know thou hast told me
 To love thee no more,
And I still must obey
 Where I once did adore.

DROP one pearl in memory's casket for your friend.

———:o:———

PASSING through life's field of action,
    Lest we part before its end,
Take within your modest volume,
    This memento from a friend.

———:o:———

OFT as thine eye shall fondly trace
    These simple lines I sketch for thee,
Whate'er the time, where'er the place,
    O think of me.

———:o:———

ONE struggle more, and I am free
    From pangs that rend my heart in twain;
One last long sigh to love and thee,
    Then back to busy life again.

———:o:———

I ask not a life for thee,
    All radiant as others have done;
But that life may have just enough shadow
    To temper the glare of the sun.

———:o:———

OH, Woman! lovely Woman! Nature made thee
To temper man; we had been brutes without you!
Angels are painted fair, to look like you;
There's in you all that we believe of heaven;
Amazing brightness, purity and truth,
Eternal joy, and everlasting love.

THE sweetest tales of human weal and sorrow,
The fairest trophies of the limner's fame,
To my fond fancy, Mary, seem to borrow
Celestial halos from thy gentle name.

———:o:———

THE bright black eye, the melting blue,
I cannot choose between the two;
But that is dearest all the while
Which means for us the sweetest smile.

———:o:———

Is thy name Mary, maiden fair?
Such should, methinks, its music be.
The sweetest name that mortals bear,
Were best befitting thee;
And she to whom it once was given
Was half of earth and half of heaven.

———:o:———

TRUST, my friend, no Siren's whisper,
Weave no web in fancy's loom,
Build no castle for the future,
For the golden days to come.

———:o:———

THERE'S music in the forest leaves
When summer winds are there,
And in the laugh of forest girls,
That braid their sunny hair.
The first wild bird that drinks the dew,
From violets of the spring,
Has music in his song, and in
The fluttering of his wing.

LIFE has more or less besetments,
　　More or less of grief and woe;
Shadows always check our pathway,
　　Sunbeams only come and go.

———:o:———

MAY peace enfold thee in her downy wing,
　　Pure songs around thee weave a fairy spell,
To heaven thy heart's deep longing cling,
　　And happiness forever with thee dwell.

———:o:———

I PRAY the prayer of Plato old:
　　God make the beautiful within ;
And let thine eyes the good behold
　　In everything save sin.

———:o:———

THEY say that love had once a book,
　　(Tne urchin likes to copy you),
Where all who came the pencil took,
　　And wrote—like us—a line or two.

'Twas innocence, the maid divine,
　　Who kept this volume bright and fair,
And saw that no unhallowed line
　　Or thought profane should enter there.

———:o:———

MAY the blessing of God be upon thee,
May the Sun of Glory shine 'round thy bed,
May the gates of plenty, honor and happiness be
　　open to thee.

THE crimson glow of modesty o'erspread
Her cheek, and gave new lustre to her charms.

——:o:——

THIS book may fall assunder,
　　Its pages dim with age;
The ink may lose its lustre
　　Upon each shining page;
But she who writes these verses
　　Shall ever, ever be,
Through all the world's reverses,
　　A faithful friend to thee.

——:o:——

FOR mine is the lay that lightly floats,
And mine are the murmuring, dying notes
That fall as soft as snow on the sea,
And melt in the heart as instantly!
And the passionate strain that, deeply going,
Refines the bosom that it trembles through,
As the musk-wind over the water blowing,
Ruffles the wave, but sweetens it too!

——:o:——

I WANT a warm and faithful friend,
　　To cheer the adverse hour;
Who ne'er to flatter will descend,
　　Nor bend the knee to power;
A friend to chide me when I'm wrong;
　　My inmost soul to see;
And that my friendship prove as strong,
　　For her as hers for me.

MAY Heaven on you its choicest blessings shower
Is the sincere wish of your friend.

——:o:——

THERE is a bud in life's dark wilderness,   [tress ;
Whose beauties charm, whose fragrance soothes dis-
There is a beam in life's o'erclouded sky,
That gilds the starting tear it cannot dry;
That flower, that lonely beam, on Eden's grove
Shed the full sweets and heavenly light of love.
Alas! that aught so fair could lead astray
Man's wavering foot from duty's thornless way.
Yet, lovely Woman! yet thy winning smile,
That caused our cares, can every care beguile ;
And thy soft hand amid the maze of ill
Can rear one blissful bower of Eden still.

——:o:——

THROUGH days of light and gladness,
　　Through days of love and life,
Through smiles and joy and sunshine,
　　Through days with beauty rife;

The Lord of life and glory,
　　The king of earth and sea,
The Lord who guarded Israel,
　　Keep watch, sweet friend, o'er thee.

——:o:——

To all married men be this caution,
Which they should duly tender as their life,
Neither to doat too much, nor doubt a wife.

IN the golden chain of friendship regard me as a
    link.

——:o:——

SHE that would raise a noble love, must find
Ways to beget a passion for her mind;
She must be that which she to the world would seem;
For all true love is grounded on esteem;
Plainness and truth gain more a generous heart,
Than all the crooked subtleties of art.

——:o:——

——, I'll write a line or two
    On this fair page for thee,
And though I can't the rest outdo,
    Yet this must do for me.

——:o:——

LET fate do her worst, there are relics of joy,
Bright dreams of the past, which she cannot destroy;
Which come in the night time of sorrow and care,
And bring back the features that joy used to wear.

——:o:——

As half in shade, and half in sun,
    This world along its path advances,
Oh! may that side the sun shines on
    Be all that ever meets thy glances;
May Time, who casts his blight on all,
    And daily dooms some joy to death,
On thee let years so gently fall
    They shall not crush one flower beneath.

AMONG the many friends who claim
  A kind remembrance in thy heart,
I, too, would add my simple name
    Among the rest.

————:o:————

OFT to the woods at close of day,
The star of eve directs my way.
To fairy forms my woes I tell,
And mingle plaints with Philomel.
Sweet bird! trill out thy notes so clear,
And waft the sound to ————'s ear,
And tell her, since like thee I pine,
To hear thy woes and pity mine.

————:o:————

I LOOK upon the fading flowers
  Thou gavest me, lady, in thy mirth,
And mourn, that with the perishing hours
  Such fair things perish from the earth;
For thus I know the moment's feeling
  Its own light web of life unweaves,
The dearest trace from memory stealing,
  Like perfume from their dying leaves,—
The thought that gave it, and the flower,
Alike the creatures of an hour.
And thus it better were, perhaps,—
  For feeling is the nurse of pain,
And joys that linger in their lapse
  Must die at last,—and so are vain.

Is it vain in life's wide sea,
To ask you to remember me?
Undoubtedly it is my lot
Just to be known and then—forgot.

———:o:———

Not purple violets in the early spring
Such graceful sweets, such tender beauties bring;
The orient blush which does thy cheeks adorn,
Makes coral pale—vies with the rosy morn.

———:o:———

She was knowing in all needlework,
And shone in dairy and in kitchen too,
As in the parlor

———:o:———

In after years when you recall
    The days of pleasures past,
And think of joyous hours and all
    Have flown away so fast,
When some forgotten air you hear
    Brings back past scenes to thee,
And gently claims your listening ear ;
    Keep one kind thought for me.

———:o:———

While her laugh, full of life, without any control,
But the sweet one of gracefulness, rung from her soul.
And where it most sparkled, no glance could discover,
In lip, cheek, or eyes, for she brighten'd all over,
Like any fair lake that the breeze is upon,
When it breaks into dimples, and laughs in the sun.

MAY Future, with her kindest smile,
  Wreath laurels for thy brow;
May loving angels guard and keep thee
  Ever pure as thou art now.

————:o:————

YES, ————, I will write my name
  In here, as you request ;
And, if to you it's all the same,
I'll add a line—though rather tame—
  For Critic's eyes, as my bequest.

  My wishes and my hopes for you,
    Find glad expression here ;
  Although, indeed, it's very true,
  There is no room for all that's due
    To one we hold so dear.

————:o:————

        THE world would be lonely,
The garden a wilderness left to déform,
If the flowers but remember'd the chilling winds
  only
And the fields gave no verdure for fear of the storm

————:o:————

DIE when you will, you need not wear
At heaven's court a form more fair
  Than beauty here on earth has given;
Keep but the lovely looks we see—
The voice we hear—and you will be
  An angel *ready made* for heaven.

MAY your days in joy be passed
With friends to bless and cheer.
And each year exceed the last
In all that earth holds dear.

————:o:————

LULL'D in the countless chambers of the brain,
Our thoughts are link'd by many a hidden chain;
Awake but one, and lo! what myriads rise!
Each stamps its image as the other flies!

————:o:————

ALL the blessings of this life are worth nothing
without the sunshine of hope for a bright and lasting
future. My wishes are these for thee.

————:o:————

WERE mine the power, I'd twine for thee
A crown of jewels rare;
Each gem should be a kingdom,
Each pearl an humble prayer.

————:o:————

MAY you live in bliss, from sorrow away,
Having plenty laid up for a rainy day;
And when you are ready to settle in life,
May you find a good husband and make a good wife.

————:o:————

SOON as thy letters trembling I unclose,
That well known name awakens all my woes.
Oh, name forever sad! forever dear!
Still breath'd in sighs, still usher'd with a tear!

NOT for the summer hour alone,
  When skies resplendent shine,
And youth and pleasure fill the throne,
  Our hearts and hands we twine;
But for those stern and wintry days
  Of peril, pain, and fear,
When Heaven's wise discipline doth make
  This earthly journey drear.

————:o:————

I BLESS thee for the noble heart,
  The tender and the true,
Where mine hath found the happiest rest
  That e'er fond woman knew;
I bless thee, faithful friend and guide,
  For my own, my treasur'd share,
In the mournful secrets of thy soul,
  In thy sorrow and thy care.

————:o:————

THERE is a small and simple flower
  That twines around the humblest cot,
And in the sad and lonely hours
  It whispers low: " Forget me not."

————:o:————

THOUGH fools spurn Hymen's gentle powers,
We, who improve his golden hours,
By sweet experience know
That marriage, rightly understood,
Gives to the tender and the good
A paradise below.

ACCOMPLISHMENTS are native to her mind,
　　Like precious pearls within a clasping shell,
And winning grace her every act refined,
　　Like sunshine, shedding beauty where it fell.

———:o:———

THEN come the wild weather—come sleet or come
　　snow,
We will stand by each other, however it blow;
Oppression and sickness, and sorrow and pain,
Shall be to our true love as links to the chain.

———:o:———

DOST thou know, love, that thy smile
　　Makes the whole world bright for me,
Just as sunrise pours a sudden
　　Purple glory on the sea.
Ah! had I that power, ever
　　Should the world look bright to thee.

———:o:——

HERE'S a sigh for those who love me,
　　And a smile for those who hate;
And whatever sky's above me,
　　Here's a heart for every fate.

———:o:——

OH, happy state! when souls each other draw,
When love is liberty, and Nature law!
All then is full, possessing and possess'd,
No craving void left aching in the breast.
Ev'n thought meets thought, ere from the lips it part,
And each warm wish springs mutual from the heart.

It may occur in after life
That you, I trust, a happy wife,
Will former happy hours retrace,
Recall each remembered face.
At such a moment I but ask—
I hope 'twill be a pleasant task—
That you'll remember as a friend
One who'll prove true e'en to the end.

——:o:——

My autograph? Why, certainly, my dear;
I wish its market value was more clear.
You still should have it, for my will is good—
I'd give a kingdom to you if I could.
What more could she have purchased for a smile,
That other queenly sorceress of the Nile?

——:o:——

Like Raleigh I would praise my queen,
On crystal with a diamond keen ;
But lack the diamond and the glass,—
So give you these and let those pass.
No queen that ever trod the earth
Had more of woman's genuine worth
Than thee, fair lady, bright and pure,
For whom I pen this signature.

——:o:——

I would not blot this page, but I would like to
make a spot large enough to hold you to remembrance of your friend.

LOVE.

LOVE is a subject to himself alone,
And knows no other empire than his own.

——:o:——

LOOK how the blue-eyed violets
  Glance love to one another!
Their little leaves are whispering
  The vows they may not smother.
The birds are pouring passion forth
  In every blossoming tree;—
If flowers and birds talk love, lady,
             Why not we?

——:o:——

WHY should I blush to own I love?
'Tis Love that rules the realms above.
Why should I blush to say to all
That virtue holds my heart in thrall?

Why should I seek the thickest shade,
Lest Love's dear secret be betrayed?
Why the stern brow deceitful move,
When I am languishing with love?

Is it a weakness thus to dwell
On passion that I dare not tell?
Such weakness I would ever prove.
'Tis painful, but 'tis sweet to love !

THE dart of Love was feather'd first
    From Folly's wing, they say,
Until he tried his shaft to shoot
    In Beauty's heart one day;
He miss'd the maid so oft, 'tis said,
    His aim became untrue,
And Beauty laugh'd, as his last shaft
    He from his quiver drew;
"In vain," said she, "you shoot at me,
    You little spiteful thing—
The feather on your shaft I scorn,
    When pluck'd from Folly's wing."

But Cupid soon fresh arrows found
    And fitted to his string,
And each new shaft he feathered from
    His own bright glossy wing;
He shot until no plume was left
    To waft him to the sky.
And Beauty smil'd upon the child,
    When he no more could fly;
"Now, Cupid, I am thine," she said,
    "Leave off thy archer play,
For Beauty yields—when she is sure
    Love will not fly away."

———:o:———

HAVE I not managed my contrivance well,
To try your love and make you doubt of mine?

I HOLD it true, whate'er befall—
  I feel it when I sorrow most—
  'Tis better to have loved and lost,
Than never to have loved at all.

————:o:————

THE cold in clime are cold in blood,
  Their love can scarce deserve the name;
But mine was like the lava-flood
  That boils in Ætna's breast of flame.

———— :o:————

YES! Love indeed is light from heaven,
  A spark of that immortal fire
With angels shared—to mortals given,
  To lift from earth our low desire.
Devotion wafts the mind above,
But heaven itself descends in love;
A feeling from the Godhead caught,
To wean from self each sordid thought;
A ray of Him who formed the whole;
A glory circling round the soul.

————:o:————

THERE ever is a form, a face
  Of maiden beauty in my dreams,
Speeding before me, like the race
  To ocean of the mountain streams,—
With dancing hair and laughing eyes,
That seem to mock me as it flies.

Spring has no blossom fairer than thy face;
  Winter no snow-wreath purer than thy mind;
The dewdrop trembling to the morning beam
  Is like thy smile—pure, transient, heaven-refin'd.

————:o:————

Oh, how the passions, insolent and strong,
Bear our weak minds their rapid course along ;
Make us the madness of their will obey;
Then die, and leave us to our griefs a prey.

————:o:————

The light that beams from Woman's eye,
  And sparkles through her tear,
Responds to that impassion'd sigh
  Which love delights to hear.
'Tis the sweet language of the soul,
  On which a voice is hung,
More eloquent than ever stole
  From saint's or poet's tongue.

————:o:————

I have heard of reasons manifold
  Why Love must needs be blind ;
But this the best of all I hold—
  His eyes are in his mind.

What outward form and features are
  He guesseth but in part ;
But what within is good and fair
  He seeth with his heart.

SUNS may darken,—heaven be bow'd,—
   Still unchanged shall be,
Soul-deep here that moonlit cloud,
   To which I looked with THEE.

———:o:———

     LOVE is not love
Which alters when it alteration finds,
Or bends with the remover to remove;
O no! it is an ever fixed mark,
That looks on tempests, and is never shaken;
It is the star to every wandering bark,   [taken.
Whose worth's unknown,. although his height be

———:o:———

LOVE! What a volume in a word! an ocean in a tear!
A seventh heaven in a glance! a whirlwind in a sigh!
The lightning in a touch—a millennium in a moment!
What concentrated joy, or woe, in blest or blighted
    love!

———:o:———

ALTHOUGH my heart, in earlier youth,
   Might kindle with more wild desire,
Believe me, it has gained in truth
   Much more than it has lost in fire;
The flame now warms my inmost core,
   That then but sparkled on thy brow;
And though I seem'd to love thee more,
   Yet, oh, I love thee better now.

ALMIGHTY love! what wonders are not thine!
Soon as thy influence breathes upon the soul,
By thee the haughty bend the suppliant knee,
By thee the hand of avarice is opened
Into profusion; by thy power the heart
Of cruelty is melted into softness;
The rude grow tender, and the fearful bold.

———:o:———

FOR me I'm woman's slave confessed—
Without her, hopeless and unblest;
And so are all, gainsay who can,
For what would be the life of man,
If left in desert or in isle,
Unlighted up by beauty's smile?
Even tho' he boasted monarch's name,
And o'er his own sex reign'd supreme,
With thousands bending to his sway,
If lovely Woman were away,
What were his life?   What could it be?
A vapor on a shoreless sea;
A troubled cloud in darkness toss'd,
Amongst the waste of waters lost;
A ship deserted in the gale,
Without a steersman or a sail,
A star, or beacon-light before,
Or hope of heaven evermore;
A thing without a human tie,
Unloved to live,—unwept to die.

I BLESS thee for kind looks and words
   Shower'd on my path like dew;
For all the love in those deep eyes,—
   A gladness ever new!
For the voice which ne'er to mine replied,
   But in kindly tones of cheer:
For every spring of happiness
   My soul hath tasted here!

————:o:————

I KNOW a passion still more deeply charming
Than fever'd youth e'er felt; and that is Love,
By long experience mellow'd into Friendship.
How far beyond that froward child of fancy!
With beauty pleased awhile, anon disgusted,
Seeking some other toy; how far more noble
Is that bright offspring of unchanging reason,
That fonder grows with age, and charms forever.

————:o:————

So like the chances are of Love and War,
That they alone in this distinguished are:
In Love, the victors from the vanquished fly—
They fly that wound, and they pursue that die.

————:o:————

DOUBT thou the stars are fire;
   Doubt that the sun doth move;
Doubt Truth to be a liar;
   But never doubt I love!

OH, how bitter a thing it is to look
Into happiness through another man's eyes!

————:o:————

THERE are in love the extremes of touch'd desire,—
The noblest brightness or the coarsest fire!
In vulgar bosoms vulgar wishes move:
Nature guides choice, and as men think they love.
In the loose passion men profane the name,
Mistake the purpose, and pollute the flame:
In nobler bosoms friendship's form it takes,
And sex alone the lovely difference makes.

————:o:————

LET grace and goodness be the principal load-
stone of thy affections. For love which hath ends,
will have an end; whereas that which is founded
on true Virtue, will always continue.

————:o:————

LOVE is a pearl of purest hue,
    But stormy waves are round it;
And dearly may a woman rue
    The hour that first she found it.

————:o:————

YE flowers that droop, forsaken by the spring;
YE birds that, forsaken by the summer, cease to
        sing;
Ye trees that fade when autumn heats remove,
Say, is not Absence death to those who love?

LET no one say that there is need
  Of time for love to grow;
Ah, no! the love that kills indeed,
  Despatches at a blow.

——:o:——

BY every hope that earthward clings,
By faith that mounts on angel-wings,
By dreams that make night-shadows bright,
And truths that turn our day to night,
By childhood's smile and manhood's tear
By pleasure's day and sorrow's year,
By all the strains that fancy sings,
And pangs that time so surely brings,
For joy or grief, for hope or fear,
For all hereafter as for here,
In peace or strife, in storm or shine,
My soul is wedded unto thine!

——:o:——

GOD gives us love. Something to love
  He lends us; but when love is grown
To ripeness, that on which it throve
  Falls off, and love is left alone.

——:o:——

LOVE is to my impassion'd soul
  Not, as with others, a mere part
Of existence; but the whole—
  The very life-breath of my heart.

THE world! ah, Fanny! love must shun
   The path where many rove;
     One bosom to recline upon,
     The heart to be his only one,
   Are quite enough for love.

————:o:————

'T WAS but a moment; and yet in that time
She crowded th' impressions of many an hour;
Her eye had a glow, like the sun of her clime,
Which wak'd ev'ry feeling at once into flower!

————:o:————

THERE'S not a wind but whispers of thy name,
And not a flower that grows beneath the moon
But in its hues and fragrance tells a tale
Of thee, my love.

————:o:————

WHEN, ————, I confess my pain,
   In gentle words you pity show;
But gentle words are all in vain:
   Such gales my flame but higher blow.
Ah, ————, would you cure the smart
   Your conquering eyes have keenly made,
Yourself upon my bleeding heart,
   Yourself, fair ————, must be laid.
Thus, for the viper's sting we know
   No surer remedy is found
Than to apply the torturing foe,
   And squeeze his venom on the wound.

THEY sin who tell us love can die;
With love all other passions fly,—
All others are but vanity.
In heaven ambition cannot dwell,
Nor avarice in the vaults of hell;
Earthly these passions of the earth,
They perish where they have their birth;
But love is indestructible;
Its holy flame forever burneth;
From heaven it came, to heaven returneth.

——:o:——

AH; me! how deep the poison lies
Which late I drank from ——'s eyes!
It burns, it spreads; each tortured vein
Throbs with the agonizing pain.

——:o:——

FOR several virtues
Have I lik'd several women; never any
With so full soul, but some defect in her
Did quarrel with the noblest grace she owed,
And put it to the foil: but you, oh you,
So perfect, and so peerless, are created
Of every creature's best!

——:o:——

I NEED not say how, one by one,
    Love's flowers have dropp'd from off love's chain;
Enough to say that they are gone,
    And that they cannot bloom again.

SEEK for a bosom all honest and true,
  Where love once awaken'd will never depart;
Turn, turn to that breast, like the dove to its nest,
  And you'll find there's no home like the home in
    the heart.

——:o:——

I DEEM'D that time, I deem'd that pride,
  Had quench'd at last my boyish flame;
Nor knew, till seated by thy side,
  My heart in all, save hope, the same.

——:o:——

THEY that Love had once a book
  (The urchin likes to copy you),
Where all who came the pencil took,
  And wrote, like us, a line or two.

——:o:——

'T WAS Innocence, the maid divine,
  Who kept this volume bright and fair,
And saw that no unhallowed line
  Or thought profane should enter there.

——:o:——

BENEATH the touch of Hope, how soft,
  How light the magic pencil ran!
Till Fear would come, alas! as oft,
  And, trembling, close what Hope began.

——:o:——

LOVE is, or ought to be, our greatest bliss;
Since every other joy, how dear soever,
Gives way to that, and we leave all for love.

HUMOROUS.

MAY you always have enough and plenty for each
  day;
May you never have enough to waste or throw
  away;
May you live long enough your debts to pay;
May you never live so long as to be in other people's
  way.

———:o:———

To knit and spin was once a girl's employment;
But now to dress and have a beau is all a girl's enjoyment.

———:o:———

REMEMBER me when far away,
 And only half awake;
Remember me on your wedding-day,
 And send a piece of cake.

———:o:———

———— is your name,
 Single is your station,
Happy be the little man
 That makes the alteration.

———:o:———

REMEMBER me, is all I ask,
And, if remembrance be a task,
 Forget me.

36C

MAY your coffee and slanders against you be
ever the same—without grounds.

——:o:——

ROUND went the autograph; hither it came,
For me to write in; so here's my name.

——:o:——

THE world is full of fools,
    And he who would none view,
Must shut himself in a cave,
    And break his mirror, too.

——:o:——

SOME folks are constantly wishing;
    I could never get much for a wish,
But should you ever go a fishing,
    May your net be filled with fish.

——:o:——

OH, for a home in Zululand, or Arctic regions cold,
A peasant's cot or hermit's hut, midst solitude un-
    told,
With Kaffirs or with Hottentots, in Egypt or Leone;
'Twere bliss to live in *any* spot where albums are
    unknown.

——:o:——

THANKSGIVING-DAY again is here,
    And turkey is the leading question;
I wish, with heartiness sincere,
    That you may have a good digestion.

I MOST sincerely wish that you
May have many friends, and who,
No matter what you are passing through,
Will stick as close as good, strong glue.

————:o:————

LIFE'S a jest, and all things show it;
I thought so once, and now I know it.

————:o:————

ON this page I'll write,
Simply to indite
My name as your friend.

————:o:————

OH! love is such a strange affair;
So strange to all.
It cometh from above
And lighteth like a dove
On some.
But some it never hits
Unless it gives them fits.
Oh, hum.

————:o:————

SOME write for pleasure, some write for fame;
But I write simply to sign my name.

————:o:————

OH, wayward mortal who these books invented,
Why wast thou not by some kind hand prevented?
And thereby kept from many a luckless swain
The direful knowledge that he lacked a brain—
Lacked it, at least, where poetry was needed,
Like the poor wight who here has not succeeded.

REMEMBER me when "far, far off,
Where the woodchucks die of whooping-cough."

————:o:————

EVER be content with thy lot, especially if it be
a corner lot.

————:o:————

I'M in a quandary how to compose
Doggerel rhymes and ditties for those
Albums so freely thrust under my nose.
Vain 'tis to strive 'gainst the Miss who decrees,
An original poem, if you please,"
From your dull brain you must squeeze
Fain would I fly—I care not where;
Lend me your wings, O angels fair,
Encounter another album I do not dare.
Can it be that there is no country bright,
Kept securely free from albums' blight?
'TIS but a trifle that you ask,
    But this you will admit,
That trifles, more than greater tasks
    Will sometimes strain our wit,
I wish thee health, and wealth, and joy,
    As others have before;
And were I in poetic mood,
    I'd surely wish thee more.

————:o:————

HE who complies against his will
Is of his own opinion still.

I WRITE here a name which I hope shall be known
To all of the ages which follow my own.
" How conceited ! " you say; but my lines shall
     remain,
'Tis my hope, you'll discover, Not I, that is vain.

————:o:————

MAY you always be happy,
     And live at your ease;
Get a kind husband,
     And do as you please.

————:o:————

WHEN on this page you chance to look,
Just think of me and close the book.

————:o:————

AS sure as comes your wedding day,
     A broom to you I'll send;
In *sunshine*, use the brushy part,
     In *storm*, the other end.

————:o:————

WHEN asked in an album to write,
     I feel quite inclined to refuse;
For what should I dare to indite
     That would a young lady amuse?
Not wit, for I have none of that,
     Nor romance—my fancy is tame;
And compliments sound so flat,
     I'm forced to write merely my name.

WHAT can I write that's new
Among so very many
Pretty compliments to you?
In poetry, I fear I'd fail—
I'm very sure I'd stammer—
You cannot drive the ponderous nail
With a small ten-cent tack hammer.
Since, then, so high I cannot soar,
Nor chirp notes like the lark,
Please cancel what I've said before,
I'll simply make my mark.

———:o:———

SAILING down the stream of life,
In your little bark canoe,
May you have a pleasant trip
With just room enough for two.

———:o:———

IF a body ask a body,
In her book to write; .
If a body refuse a body,
Need a body fight?

All the lassies and the laddies
Write sweet things herein;
If a body write less sweetly,
Does a body sin?

———:o:———

IF writing in Albums remembrance insures,
With the greatest of pleasure I'll scribble in yours.

THOUGH many friends have signed their names,
  And some have left their mark,
I see a place for me remains
  To add my small remark.
My wish for thee is: joy through life;
  And bliss supreme, when someone's wife.

———:o:———

A VERSE you ask this fine day;
  Of course I'll write you one.
The task of writing finds its pay
  In joy that it is done

———:o:———

THEN be not coy, but use your time,
  And while ye may, go marry;
For having lost but once your prime
  You may forever tarry.

———:o:———

IF ever a husband you should have,
  And he this book should see,
Tell him of your youthful days,
  And kiss him once for me.

———:o:———

SOME people can be very funny;
  I never could be so.
So I'll just inscribe my name—
  It's the funniest thing I know.

IN the storms of life,
 When you need an umbrella,
May you have to uphold it
 A handsome young fellow

———:o:———

MAY your cheeks retain their dimples,
 May your heart be just as gay,
Until some manly voice shall whisper,
 " Dearest, will you name the day? "

———:o:———

Long may you live,
 Happy may you be;
When you get married
 Come and see me.

———:o:———

MAN'S love is like Scotch snuff—
You take a pinch, and that's enough.
Profit by this sage advice,
When you fall in love, think twice.

———:o:———

I WOULD that I could express my mind
To you, dear friend, in scribbling some rhyme;
But you know my failing as well as I,
And you better get another to try.

———:o:———

MAY beauty and truth,
 Keep you in youth;
Green tea and sage
 Preserve your old age.

'TIS an old maxim in the schools,
That flattery's the food of fools;
Yet now and then you men of wit
Will condescend to take a bit.

———:o:———

LIKE a lovely tree
She grew to womahood, and between whiles
Rejected several suitors, just to learn
How to accept a better in his turn.

———:o:———

YOUR love in a cottage is hungry,
   Your vine is a nest for flies;
Your milkmaid shocks the graces,
   And Simplicity talks of pies!
You lie down to your shady slumber,
   And wake with a bug in your ear;
And your damsel that walks in the morning,
Is shod like a mountaineer.

REMEMBRANCE.

REMEMBER me, I pray; but not
   In Flora's gay and blooming hour,
When every brake hath found its note,
   And sunshine smiles in every flower;
But when the falling leaf is sere,
   And withers sadly from the tree
And o'er the ruins of the year
   Cold autumn weeps,—remember me.

————:o:————

A PLACE in thy memory, dearest,
   Is all that I claim;
To pause and look back when thou hearest
   The sound of my name.

————:o:————

THERE'S not an hour
Of day, or dreaming night, but I am with thee;
There's not a wind but whispers of thy name;
And not a flower that sleeps beneath the moon,
But in its fragrance tells a tale
Of thee.

————:o:————

WHEN thou art gone, there creeps into my heart
   A cold and bitter consciousness of pain;
The light, the warmth of life, with thee depart,
   And I sit dreaming o'er and o'er again.
Thy greeting clasp, thy parting look and tone;
And suddenly I wake—and am alone!

THE hills are shadows, and they flow
　　From form to form and nothing stands;
They melt like mist the solid lands,
　　Like clouds they shape themselves and go.

But in my spirit will I dwell,
　　And dream my dream and hold it true;
For though my pen doth write adieu,
　　I cannot say for aye, farewell.

———:o:———

NO mental blossom can I give
Fit 'mid these pretty flowers to live:
No rose to rear its blushing head;
No lily from its watery bed;
No briar its sweetness round to spread;
No tuberose fragrance aye to shed.
No, Lady, hard will be my lot
Unless you'll say "Forget-me-not."

———:o:———

WHEN the golden sun is sinking,
　　And your mind from care and trouble's free;
When of others you are thinking,
　　Won't you sometimes think of me?

———:o:———

THE time is swiftly passing by
　　When we must bid adieu.
We know not when we meet again,
　　So these lines I leave with you.

FOND Memory, come and hover o'er
   This album page of my dear friend;
Enrich her from thy precious store,
   And happy recollection send
If on this page she chance to gaze,
   In years to come—where'er she be—
Tell her of earlier happy days,
   And bring her back one thought of me.

————:o:————

AH, tell me not that memory
   Sheds gladness o'er the past,—
What is recalled by faded flowers,
   Save that they did not last!

————:o:————

WHEN forced to part from those we love,
   Though sure to meet to-morrow.
We yet a kind of anguish prove,
   And feel a touch of sorrow.
But oh, what words can paint the fears,
   When from those friends we sever
Perhaps to part for month—for years—
   Perhaps to part forever.

————:o:————

FAREWELL! The leisure and the fearful time
Cuts off the ceremonious vows of love,
And ample interchange of sweet discourse,
Which so long sunder'd friends should dwell upon.
God give us leisure for these rites of love!
Once more, adieu!

COUNT not the hours while their silent wings
    Thus waft them in fairy flight;
For feeling, warm from her dearest springs,
    Shall hallow the scene to-night.
And while the music of joy is here,
    And the colors of life are gay,
Let us think on those that have loved us dear—
    The friends who are far away.

———:o:———

THEY tell me 'tis decided, you depart:
    'Tis wise, 'tis well, but not the less a pain;
I have no further claim on your young heart,
    Mine is the victim, and would be again.
To love too much has been the only art
    I used.   I write in haste, and if a stain
Be on this sheet, 'tis not what it appears,
My eyeballs burn and throb, but have no tears

———:o:———

LET me, then let me dream
    That love goes with us to the shore unknown:
So o'er the burning tear a heavenly gleam
    In mercy shall be thrown.

———:o:———

FAREWELL, oh farewell, but whenever you give
    A thought to the days that are gone,
Of the bright sunny things that in memory live,
    Let a thought of the writer be one.

FAREWELL, oh farewell, but whenever you give
   A thought to the days that are gone,
Of the bright sunny things that in memory live
   Let a thought of the writer be one.
The hope is but humble—he asks but a share,
   But a part of *thy memories* to be,
While no *future* to *him* can in rapture compare
   To the past, made enchanting by thee.

———:o:———

ACCEPT, my friend, these lines from me,
They show that I remember thee,
And hope some thought they will retain,
Till you and I shall meet again.

———:o:———

ENOUGH, that we are parted—that there rolls
A flood of headlong fate between our souls,
Whose darkness severs me as wide from thee
As hell from heaven, to all eternity.

———:o:———

FOND Memory, come and hover o'er
   This album page of my fair friend;
Enrich her from thy precious store,
   And happy recollections send.
If on this page she chance to gaze
   In years to come—where'er she be—
Tell her of earlier happy days,
   And bring her back one thought of me.

FAREWELL! Thou hast trampled love's faith in the
　　dust,
Thou hast torn from my bosom its hope and its
　　trust;
Yet, if thy life's current with bliss it would swell,
I would pour out my own in this last fond farewell.

————:o:————

BE always kind-hearted,
　　Do good deeds without end,
But never forget,
　　Your affectionate friend.

————:o:————

AH, tell me not that memory
　　Sheds gladness o'er the past:
What is recall'd by faded flowers
　　Save that they do not last?
Were it not better to forget,
Than but remember and regret?

————:o:————

KEEP me in remembrance,
If in the darkness
　　I should stray afar,
　　　Like some lost traveler
　　With no guiding star.
Be then still my true,
　　Sincere, and loving friend,
And o'er all ills and
　　Trials to my life's end
　　　Keep me in remembrance.

Accept my friend these lines from me,
They show that I remember thee,
And hope some thought they will retain
Till you and I shall meet again.

———:o:———

Oh, Memory! thou fond deceiver,
  Still importunate and vain,
To former joys recurring ever,
  And turning all the past to pain;
Thou, like the world, th' opprest oppressing,
  Thy smiles increase the wretch's woe!
And he who wants each other blessing
  In thee must ever find a foe.

———:o:———

Methinks that many years have flown
  And in a large arm-chair,
——— is sitting older grown
  With silver in her hair.

And thus she muses, as she wipes
  Her glasses o'er and o'er:
I wonder if my album keeps
  The memories of yore.

She turns the pages through and through
  With many a sigh and kiss,
When suddenly she stops and says,
  Who could have written this?

HAIL, memory, hail! In thy exhaustless mine,
From age to age unnumber'd treasures shine!
Thought and her shadowy brood thy call obey,
And place and time are subject to thy sway!

———:o:———

FAREWELL! God knows when we shall meet again!
I have a faint cold fear thrills through my veins,
That almost freezes up the heat of life.
Art thou gone so? My love! my lord! my friend!
I must hear from thee ev'ry day i' the hour,
For in a minute there are many days!
Oh, by this count I shall be much in years,
Ere I again behold my Romeo!

———:o:———

IN this world of change and sorrow when shall
we meet again?

———:o:———

WITH a heart free from care, and my home in the
    West,
I'll pace the broad deck with a light throbbing breast,
Yet still as I dream of those days that are gone,
Of the gay happy hours in my own native home,
Far, far o'er the wave my heart wanders there
To its shrine of devotion, where youth, free from
    care,
We spent such golden hours of innocence and glee
With you and dear companions, so pray remember
    me.

COME, flattering memory! and tell my heart
How kind she was, and with what pleasing art
She strove its fondest wishes to obtain,
Confirm her power, and faster bind my chain.

————:o:————

THOUGH many miles apart
　　Our homes may prove to be,
YET in the recess of your heart
　　Keep one kind thought of me.

————:o:————

FARE thee well!　Yet think a while
　　On one whose bosom bleeds to doubt thee;
Who now would rather trust thy smile,
　　And die with thee, than live without thee.

————:o:————

THROUGH time we'll change, and then,
　　This little book will somewhat bind us;
You'll take it up, and think of me,
　　And all the joys we've left behind us.

————:o:————

"FORGET me not" when death shall close
These eyelids in their last repose,
And murm'ring breezes softly wave
Perchance the grass upon my grave.
Whate'er thy age and lot may be,
Long as thy life shall last, remember me.

I HEARD thy low-whispered farewell, love,
And silently saw thee depart;—
Ay, silent;— for how could words tell, love,
The sorrow that swelled in my heart?
They could not.   Oh, language is faint,
When passion's devotion would speak;
Light pleasure or pain it may paint,
But with feelings like ours it is weak!
Yet tearless and mute though I stood, love,
Thy last words are thrilling me yet,
And my heart would have breathed, if it could love,
And murmured, "Oh, do not forget!"

———:o:———

"FORGET me not" when pleasure's snare
Would keep you from the house of prayer.
"Forget me not" in feeble age,
E'en let me then your thoughts engage.

———:o:———

IF ever love's fondest prayer brought blessings
from on high, thou shalt be blessed.   Friend! farewell!   To him on whom thy cheerful hope relies,
whose arm sustains thee, and whose promise soothes
—my faith commends thee—may'st thou still receive grace for grace, and love for love; and guid-
ance through this wilderness of tears! till thou possess thy Crown of Life.

———:o:———

ON this leaf, in memory prest.
May my name forever rest.

OH! think of me some day
When I am far away;
I'll pray thy days be long
And joyous as the song
Of sweet birds singing near,
Thy heart with love to cheer.

———:o:———

FAREWELL; how oft that sound of sadness,
    Like thorns of sorrow pierce the heart,
And hush the harp tones of its gladness,
    And tear the bleeding chords apart.

Farewell! and if by distance parted
    We see each other's face no more,
Ah! may we with the faithful-hearted
    Meet beyond this parting shore.

———:o:———

FAREWELL! perhaps forever,
Beloved one adieu!
Wilt thou this token please to take,
And keep it long for friendship's sake;
And when these lines you chance to see,
Remember that they came from me.

———:o:———

THESE few lines to you are tendered,
    By a friend sincere and true;
Hoping but to be remembered
    When I'm far away from you.

WE will revive those times, and in our memories
Preserve, and still keep fresh, like flowers in water,
Those happier days; when at our eyes our souls
Kindled their mutual fires, their equal beams
Shot and return'd, till link'd and twin'd in one,
They chain'd our hearts together.

———:o:———

"FORGET me not" when far away
Amidst a thoughtless world you stray
"Forget me not" when fools would win
Your footsteps to the paths of sin.
"Forget me not" when urged to wrong
By fashions and temptations strong.

———:o:———

STILL o'er these scenes my memory wakes,
   And fondly broods with miser care:
Time but the impression deeper makes,
   As streams their channels deeper wear.

MISCELLANEOUS.

WE bask in Friendship's smile,
And pure affection glows with gladdening light,
As life's extending path is often bright
    And beautiful the while.

But if a stormy wave
Break on our path and change the pleasing scene,
Disturb the sea of life, so late serene,
    Friendship may find a grave.

Such is the changeless love,
The pure affection of that lasting Friend
Whose smile imparts a joy that ne'er shall end–
    A boon from Heaven above;

Whatever be our lot,
Sickness or health, or trial's darkest hour;
If friends forsake, and tempests o'er us lower,
    That Friend forsaketh not.

———:o:———

I CARE not much for gold or land;
    Give me a mortgage here and there,
Some good bank stock—some note of hand
    Or trifling railroad share;
I only ask that Fortune send
    A little more than I can spend.

———:o:———

YOURS sincerely—although merely—

Look forward what's to come, and back what's past,
Thy life will be with praise and prudence graced;
What loss or gain may follow, thou may'st guess;
Thou then wilt be secure of the success.

————:o:————

Each to your chaplet brings a flower,
To please you in an idle hour.
Some bring a violet, some a rose;
Some poppy blossoms, for repose;
Some lilies white, some eglantine,
And some the climbing passion vine.
The simplest blossom suits me best,
So here's my primrose with the rest.

————:o:————

Sweet beauty sleeps upon thy brow,
And floats before my eyes;
As meek and pure as doves art thou,
Or beings of the skies.

————:o:————

Accept, dear friend, the trifle that ı write—
The simple tribute of a faithful wight
Who knows thy worth, and far esteems it more
Than the rich diamond from Golconda's store.

————:o:————

He who does good to another does also good to
himself—not only in the act but in the consciousness
of well-doing is his reward.

SPITE of all the fools that pride has made,
'Tis not on man a useless burthen laid:
Pride has ennobled some, and some disgraced;
It hurts not in itself, but as 'tis placed;
When right, its views know none but virtue's bound;
When wrong, it scarcely looks one inch around.

————:o:————

DUTY has pleasures with no satiety;
Duties fulfilled are always pleasures to the memory;
Duty makes pleasure doubly sweet by contrast.

————:o:————

ROUND went the book, and here it came,
In it for me to write my name;
I would write better, if I could,
But Nature said I never should.

————:o:————

THERE are ten thousand tones and signs
We hear and see, but none defines—
Involuntary sparks of thought
Which strike from out the heart o'erwrought,
And form a strange intelligence
Alike mysterious and intense;
Which link the burning chain that binds
Without their will, young hearts and minds,
Conveying, as the electric wire,
We know not how, the absorbing fire.

————:o:————

HE ought not to pretend to friendship's name,
Who reckons not himself and friend the same.

THE love of praise, how'er concealed by art,
Reigns, more or less, and glows in every heart:
The proud to gain it toils on toils endure,
The modest shun it but to make it sure.

————:o:————

OF all the causes which conspire to blind
Man's erring judgment, and misguide the mind,
What the weak head with strongest bias rules,
Is pride, the never-failing vice of fools.

————:o:————

WHEN two friends part, they should lock up one
ancther's secrets, and interchange their keys.

————:o:————

IN future years should trusted friends
    Depart like summer birds;
And all the comfort memory lends,
    Is false and honeyed words,
Turn then to me, who fain would prove
    However thy lot be cast,
That naught his heart can ever move
    From friendship of the past.

————:o:————

A FRIEND is gold: if true, he'll never leave thee;
Yet both, without a touchstone, may deceive thee.

————:o:————

LET us try to be happy; we may if we will
Find some pleasure in life to o'erbalance the ill.
There was never an evil, if well understood,
But what, rightly managed, would turn to a good.

THE soul of music slumbers in the shell,
Till wak'd and kindled by the master's spell;
And feeling hearts—touch them but lightly—pour
A thousand melodies unheard before.

————:o:————

MAY all go well with you! May life's short day
glide on peaceful and bright, with no more clouds
than may glisten in the sunshine, no more rain than
may form a rainbow; and may the veiled one of
heaven bring us to meet again.

————:o:————

I THINK of thee when morning springs
    From sleep, with plumage bath'd in dew;
And, like a young bird, lifts its wings
    Of gladness on the welkin blue:
And when, at noon, the breath of love
    O'er flower and stream is wandering free,
And sent in music from the grove,
    I think of thee—I think of thee.

I think of thee, when, soft and wide,
    The evening spreads her robes of light,
And, like a young and timid bride,
    Sits blushing in the arms of night:
And when the moon's sweet crescent springs
    In light o'er heaven's wide waveless sea,
And stars are forth, like blessed things.
    I think of thee—I think of thee,

FAVOR is deceitful and beauty is vain, but a woman that feareth the Lord she shall be praised. —PROV. XXXI, 30.

——:o:——

THERE'S not a look—a word—of thine
    My soul hath e'er forgot:
Thou ne'er hast bid a ringlet shine,
Nor given thy locks one graceful twine,
    Which I remember not.

——:o:——

MAN hath a weary pilgrimage,
    As through the world he wends;
On every stage, from youth to age,
    Still discontent attends.
With heaviness he casts his eye
    Jpon the road before,
And still remembers, with a sigh,
    The days that are no more.

——:o:——

PURCHASE not friends by gifts.   When thou ceasest to give, such will cease to love.

——:o:——

OUR lives are albums written through
With good or ill—with false or true—
And, as the blessed angels turn
    The pages of our years,
God grant they read the good with smiles,
    And blot the bad with tears.

I WOULD add a fresh flower to the varied bouquet
That blushes and blooms in these pages to-day;
But I fear that my efforts could only succeed
In producing a coarse and valueless weed
That some gardener—cold critic, from pity exempt—
Might uproot, and then throw it aside with contempt.

————:o:————

LOOK upward and onward. We learn to climb
by keeping our eyes, not on the valleys that lie
behind, but on the mountains that rise before us.

————:o:————

LET us be kind to each other!
The night's coming on,
When friend and when brother
Perchance may be gone!
Then, midst our dejection,
How sweet to have earned
The blest recollection
Of kindness returned.

————:o:————

COMMEND but sparingly whom thou dost love;
But less condemn whom thou dost not approve;
Thy friend, like flattery, too much praise doth wrong,
And too sharp censure shows an evil tongue.

————:o:————

OH, reason not the need; our basest beggars
Are in the poorest thing superfluous;
Allow not nature more than nature needs;
Man's life is cheap as beast's.

FRIENDSHIP is power and riches all to me;
Friendship's another element of life;
Water and fire not of more general use
To the support and comfort of the world
Than Friendship to the being of my joy;
I would do everything to serve a friend.

————:o:————

IN the evening of life, cherish the remembrance of
those who loved thee in its morning.

————:o:————

THE saints will aid, if men will call;
For the blue sky bends over all.

————:o:————

A GENTLE word is never lost;
    Oh! never, then, refuse one;
It cheers the heart when tempest-tossed,
    And lulls the cares that bruise one;
It scatters sunshine o'er our way,
    And turns our thorns to roses;
It changes weary night and day,
    And hope and love discloses.

————:o:————

AT your command these artless numbers flow
(Tho' verdant laurels ne'er will crown my brow);
Unskillful, yet submissive, I obey,
Pleased with my task, since you direct my lay.
Oh, may my lines an easy freedom gain—
Truthful each note, and gentle every strain.

BEWARE of sudden friendship; 'tis a flower
That thrives but in the sun; its bud is fair,
And it may blossom in the summer hour,
But winter's withering tempests will not bear.
True Friendship is a tree, whose lasting strength
Is slow of growth, but proves, whate'er befall,
Through life our hope and haven, and at length
Yields but to death—the power that conquers all.

———:o:———

WITHIN this book, so pure and white,
Let none but friends presume to write;
And may each line with friendship given,
Direct the reader's thoughts to heaven.

———:o:———

EVE,
With all the fruits of Eden blest
Save only one, rather than leave
That one unknown, lost all the rest.

LEARN to win a lady's faith
Nobly, as the thing is high;
Bravely, as for life and death,
With a loyal gravity.
Lead her from the festive boards,
Point her to the starry skies,
Guard her by your truthful words,
Pure from courtship's flatteries.

———:o:———

MAY that love which has always existed grow
stronger.

AND on, with many a step of pain,
  Our weary race is sadly run;
And still, as on we plod our way,
  We find, as life's gay dreams depart,
To close our being's troubled day,
  Nought left us but a broken heart.

———:o:———

HAVE Hope.   Though clouds environ now,
  And gladness hides her face in scorn,
Put thou the shadow from thy brow;
  No night but hath its morn.

———:o:———

I AM as constant as the northern star—
Of whose true fixed and resting quality,
There is no fellow in the firmament.

———:o:———

WHEN winsome ———, beautiful and young,
Rolls the soft accents from her tuneful tongue,
In admiration stand the list'ners round,
And feel the spell of beauty and of sound.
The miser, rapt, forgets the gainful plan—
The beau his compliments, and the coquette her fan.
E'en ———'s tongue yields to her wondering ear,
And deigns for once another's voice to hear.
Such power has music when with beauty joined;
Not to be charmed, is to be deaf and blind.

———:o:———

FRIENDSHIP is a strong and habitual inclination in two persons to promote the good and happiness of each other.

NOT to go back is somewhat to advance.

————:o:————

MAIDEN, through every change the same
　　Sweet semblance thou may'st wear;
Ay, scorch thy very soul with shame,
　　Thy brow may still be fair;
But if thy lovely cheek forget
　　The rose of purer years,—
Say, does not memory sometimes wet
　　That changeless cheek with tears?

————:o:————

THANKS to the human heart by which we live,
　　Thanks to its tenderness, its joys and fears;
To me the meanest flower that blows can give
　　Thoughts that do often lie too deep for tears.

————:o:————

CARE that is entered once into the breast,
Will have the whole possession ere it rest.

————:o:————

BEAUTIFUL!　Yes, but the blush will fade,
　　The light grow dim which the blue eyes wear;
The gloss will vanish from curl and braid,
　　And the sunbeam die in the waving hair.
Turn from the mirror, and strive to win
　　Treasures of loveliness still to last;
Gather earth's glory and bloom within,
　　That the soul may be bright when youth is past.

A SMOOTH sea never made a skillful mariner.

———:o:———

HER cheek had the pale pearly pink
Of sea-shells, the world's sweetest tint, as though
She lived, one-half might deem on roses sopp'd
In silver dew.

———:o:———

THEN gently scan your brother man,
    Still gentler sister woman;
For though they gang a kennie wrang,
    To step aside is human.

———:o:———

AS o'er the cold sepulchral stone
    Some name arrests the passer-by,
Thus, when thou view'st this page alone,
    May mine attract thy pensive eye!

And when by thee that name is read,
    Perchance in some succeeding year,
Reflect on me as on the dead,
    And think my heart is buried here.

———:o:———

OH, as the bee upon the flower, I hang
Upon the honey of thy eloquent tongue.

———:o:———

THAT ye might walk worthy of the Lord unto
all pleasing, being beautiful in every good work,
and increasing in the knowledge of God, is the wish
of your friend.

HE is a coward who will not turn back,
When first he discovers he's on the wrong track.

————:o:————

THERE'S beauty all around our paths,
   If but our watchful eyes
Can trace it midst familiar things
   And through their lowly guise.

————:o:————

THINK much, speak little, write with care.

————:o:————

WITHIN the oyster's shell uncouth
   The purest pearl may hide;
Trust me you'll find a heart of truth
   Within that rough outside.

————:o:————

'TIS the mind that makes the body rich:
And as the sun breaks through the darkest clouds,
So honor appeareth in the meanest habit.

————:o:————

YOURS sincerely, in the bonds of friendship.

————:o:————

WHAT doth the poor man's son inherit?
   Stout muscles and a sinewy heart;
A hardy frame, a hardier spirit;
   King of two hands, he does his part
   In every useful toil and art;
A heritage, it seems to me,
A king might wish to hold in fee.

A LITTLE body often harbors a great soul.

——:o:——

'TIS not the fairest form that holds
The mildest, purest soul within;
'Tis not the richest plant that folds
The sweetest breath of fragrance in.

——:o:——

GET but the truth once uttered, and 'tis like
A star new-born, that drops into its place,
And which, once circling in its placid sound,
Not all the tumult of the earth can shake.

——:o:——

BE good, do good, and you will be happy.

——:o:——

JOY'S opening buds, affection's glowing flowers,
Once lightly sprang within thy beaming track.
O! life was beautiful in those lost hours!
And yet you cannot wish to wander back;
Nay! thou may'st love in loneliness to think
On pleasures past, though never more to be;
Hope links thee to the future, but the link
That binds thee to the past is memory.

——:o:——

OF all the passions that possess mankind,
The love of novelty rules most the mind:
In search of this, from realm to realm we roam;
Our fleets come fraught with ev'ry folly home.

THE heart that is deceived or betrayed need not augment its anguish by self-reproach.

——:o:——

THE book of Nature, and the print
 Of beauty on the whispering sea,
Give ayc to me some lineament
 Of what I have been taught to be.
My heart is harder, and perhaps
 My manliness hath drunk up tears;
And there's a mildew in the lapse
 Of a few swift and chequer'd years;
But Nature's book is even yet
With all my mother's lessons writ.

——:o:——

FRIENDSHIP, which, once determined, never swerves;
Weighs ere it trusts, but weighs not ere it serves;
And soft-eyed Pity, and Forgiveuess bland,
And melting Charity, with open hand;
And artless love, believing and believed;
And honest Confidence, which ne'er deceived;
And Mercy, stretching out ere Want can speak,
To wipe the tear which stains Affliction's cheek.

——:o:——

THICK waters show no images of things;
 Friends are each other's mirrors, and should be
Clearer than crystal or the mountain springs,
 And free from cloud, design, or flattery.
For vulgar souls no part of friendship share;
Poets and friends are born to what they are.

BRIGHT sunny hope, thy radiant beam
Smiles sweetly on life's troubled dream.

————:o:————

Is this a time to be cloudy and sad,
  When our mother Nature laughs around?
When even the blue deep heavens look glad,
  And gladness blooms from the blossoming ground?

————:o:————

MUSIC!—Oh, how faint, how weak,
  Language fades before thy spell!
Why should feeling ever speak
  When thou canst breathe her soul so well?
Friendship's balmy words may feign,—
  Love's are e'en more false than they!
Oh, 'tis only music's strain
  Can sweetly soothe, and not betray!

————:o:————

USEFUL and steady may thy life proceed,
    Mild every word,
Good-natured every deed.
    Never with one thou lovest contend,
      But bear a thousand frailties
From your friend.

————:o:————

WHEN the world has spent its frowns and wrath,
  And cares are sorely pressing,
'Tis sweet to turn from our roving path,
  And find a fireside blessing.

WHAT'S in a name?   That which we call a rose;
By any other name would smell as sweet.

———:o:———

IN the course of our reading we should lay up
in our minds a store of goodly thoughts in well-
wrought words, which shall be a living treasure of
knowledge always with us, and from which, at various times, and amidst all the shifting circumstances,
we might be sure of drawing some comfort, guid-
ance and sympathy.

———:o:———

ONE long sweet spring be thine
With buds still bursting forth,
Fresh blossoms every hour,
And verdure fair and new.
Peace be thy gentle guest,
Peace, holy and divine,
God's blessed sunlight still
Upon thy pathway shine.

———:o:———

WELL chosen friendship, the most noble
Of virtues, all our joys makes double,
And into halves divides our trouble.

———:o:———

AS sunshine and rain, pleasure and pain,
    Each day on some must fall,
So the wise thing to do, if we only knew,
    Is to make the best of it all.

THE older the ruin, the greener the moss.
The older the friendship, the keener the loss.

————:o:————

'TIS beauty that doth make woman proud,
'Tis virtue that doth make her most admired,
'Tis modesty that makes her seem divine.

————:o:————

WHAT will it matter,
                    By and by,
Whether our path below was bright,
Whether it shone through dark or light—
    Under a gray or golden sky—
        What will it matter,
                    By and by?

————:o:————

THE little bee so silently
    Gathers honey from the flower,
So may you as quietly
    Find pleasure in each hour.

————:o:————

IF I should make a wish for you it would be this:
I wish you a large share of success in your pursuit
of happiness; may your efforts in the direction of
right bring abundant reward.   I would not wish
your pathway to be over flowers only; God made
the rose and thorn to go together; let us not separ-
ate them, but with you may the roses be many and
the thorns few.

WHOEVER thinks a faultless piece to see,
Thinks what ne'er was, nor is, nor ne'er can be.

———:o:———

HOW music charms!
How meter warms!
Parent of actions good and brave!
How vice it tames,
And worth inflames,
And holds proud empire o'er the grave!

———:o:———

MAY you always have a full share,
With a surplus on the shelf,
And ever be ready to share
With those who have less than yourself.

———:o:———

BUT the gentlest of all are those sounds full of feel-
ing,
That soft from the lute of some lover are stealing,—
Some lover who knows all the heart-touching power
Of a lute and a sigh in the magical hour.

———:o:———

THERE is a jewel which no Indian mine can buy,
No chemic art can counterfeit;
It makes men rich in greatest poverty,
Makes water wine, turns wooden cups to gold,
The homely whistle to sweet music's strain;
Seldom it comes—to few from Heaven sent—
That much in little— all in nought—Content.

MUSIC hath charms to soothe the savage breast,
To soften rocks, and bend the knotted oak

———:o:———

ON this page of your album I scribble,
  Now, remember, no critic must see,
But once in a while peep at it yourself,
  Then remember 'twas scribbled by me

———:o:———

HAVE Faith.   Where'er thy bark is driven,
  The calm's disport. the tempest's mirth—
Know this.   God rules the hosts of heaven,
  The inhabitants of earth.

———:o:———

YES, I have left the golden shore,
  Where childhood 'midst the roses play'd:
Those sunny dreams will come no more,
  That youth a long bright Sabbath made.
Yet while those dreams of memory's eye
  Arise in many a glittering train,
My soul goes back to infancy,
  And hears my mother's song again!

———:o:———

PERFORM your duties without fear,
  Will make your pathway bright and clear;
Falter, stop, and leave undone,
  Will make it like the clouded sun.

———:o:———

A GOOD name is rather to be chosen than great
riches.

SWEET is the image of the brooding dove!
Holy as heaven a mother's tender love!
The love of many prayers, and many tears,
Which changes not with dim declining years,—
The only love, which, on this teeming earth,
Asks no return for passion's wayward birth.

———:o:———

"LIFE is real—life is earnest;
    And the heroine in the strife
Is the one who leaves the future—
    Living but the present life—
Lives it truly, nobly, grandly,
    Thus prepares for coming fate,
Strives to make her living perfect;—
    Learns to labor and to wait.

———:o:———

It never pays to wreck the health
    In drudging after gain;
And he is sold who thinks that gold
    The cheapest bought with pain.
        An humble lot,
        A cosy cot,
Have tempted even kings;
        For station high,
        That wealth will buy,
Not oft contentment brings.

———:o:———

As perfume is to the rose, so is good **nature** to
the lovely.

THE violet droops its soft and bashful brow,
  But from its heart sweet incense fills the air:
So rich within—so pure without—art thou,
  With modest mien and soul of virtue rare.

————:o:————

FAITH is the star that gleams above,
  Hope is the flower that buds below;
Twin tokens of celestial love
  That out from Nature's bosom grow;
And still alike, in sky, on sod,
That star and blossom ever point to God.

————:o:————

THE moon!   She is the source of sighs,
  The very face to make us sad,—
If but to thing in other times
  The same calm quiet look she had.

————:o:————

LONGEST joys won't last forever—
  Make the most of every day;
Youth and beauty Time will sever,
  But Content hath no decay.

————:o:————

WHEN things don't go to suit you,
  And the world seems upside down,
Don't waste your time in fretting,
  But drive away the frown.

————:o:————

GOD give you many days, and may your whole
life be spotless and pure, giving beauty through all
the changes, even when the leaf has turned brown
and the fruit has ripened.

HOURS are golden links—God's token—
Reaching heaven but one by one;
Take them, lest the chain be broken
Ere thy pilgrimage be done.

———:o:———

YET, oh yet, thyself deceive not,—
    Love may sink by slow decay;
But by sudden wrench, believe not
    Hearts can thus be torn away.

———:o:———

OLD friends and true friends!
Don't talk to me of new friends;
        The old are the best,
        Who stand the test,
Who book their name as *through* friends.

———:o:———

FRIEND after friend departs;
    Who hath not lost a friend?
There is no union here of hearts
    That finds not here an end.
Were this frail world our only rest,
    Living or dying, none were blest.

Thus star by star declines,
    Till all are passed away,
As morning high and higher shines
    To pure and perfect day;
Nor sink those stars in empty night,
    They lose themselves in heaven's own light.

YE are stars of the night, ye are gems of the morn,
Ye are dewdrops whose lustre illumines the thorn;
And rayless that night is, that morning unblest,
When no beams in your eye light up peace in the
     breast.
And the sharp thorn of sorrow sinks deep in the
     heart,
Till the sweet lip of Woman assuages the smart;
'Tis hers o'er the couch of misfortune to bend
In fondness a lover, in firmness a friend;
And prosperity's hour, be it ever confessed,
From Woman receives both refinement and zest;
And adorn'd by the bays or enwreath'd with the
     willow,
Her smile is our meed, and her bosom our pillow.

———:o:———

AGE and youth both have their dreams.   Youth
looks at the possible age, age at the probable.

———:o:———

CONTENTMENT is a pearl of great price, and
whoever procures it at the expense of ten thousand
desires, makes a wise and happy purchase.

———:o:———

THERE is seldom a line of glory written upon
earth's face, but a line of suffering runs parallel with
it; and they that read the lustrous syllables of the
one, and stoop not to decipher the spotted and worn
inscription of the other, get the least half of the lesson that earth has to give.

WHY do I weep? To leave the vine
　　Whose clusters o'er me bend;
The myrtle—yet, oh, call it mine!—
　　The flowers I lov'd to tend.
A thousand thoughts of all things dear,
　　Like shadows o'er me sleep;
I leave my sunny childhood here,—
　　Oh, therefore let me weep!

————:o:————

How brilliant and mirthful the light of her eye,
Like a star glancing out from the blue of the sky!

————:o:————

THE tissues of the Life to be,
　　We weave with colors all our own;
And in the field of Destiny,
　　We reap as we have sown.

————:o:————

HONOR thy parents, to prolong thine end;
With them, though for a truth, do not contend;
Though all should truth defend, do thou lose rather
The truth a while, than lose their love forever;
Whoever makes his father's heart to bleed,
Shall have a child that will revenge the deed.

————:o:————

WHILE the fading flowers of pleasure,
　　Spring spontaneous from the soil;
Thou wilt find the harvest's treasure
　　Yields alone to patient toil.

THE light of friendship, like phosphorus, is seen
most plainly when all around is dark.

———:o:———

THE means that heaven yields must be embrac'd,
And not neglected; else, if heaven would,
And we will not, heaven's offer we refuse,
The proffer'd means of succor and redress.

———:o:———

ASK the poor pilgrim on this rude world cast,
His grizzled locks distorted in the blast;
Ask him what accent soothes, what hand bestows
The cordial bev'rage, garment and repose.
O, he will dart a spark of ancient flame,
And clasp his tremulous hands, and Woman name.
Peruse the sacred volume; Him who died
Her kiss betray'd not, nor her tongue denied;
While even the Apostle left Him to His doom,
She linger'd round His cross and watched His tomb.

———:o:———

GEMS of price are deeply hidden
'Neath the rugged rocks concealed ;
What would ne'er come forth unbidden,
To thy search may be revealed.

———:o:———

MISS not the occasion: by the forelock take
That subtle Power, the never-halting Time,
Lest a mere moment's putting-off should make
Mischance almost as heavy as a crime.

IN times of prosperity our friends are many,
But the time of adversity tries and proves them.

———:o:———

OPINION is that high and mighty dame
Which rules the world: and in the mind doth frame
Distaste or liking; for in human race,
She makes the fancy various as the face.

———:o:———

HOW much there is self-will would do,
    Were it not for the dire dismay
That bids ye shrink as ye suddenly think
    Of " what will my neighbors say? "

———:o:———

THE sunshine of the heart be mine,
    That beams a charm around;
Where'er it sheds its ray divine,
    Is all enchanted ground!
No fiend of care may enter there,
    Tho' Fate employ her art—
Her power, tho' mighty, bows to *thine!*
    Bright sunshine of the heart!

———:o:———

Do all the good you can,
To all the people you can,
In all the ways you can,
Just as long as you can

———:o:———

MAY there be just clouds enough o'er your life
to cause a glorious sunset.

THY beauty, not a fault is there!
   No queen of Grecian line
E'er braided more luxuriant hair
   O'er forehead more divine!
The light of midnight's starry heaven
   Is in those radiant eyes,—
The rose's crimson life has given
   That check its glowing dies.
And yet I love thee not: thy brow
   Is but the sculptor's mould;
It wants a shade—it wants a glow—
   It is less fair than cold.

———:o:———

IF you have found the "pearl of great price," all
the bliss of heaven will be yours.

——— :o:———

ACCOMPLISHMENTS were native to her mind,
   Like precious pearls within a clasping shell;
And winning grace her every act refined,
   Like sunshine shedding beauty where it fell.

———:o:———

STRIVE to keep the "Golden Rule,"
And learn your lessons well at school.

———:o:———

IN this wide world, the fondest and the best
Are the most tried, most troubled, and distressed.

———:o:———

WE could count time by heart-throbs; he most
lives who thinks most, speaks the noblest, acts the
best.

Love all, trust a few,
Do wrong to none; be able for thine enemy
Rather in power than use; and keep thy friend
Under thine own life's key: be check'd for silence,
But never taxed for speech.

————:o:————

The proudest motto for the young,—
   Write it in lines of gold
Upon thy heart, and in thy mind
   The stirring words enfold;
And in misfortune's dreary hour,
   Or fortune's prosperous gale,
'Twill have a holy, cheering power,—
   "There's no such word as *fail!*"

————:o:————

The massive gates of circumstance
   Are turned upon the slightest hinge,
And thus some seeming pettiest chance,
   Oft gives the life its after tinge.

————:o:————

Alas! why sit I here, committing jokes
On social pleasures and good-humor'd folks,
That see far better with their trusting eyes,
Than all the blinkings of the would-be wise?
Albums are, after all, pleasant inventions,   [tions,
Make friends more friendiy, grace one's good inten-
Brighten dull names, give great ones kinder looks,
Nay, now and then produce right curious books,
And make the scoffer (now the case with me)
Blush to look round on deathless company.

To persevere in one's duty and be silent, is the best answer to calumny.

————:o:————

Will I not in your album write?
   Yes, ————, on this spotless page
The Muse may trace in colors bright
   Some lesson worthy of a sage.
'Tis not in heavy tomes alone
That wisdom's maxims may be known.

The pale star, fading in the skies,
   May preach a sermon to the heart;
The flower that blossoms and then dies
   May tell how loved ones meet and part;
The streams meand'ring to the sea
May guide us to eternity.

————:o:————

We ourselves shape the joy and fears
   Of which the life to come is made,
And fill our future atmosphere
   With sunshine or with shade.

————:o:————

Stick to your aim! The mongrel's hold will slip;
But only crowbars loose the bulldog's lip!
Small as he looks, the jaw that never yields
Drags down the bellowing monarch of the fields.

————:o:————

Alas! too well, too well they know
The pain, the penitence, the woe
That passion brings down on the best,
The wisest, and the loveliest.

FLING wide the portals of your heart!
Make it a temple set apart
From earthly use, for Heaven's employ—
Adorned with prayer and love and joy;
So shall your Sovereign enter in
And new and noble life begin.

——:o:——

OH, Passion's words are faithless things,
　And Love disowns them ere they fall;
It is the reckless tongue that stings,
　The tongue that knows not reason's thrall.

——:o:——

THE brave man is not he who feels no fear,
For that were stupid and irrational;
But he whose noble soul its fears subdues,
And bravely dares the danger nature shrinks from.

——:o:——

TO Woman, whose best books are human hearts,
Wise Heaven a genius less profound imparts;
His awful—hers is lovely; his should tell
How thunderbolts, and hers how roses fell.
Her rapid mind decides while his debates;
She feels a truth that he but calculates.
He, provident, averts approaching ill;
She snatches present good with ready skill.
That active perseverance his, which gains;
And hers, that passive patience which sustains.

———:o:———

THOSE that want friends must show themselves
friendly.

Our lives are rivers, gliding free
To that unfathom'd, boundless sea,
    The silent grave!
Thither all earthly pomp and boast
Roll, to be swallow'd up and lost
    In one dark wave.

————:o:————

Every young man is now a sower of seed on the field of life. The bright days of youth are the seed-time. Every thought of your intellect, every emotion of your heart, every word of your tongue; every principle you adopt, every act you perform, is a seed whose good or evil fruit will prove bliss or bane of your after life.

————:o:————

There are a thousand nameless ties,
    Which only those who feel them know,—
Of kindred thoughts, deep sympathies,
    And untold fancy spells, which throw
O'er ardent minds and faithful hearts
    A chain, whose charmed links so blend
That the light circlet but imparts
    Its force in these fond words—MY FRIEND.

————:o:————

As jewels encased in a casket of gold,
    Where the richest of treasure we hide,
So our purest of thoughts lie deep and untold,
    Like the gems that are under the tide.

THUS as these lines I slowly trace
 Across this spotless page,
Will time all earthly things efface,
 And passing leave behind no trace
But the vile dusts of age;
 But truth and virtue mounting high,
Shall heavenward wing their flight,
 And shine forever from the sky
Beyond the gems of night.

————:o:————

THE friend
Who smiles when smoothing down the lonely couch,
And does kind deeds, which any one can do
Who has a feeling spirit—such a friend
Heals with a searching balsam.

————:o:————

GOD'S noblest works are honest men,
 Says Pope's instructive line;
To make a lovely woman, then,
 Must surely be divine.

————:o:————

I WOULD not enter on my list
Of friends the man
Who needlessly sets foot upon a worm.
An inadvertent step may crush the snail
That crawls at evening in the public path;
But he that has humanity, forewarned,
Will tread aside and let the reptile live.

OH, let my friendship in the wreath,
  Though but a bud among the flowers,
Its sweetest fragrance round thee breathe,—
  'Twill serve to soothe thy weary hours.

———:o:———

WITH leaden foot time creeps along,
  While ——— is away;
With her, nor plaintive was the song,
  Nor tedious was the day.

Ah! envious power! reverse my doom,
  Nor double thy career;
Strain every nerve, stretch every plume,
  And rest them when she's here.

———:o:———

CAST thy bread upon the waters,
  Out upon the waves alone,
You will find it drifted to thee,
  After many days have flown.

Ever hoping and enduring,
  Ever prayerful on the way,
May you reach the golden entrance
  Opening on eternal day.

———:o:———

MAY no sorrow distress thy days,
May no griefs disturb thy nights;
May the pillow of peace kiss thy cheek,
And the pleasure of realization attend thy beau-
  tiful dreams.

FRIENDSHIP, like love, is but a name,
Unless to one you stint the flame.
The child, whom many father's share,
Hath seldom known a father's care.
'Tis thus in friendships: who depend
On many, rarely find a friend.

———:o:———

HELP somebody worse off than yourself, and you
will find you are better off than you fancied.

———:o:———

So live, so act, that every hour,
May die as dies the natural flower,
A self-reviving thing of power;
That every word and every deed,
May bear within itself the seed
Of future good in future need.

———:o:———

LET others sing the toils of state,
That ceaseless urge the aspiring great;
Others again, in pompous verse,
The warrior's actions may rehearse;
Me the soft god of soft desires
A gentler theme of verse inspires;
Of ———'s charms he bids me sing,
And strike for her the trembling string.
Forgive me, gentle god of love,
If once I disobedient prove,
Of ———'s charms how can I sing?
Too low my voice, too weak the string!

IF we were but as ready to look to the light,
As we are to sit moping because it is night,
We would own it a truth, both in word and in deed,
That who tries to be happy is sure to succeed.

————:o:————

ONE by one thy griefs will meet thee,
Do not fear an armed band;
One will fade as others greet thee,
Shadows passing through the land.

————:o:————

BEWARE of doubt! Faith is the subtle chain
Which binds us to the Infinite: the voice
Of a deep life within, that will remain
Until we crowd it thence.

————:o:————

OF all the gifts which heaven bestows,
There is one above all measure,
And that's a friend; 'midst all our woes
A friend is found a treasure.

To thee I give this sacred name,
For thou art such to me,
And ever proudly will I claim
To be a friend of thee.

THE END.

www.ingramcontent.com/pod-product-compliance
Lightning Source LLC
Chambersburg PA
CBHW032312280326
41932CB00009B/790